Afro-Orientalism

Afro-Orientalism

Bill V. Mullen

University of Minnesota Press
Minneapolis • London

Part of chapter 1 first appeared in *positions: east asia cultures critique* 11, no. 1 (Spring 2003): 217–40, and as the chapter "W. E. B. Du Bois, *Dark Princess*, and the Afro-Asian International," in *Left of the Color Line: Race, Radicalism, and Twentieth-Century Literature of the United States*, ed. Bill V. Mullen and James Smethurst (Chapel Hill: University of North Carolina Press, 2003), 87–106, copyright 2003 by the University of North Carolina Press and reprinted by permission of the publisher. Part of chapter 2 first appeared in different form in *Mediations* 22 (Spring 1999): 44–55. Part of chapter 3 first appeared in *Works and Days* 39–40, no. 20 (2002): 189–216.

Permission to quote from the Fred Ho Papers at the Archives and Special Collections, Thomas J. Dodd Research Center, University of Connecticut Libraries, and from the Robert F. Williams Papers, Bentley Historical Library, University of Michigan, is gratefully acknowledged.

"I Sing to China" and an excerpt from "The Riddle of the Sphinx," poems by W. E. B. Du Bois, reprinted with the permission of David Graham Du Bois and the W. E. B. Du Bois Foundation, Inc. Permission to quote from the poem "Roses and Revolution" by Dudley Randall is gratefully acknowledged. The poem "Slogan (Buy American)" is reprinted with permission from the author, Sonia Sanchez. The poem "Puerto Rican Woman" is reprinted with permission of the author, Alma Villegas. Lines from two poems by Esther Iverem, "Essay to X" and "Essay to Us," appear with the permission of the author. Lyric quotations from *Warrior Sister*, an opera with book and libretto by Ann T. Greene in collaboration with Fred Ho, appear with permission of Ann T. Greene.

Published by the University of Minnesota Press
111 Third Avenue South, Suite 290
Minneapolis, MN 55401-2520
http://www.upress.umn.edu

Library of Congress Cataloging-in-Publication Data

Mullen, Bill, 1959-
   Afro-Orientalism / Bill V. Mullen.
      p. cm.
Includes bibliographical references and index.
   ISBN 0-8166-3748-2 (hc : alk. paper) -- ISBN 0-8166-3749-0 (pb : alk. paper)
   1. African Americans--Relations with Asian Americans. 2. African Americans--
Intellectual life--20th century. 3. Asian Americans--Intellectual life--20th century.
4. United States--Race relations. 5. American literature--20th century--
History and criticism. 6. American literature--African American authors.
7. Race relations in literature. 8. Racism in literature. 9. Imperialism in literature.
I. Title.
   E185.615.M75 2004
   305.896'073--   dc22   2004014985

Printed in the United States of America on acid-free paper

The University of Minnesota is an equal-opportunity educator and employer.

12 11 10 09 08 07 06 05 04   10 9 8 7 6 5 4 3 2 1

Contents

Acknowledgments   vii

Introduction: Afro-Orientalism and Other Tales
of Diaspora   xi

1. **W. E. B. Du Bois's Afro-Asian Fantasia**   1

2. **The Limits of Being Outside:
   Richard Wright's Anticolonial Turn**   43

3. **Transnational Correspondence:
   Robert F. Williams, Detroit,
   and the Bandung Era**   73

4. **"Philosophy Must Be Proletarian":
   The Dialectical Humanism of
   Grace Lee and James Boggs**   113

5. **Making Monkey Signify:
   Fred Ho's Revolutionary Vision Quest**   163

Appendix: Fred Ho Discography   205

Notes   207

Index   229

Acknowledgments

I owe this book to my students in the People's Republic of China. This project was conceived in 1985 as they and I decoded James Baldwin's "Fifth Avenue Uptown: A Letter from Harlem" at a moment when even a policy of open doors couldn't shed light on that corner of the United States. Particularly inspiring in that course at the Changsha Railway Institute was Xiao Xiao Yu, as were the friendship and support of colleagues Chen Xiao Chen, Ren, and their son Kenny. The project deepened with the assistance of a Fulbright award to Wuhan University in the PRC, where students in a graduate course began to theorize their own Afro-Orientalism while reading Claude McKay's revolutionary sonnets and Richard Wright's *Black Boy*. Zhu Ying, a brilliant and gracious woman, wrote her MA thesis on Toni Morrison out of that course.

My family also lives in every page of this book, particularly my grandfather John J. Mullen, who opened the first door between the Harlem Irish and this project. Liz Petrasovic has been a strong, caring, and patient partner through the long march of authorship. Max Mullen is eleven now and already a polyrhythmist and polyculturalist. He plays backbeat behind this story.

A number of institutions and libraries have been exceedingly generous in support of this book. Youngstown State University granted both a sabbatical leave in 1998 and a research professorship. The University of Texas–San Antonio provided a faculty summer grant and support for two superb research assistants. The Bentley Historical Library at the University of Michigan provided a Bentley travel grant for use of the Robert Franklin Williams Papers. Roger Buckley at the Asian American Studies Institute at the University of Connecticut made possible my research into the Fred Ho Papers at the Thomas J. Dodd Center. The faculty and students at UConn, especially Roger and program assistant Fe Delos-Santos, were especially generous to me during my visit to the institute—special thanks to them. Other support came from the Walter Reuther Library in Detroit and the Tamiment Library at New York University. My thanks to the staffs at each of these facilities for their generous assistance with collections. Still other timely help came from the CISA Crossroads in the Americas Lecture Series, which allowed me to present developing work from this project in lecture form at Hampshire College. Special thanks to Eric Schocket for his efforts to bring me there and to Michelle Stephens for thoughtful and provocative exchange about Robert Williams and the idea of Afro-Orientalism.

Other people close to this project are owed heartfelt thanks for their generosity with materials and time with interviews, especially Grace Lee Boggs and members of the Grace and James Boggs Center in Detroit, including Scott Kurashige, Jim Embry, Rick Feldman, and Shea Howell. Fred Ho made available materials that were otherwise difficult or impossible to discover. Herb Boyd and Kalamu ya Salaam gave generously of themselves in interviews conducted for this book. Their lived history is the history I seek to resurrect. I was lucky to spend time talking with Marty Glaberman about *Facing Reality* and facing reality before he passed. Marty connects people and ideas in this book in the same way he did as a writer and organizer.

Doug Armato has been a fabulously supportive and patient editor for this book; Gretchen Asmussen at the University of Minnesota Press guided the manuscript flawlessly. Other journals, presses, and editors have also given their much-appreciated critical attention to early versions of this work and deserve all thanks: Ron Strickland and Amitava Kumar at *Mediations* helped shape an early version of my chapter on Richard Wright; Mike Sell gave a careful reading to an early draft of the chapter on Robert Williams and Detroit and shepherded to publication an important journal issue on transnationalism and the 1960s. Andrew Jones and Nikhil Pal Singh, along with two anonymous readers, gave expert response and encouragement to an early version of my work on W. E. B. Du Bois and *Dark Princess*. Their special issue of *positions*, "The Afro-Asian Century," is an important moment of scholarship. I share their debt to writer and editor Joe Wood, who introduced me to the "yellow Negro" and was a beam of light and honesty during his too-short time in this world. Finally, Greg Meyerson and David Siars offered excellent advice on a related piece of work that improved the final direction of this book.

A number of friends and comrades from Youngstown were steady sources of joy and support during the time this book was coming into being. Nawal Amar, Barbara Brothers, Beverly Gray, Dale Harrison, Julian Madison, Gail Okawa, Sue and Gary Sexton, Homer Warren, and Bob Weaver kept me close to this material and alive to its important questions. My friend and mentor Mark Shutes died during the writing of this book; we miss him still. Alice and Staughton Lynd and fellow members of the Youngstown Prison Forum, Ed Wells and Jim Jordan, were the best of friends and best hope in my time with them. Morris Slavin and his late wife Sophie were guardian angels to good people and good ideas. Morris remains a standard of integrity and scholarship.

Here in San Antonio a cohort of colleagues keeps a collective flame burning beneath shared ideas and worthy political goals. *Mil gracias* to Bernadette Andrea, Norma Cantú, Sue Hum, Louis Mendoza, Mona Narain, Ben Olguin, and Sonia Saldívar-Hull. Our many dinners and conversations have deepened my apprehension of the boundaries and borders of this project. Also inspirational to my better ideas were members of the UTSA Progressive Faculty Association. Their continued good works and intellectual influences are, I hope, reflected in this book. Finally, members of the Young Scholars Group at UTSA, including Juliet Langman, Anne Hardgrove, and Dan Engster, provided helpful feedback on early portions of this work.

Elsewhere around the country, folks who are more than scholars and more than friends sharpened my thinking on this project through conversation, question, encouragement, and exchange. They merit a special place in these acknowledgments: Mark Dery, Barbara Foley, Marcial Gonzalez, Pat Keeton, Margot Mifflin, and Jim Smethurst. Alan Wald deserves special thanks for his help enabling my research in Ann Arbor. Still other scholars with whom I am in more-silent conversation but to whom major intellectual debts and thanks are owed include Aijaz Ahmad, Muhammad Ahmed, Herbert Aptheker, Grace Boggs, Morris Dickstein, Arif Dirlik, Brent Edwards, Betsy Esch, Gerald Horne, Evelyn Hu-dehart, Robin D. G. Kelley, Bill Maxwell, Tiffany Patterson, Vijay Prashad, Mary Helen Washington, and Lisa Yun. Their strong shoulders have allowed me to see further and, I hope, more clearly. Still other influences are acknowledged throughout the text.

I hope the flaws in *Afro-Orientalism* will be improved on by its readers, who in a perfect world (or in the process of making it) will rewrite this story, fill in its gaps, sharpen its stances, deepen its understandings. More immediately, I hope the book takes its place in a conversation with high stakes about means of challenging the current moment of U.S. imperialist venturing. I had originally intended a postscript that would try to draw a line between Afro-Orientalism, 9/11, and the pending U.S. attack on Iraq. Everything has changed since that first effort. The verbal shadow of Amiri Baraka—"Who want the world like it is"— hangs over my own post–September 11 prefaces and conclusions. Yet I continue to draw from the example and work of friends and figures and family highlighted in these acknowledgments inspiration for struggle— on the page, in the classroom, and in the public arena. Bad times have brought out their beauty and brilliance, resolve and patience, love and tenacity. It is to them that this book is dedicated.

Afro-Orientalism
and Other Tales of Diaspora

> The problem of the twenty-first century is to re-invent political
> practices that account for new social problems without forgetting
> those that we have inherited from the past.
>
> —Arif Dirlik, *Amerasia Journal*

In his 1941 collaborative photodocumentary *12 Million Black Voices,* a
study of African American migration to Chicago, Richard Wright casts
himself as a participant observer in this memorial description of a southern black peasantry he had not so very long ago left behind. Recalling
Jim Crow life in rural Mississippi as a persisting nightmare—"as though
the Lords of the Land had waved a magic wand and cast a spell upon us,
a spell from which we cannot awaken"—Wright recounts moments of
abjection and reverie expressed in secular songs sung by black families
behind closed doors. Some tunes, he remembers, protest the indiffer-
ence of poor whites to black suffering. Still other times, he writes, songs
emerge "when we feel self-disgust at our bare lot, when we contemplate
our lack of courage in the face of daily force." In these moments, "we
are seized with a desire to escape our shameful identification; and, over-
whelmed emotionally, we seek to become protectively merged with the
least-known and farthest removed race of men we know; yes, when we
weigh ourselves and find ourselves wanting, we say with a snicker of
self-depreciation":

> White folks is evil
> > And niggers is too
> So glad I'm a Chinaman
> > I don't know what to do . . .[1]

Wright moves swiftly past this knowing and ironic memory, but we should not. In addition to disclosing a poignant example of resistance culture, this peasant spiritual's playful positing of an imaginary Asianness as a fleeting antidote for African American suffering should resonate in multiple ways for readers familiar with twentieth-century geopolitics and writings on race. From the moment of his 1900 declaration that the problem of the twentieth century would be the problem of the *world* color line, W. E. B. Du Bois hoped for just such radically imaginative (if more healthily assertive) linkages between and among people of color in response to white Western domination. Indeed, it was the Japanese victory over Russia in 1904, the century's first major victory over a white nation by a colored one, that moved Du Bois to declare Asia the fraternal twin of Africa in the struggle to decolonize the modern world, and contributed to his lifelong interest in Asian politics and culture. Second, Wright's signifying snippet resonates with and anticipates contemporary academic deliberations on racial identity. Choked by Jim Crow segregation, black sharecroppers attacked racial binarism with a creative double consciousness. Implicit in their critique of brutalizing Jim Crow norms is a satirical and strategic antiessentialism that sees race, and racism, as being devalued once the possibility of an ulterior miscegenation—colored mixing—is thinkable, if not allowable. Thinking dialectically, as this vernacular syllogism invites us to do, China and the Chinaman represent an imaginary "third way" out of the crushing oppositional hierarchies of the American South's peculiarly brutal history. Asia's distance in this parable is its utopian attraction, far removed, literally and figuratively, from the sphere of Western power. Its surprising appearance in a Mississippi folk song is a prime example of what Robin D. G. Kelley has called, in a different context, the "freedom dreams" of the black radical imagination.[2]

Yet the temptation to make a fetish of this local anecdote, to inflate it to world-historical or world-biographical significance, might also be tempered by another critical problem it evokes, namely, the tendency of Western speakers to conjure Asia primarily for the purposes of delineating Occidental problems and desires. In his still-dominative study of the subject, Edward Said writes: "To the Westerner . . . the Oriental was always like some aspect of the West; to some of the German Romantics, for example, Indian religion was essentially an Oriental version of Germano-Christian pantheism. Yet the Orientalist makes it his work to be always converting the Orient from something into something else: he does this for himself, for the sake of his culture, in some cases for what he believes is the sake of the Oriental."[3]

Said's invitation to understand Orientalism as both an oppressive discursive trend in Western thought and a specific embodiment of local subjectivities has for understandable reasons been most often applied by scholars to a range of texts reflective of imperialism's visible hand. Yet interrogating the stratagems for "converting the Orient from something into something else" in this subaltern parable from *12 Million Black Voices* yields results resonant of, if not intended by, his formulation. The desire of poor black singers to become "protectively merged with the least-known and farthest removed race of men we know" suggests not just a shameful recognition of the deleterious consequences of racist restriction —Wright calls it "self-depreciation"—but a negative affirmation of knowing this unknowing as the starting point for rethinking and reordering the world. To see this cognitive process more fully and self-consciously realized, we can turn to *The Autobiography of Malcolm X*. In the famous section of the text called "Saved," where he learns to read, Malcolm Little crystallizes his social, racial, and intellectual dislocation as a political prisoner in the United States by noting that the prison library books he first attempts to read "might as well have been in Chinese."[4] As he enters literacy, Malcolm equates words with facts—"the dictionary is like a miniature encyclopedia" (267), and within pages he is discoursing on a new map of knowledge whose intellectual geography collapses East and West, Asian and African: he discovers almost simultaneously J. A. Rogers's *Sex and Race* and Carter Woodson's *Negro History*, as well as Will Durant's *The Story of Oriental Civilization* and Mahatma Gandhi's account of decolonization. Malcolm thunders against British rule in India, noting that "excepting the African slave trade, nowhere has history recorded any more unnecessary bestial and ruthless human carnage than the British suppression of the non-white Indian people" (272). Malcolm's reading is also framed by and confirms his newfound appreciation, via the tutelage of Elijah Muhammad, that he is himself a descendant of the "Asiatic Black Man." This intellectual identification is incited by sources disclosing that "even . . . Socrates was initiated into some of the Egyptian mysteries," a metonymy for Malcolm's own prison education. This revelation also nudges him to the deeper, if more hazardous, assertion that "most Occidental philosophy had been largely borrowed from the Oriental thinkers" (274). On the final page of the autobiography, Malcolm swears a commitment to study not just "the basic African dialects" but Chinese and Arabic: "it looks as if Chinese will be the most powerful political language of the future," and Arabic will be its most powerful "spiritual language" (499).

Malcolm's breathtaking voyage from Asia as metaphor for the inscrutability of his own racial and intellectual position in the United States to the locus of his—and black America's—precarious self-knowledge can be read as an allegory of the following question: is it possible for Orientalism to do the work of both colonizing and decolonizing the mind? Indeed, it was precisely this question that Du Bois himself asked and answered in his spectacularly rich 1935 essay "Indians and Negroes," first published in the 1935 journal *Aryan Path*. Du Bois was already well into his long career as an autodidact scholar, writer, and editor on Asia when he issued a provocative 1,500-word essay spurred by a desire to bring "understanding, sympathy and cooperation between the Negroes of America and the peoples of India." The essay began with the complaint that absent and distorted education about each race to the other was the crucible in which Western racist imperialism sustained its grasp. Negroes taught in American schools and reading books and articles by American writers, he complained, "have almost no conception of the history of India." What they do receive are sensationalistic tales of "religious frenzy, fights between Hindus and Mohammedans, the deeds of masters of magic and the wealth of Indian princes," in short, a genie's lamp of derogatory and distorting myth. By contrast, "the knowledge which Indians have of the American Negro is chiefly confined to the conventional story spread by most white American and English writers: ignorant black savages were enslaved and made to do labor which was the only thing they could do." Du Bois blamed "modern methods of gathering and distributing news" and "deliberate and purposeful propaganda" for these slights and called for the "one hundred or more weekly newspapers circulating among Negroes" to begin reporting on the history and problems of Asia. The press of India, meanwhile, "ought to welcome a number of Negro contributors with explanations of their situation there."[5] Du Bois was not speaking without precedents. As editor of *Crisis*, he had routinely written on political developments in Asia since the journal's founding in 1910. His friend and mentor Lala Lajpat Rai had spent five years living in the United States from 1914 to 1919 and had written a book on the country's social and racial relations, *United States*, for readers back in India. Du Bois likewise reminded readers that East Indians had appeared in the several Pan-African Congresses already held to that point. One year later, Du Bois would himself visit China and Japan for the first time. Du Bois's emphatic challenge to American readers, especially black readers, was to recognize perforce the need for an internal strategy of political, literary, and intellectual repudiation of Orientalism's complex mechanisms, one that he well understood folded African Americans and Asian Americans into the same discursive trap of mutual subordination and, more important, separation.

This book is about the response of a select gathering of African Americans and Asian Americans to Du Bois's call. Collectively, they represent a tradition of U.S. writing on race, nation, and empire whose insistence on resistance to the West's most geographically determined form of racism is signaled in the title of this project. Afro-Orientalism is a counterdiscourse that at times shares with its dominant namesake certain features but primarily constitutes an independent critical trajectory of thought on the practice and ideological weight of Orientalism in the Western world. Afro-Orientalism, in other words, is a signifying discourse on race, nation, and global politics constituting a subtradition in indigenous U.S. writing on imperialism, colonialism, and the making of capitalist empire. It is grounded in several specific terrains: the experience of black Americans and Asian Americans as indentured servants and slaves in the United States; the parallel routes of Western imperialism through Asia and Africa; the struggles of black and Asian Americans to be understood as global citizens in a diasporic world; the constant self-awareness on the part of African Americans that Orientalism, though a racist discourse directed primarily against Asians, discriminates against people of color everywhere; the parallel byways that African Americans and Asian Americans, Africans and Asians, have traveled in the economic and political routes of modernity; the attempt by black Americans, from the origins of the Republic, to link with larger radical and revolutionary projects originating outside the shores of the American empire; and finally, in more recent years, the efforts of scholars of African and Asian diaspora to speak of synchronous, rather than discrete, histories of Afro-Asian encounter and exchange.

Indeed, in coining what may strike some readers as a dangerous and problematic critical trope, I take my lead from the work of Chinese scholar Xiaomei Chen. In her important 1995 work *Occidentalism: A Theory of Counter-discourse in Post-Mao China*, Chen notes how twentieth-century Chinese intellectuals have themselves struggled with the legacy of Orientalism as both a "partially self-imposed" adoption of Western conceptions of racial and ethnic difference and a discourse with which to vigilantly resist and critique Western hegemony. Chen's name for this process is Occidentalism:

> As a result of constantly revising and manipulating imperialistically imposed Western theories and practices, the Chinese Orient had produced a new discourse, marked by a particular combination of the Western construction of China with the Chinese construction of the West, with both of these components interacting and interpenetrating each other.
>
> This seemingly unified discursive practice of Occidentalism exists in a paradoxical relationship to the discursive practices of Orientalism, and in fact shares with it many ideological techniques and strategies. Despite these similarities, however, Chinese Occidentalism has mainly served an ideological function quite different from that of Orientalism. Orientalism,

in Said's account, is a strategy of Western world domination, whereas . . .
Chinese Occidentalism is primarily a discourse that has been evoked by
various and competing groups within Chinese society for a variety of different ends. . . . As such, it has been both a discourse of oppression and a
discourse of liberation.[6]

Xiaomei Chen points the way to a provocative rethinking of both
Orientalism and its relationship to subaltern or marginalized populations. Akin to Homi Bhabha's notion of mimicry, her Occidentalism
offers a means of repeating with a difference the perspective, literally, of
dominance and subordination. Her work reminds us that the best critiques of, and supplements to, Saidian Orientalism, like those of Aijaz
Ahmad, Arif Dirlik, and feminist critics, to name a few, insist that post-
colonialist theory and Orientalism are themselves theoretical prisms refracting the Western capitalist patriarchal history that gave them birth.[7]
Likewise, as its own theoretical thematic in the history of the West,
Afro-Orientalism has several distinguishing features both mimetic and
original: emerging primarily, though not exclusively, from Marxian analytical contributions on colonialism and imperialism, it revises these in
accord with what it perceives as racist, or racial, absences, silences, and
gaps within the Marxist tradition. More than a fatuous and simplified
rejection of Marxism's "Orientalism," as described by some critics, or a
mutant-variety nationalism, however, this revised tradition accords primacy to an attack on Western Orientalism(s) as byproducts of Western
capitalism. It foregrounds the relationship between peoples of African
and Asian descent as a dialectical synecdoche of Western capitalist modernity, in much the manner that traditional Marxist theory has viewed
the international working class: as the agent of Western capitalism's rise
and fall. In this regard, Afro-Orientalism may be understood as a like
but different companion to the important work on hybridity championed
by many critics in postmodern and postcolonial theory. This paradigm
has been dominated by decentered or diasporic readings of literary and
historical texts, and the search for what Mary Louise Pratt has called
"contact zones" between colonized and colonizer, or similarly situated

subaltern populations.[8] Hybridity theory, if it can be so labeled, has premised its critiques of racial essentialism and absolutism on sophisticated demonstrations of racial and cultural mixing, the elaborate presentation of geographic and population intersections, and innumerable examples of cultural, ethnic, and racial crossings.

The most brilliant applicator of these principles to the historical relationship between peoples of Asian and African descent is Vijay Prashad. His books *Karma of Brown Folk* and *Everybody Was Kung Fu Fighting: Afro-Asian Connections and the Myth of Cultural Purity*, particularly the latter, provide a fantastic map dating to Vasco da Gama's disruption of racial harmony in the fifteenth-century Indian Ocean of the conduits by which peoples of African and Asian descent have found themselves in mutual struggle against Western empires. Prashad has meticulously documented ways in which people of African and Asian descent have fashioned local strategies for grassroots resistance rooted primarily in working-class institutions and cultural practices. He has done so ever mindful of dominant Western racial discourses that have situated African Americans as the negative shadow of the Asian American model minority myth. Suspicious as I am of a reductive multiculturalism that effaces and erases antiracist theory and praxis, Prashad borrows from Robin D. G. Kelley the notion of "polyculturalism" to describe the impetus for many Africans and Asians to seek mutuality. Polyculturalism, for Prashad, is the attempt to "think about the experience of race in a dialectical fashion rather than in the one-dimensional way" of both those who would ignore race altogether—what he calls the color blind, and those who would essentialize it, "race as biology," such as Afrocentrists. Prashad's essays on Afro-Asian history provide a compelling argument that the dead ends leading back into colonialist and imperialist views of race are those that stress "management of difference" over antiracism,[9] "adopt an idea of culture wherein culture is bounded into authentic zones with pure histories that need to be accorded a grudging dignity by policies of diversity," and replicate the logic of multinational capitalism by advocating cultural forms that "facilitate consumerism."[10] Prashad demonstrates, for example, that Rastafarianism as a hybrid merger of the African and East

Indian cultures of the Caribbean bespeaks a specific anti-imperialist and antiracist politics that never closes off the contact zones but recognizes their constant interpenetration. These features make polyculturalism, for Prashad, better attuned to the "struggle to dismantle and redistribute unequal resources and racist structures."[11]

Afro-Orientalism will confirm and echo Prashad's goals and ambitions while both repeating and deviating from a polycultural methodology. This owes in part to the book's more focused interest in the impact on, and relationship of, different and differing Orientalisms to struggles by writers and activists of African and Asian descent. As Arif Dirlik has again cautioned, concerning multiculturalist theory: "Orientalism itself may be a product of a consciousness already decentered. . . . There is no self-evident reason why a decentered consciousness should not find relief in culturalist fundamentalism, or the reification of ethnicity and culture; the history of orientalism provides evidence of this strong possibility."[12]

> It seems to me to be more important to question the assumptions of capitalist modernity (not merely Eurocentrism) of which orientalism is an integral expression. To the extent that they have assimilated the teleology of capitalism, recent challenges to Eurocentrism . . . have promoted rather than dislodged orientalism. What is necessary is to repudiate historical teleology in all its manifestations. This would entail the historicization of capitalist modernity itself, and the identification of alternative modernities, not in terms of reified cultures, but in terms of alternative historical trajectories that have been suppressed by the hegemony of capitalist modernity. It also requires questioning not just continental distinctions (orient/occident), but nations as units of analysis, since the latter also thrive on cultural homogenization and reification.[13]

Malcolm X's aforementioned linkage of Will Durant and J. A. Rogers is one such discovery of "alternative historical trajectories." Afro-Orientalism is rife with such moments and constitutes a self-conscious alternative modernity that, like Malcolm's education, can only define its subversive potential in terms of the West itself. Yet Malcolm's rapid slip into cultural fundamentalism—all Western philosophy is borrowed from the East—also bespeaks precisely the dangers of what Dirlik calls a "culturalist" reading of modernity, dangers also grossly on display in the tradition of Afro-Orientalism. The attempt by writers of African and Asian descent to escape the prison house of racist capitalism has created an entire "secret history" of cultural fetishization on which this book will look with a fascinated but remote eye. I am thinking of the tradition of African American writing on Asia as a place for countermythology: Moorish Science Temple and the Nation of Islam; nineteenth-century Egypto-centrism; the Afrocentric movement widely construed. Each of these movements has fallen prey rather explicitly to Dirlik's warning that multicultural challenges to Orientalism can lead to reifying definitions of culture "at the expense of the historicity of both ethnicity and culture." That said, these reifying tendencies almost always penetrate *all* Afro-Asian discourse, including those of writers I've already mentioned, and thus comprise an irrepressible aspect of the name and idea I am calling "Afro-Orientalism." In negotiating tributaries of its own language and ideas, this study will thus try to heed Evelyn Hu-DeHart's caution that, "since culturalism still runs against the evidence of difference, it can be sustained only by the reification of ethnicity and, ultimately, race."[14] I will argue that Afro-Orientalism remains most hopeful and useful and dangerous as a counterdiscourse to Western modernity precisely when it eschews the temptations of culturalism and raciology and focuses on the prize of what Dirlik calls the "teleology of capitalism." It will anchor its confidence in this method in ensuing chapters by delineating how practitioners of Afro-Orientalism have self-consciously used historical materialist and Marxist methods to avoid the pitfalls of culturalist and raciological thinking. This tradition of writing, it will be argued, constitutes its own self-conscious "alternative modernity" in Dirlik's terms, and it is toward its recovery, development, and implications that I will now turn.

Recovering Marx

What did Marx and Engels say, and when did they say it? The question has often been asked by succeeding generations of scholars interested in race and liberation. One important and influential answer, particularly for the purposes of this study, was provided by Edward Said. *Orientalism* famously uses Marx's quotation from *The Eighteenth Brumaire of Louis Bonaparte* as an epigraph: "They cannot represent themselves; they must be represented."[15] The quotation serves as shorthand for Said's contention that Marx and Engels's corpus of writing on Asia is a racist "speaking for the Other" from which *Orientalism*—and postcolonial theory—seek to awaken us. A careful if necessarily cursory reading, or rereading, of Marx and Engels's writings on colonialism reveals the strengths and weaknesses of Said's assessment and delineates how and why Afro-Orientalism is a discursive cousin to this debate.

The fate and movement of people of color under capitalism was, as is fairly well known, a bedrock of Marx and Engels's history of capital. In 1858, Marx and Engels grounded their description of "primitive accumulation," the earliest stage of capitalism, in the movement to impress and control the African, Asian, and Latin worker: "The discovery of gold and silver in America, the extirpation, enslavement, and entombment in mines of the aboriginal population, the beginning of the conquest and looting of the East Indies, the turning of Africa into a warren for the commercial hunting of black-skins, signalised the rosy dawn of the era of capitalist production. These idyllic proceedings are the chief momenta of primitive accumulation."[16]

The brunt of Marx and Engels's writings on the system of colonialism that emerged from this rosy dawn appears in their *Articles from the New York Tribune*, the paper to which they contributed as correspondents during the 1850s. The articles pay special attention to China and India. Africa, of course, was not yet colonized. Marx and Engels's writings on U.S. and British slavery during this period can be accurately if reductively summarized by the quotation in the foregoing paragraph. "A people which enslaves another people forges its own chains" was one variation on this view; another, analogous at the level of the state, was Engels's "A nation cannot become free and continue at the same time to oppress other nations,"[17] a hostile conception of nationalism predicated on its relationship to imperialism, and one to which we shall return. In general, Marx and Engels viewed slavery, like colonialism, dialectically: each of its sites had its antithesis and making either in the conditions and production efforts of the European working class or in some other place of exploitation. More complexly, though, this dialectic also inscribed and exacerbated racial and ethnic difference by sketching the world as separate spheres, a precondition, as Said notes, for Orientalist discourse: "Can one divide human reality, as indeed human reality seems to be genuinely divided, into clearly different cultures, histories, traditions, societies, even races, and survive the consequences humanly?"[18]

Marx and Engels in their writings on Asia reproduced both this epistemology and its questions, though coming to quite different conclusions from Said about what to do about it. "It may seem a very strange, and a very paradoxical assertion that the next uprising of the people of Europe, and their next movement for republican freedom and economy of government, may depend more probably on what is now passing in the Celestial Empire—the very opposite of Europe,—than on any other political cause that now exists,—more even than on the menaces of Russia and the consequent likelihood of a general European war."[19] Before proceeding further with an analysis of Marx and Engels's racial discourse, it is interesting to compare Frederick Douglass's sympathy and language evinced in his 1869 attempt to link the plight of Asian and Asian American and African American workers in the United States. "I want a home here not only for the negro, the mulatto, and the Latin races," he wrote, "but I want the Asiatic to find a home here in the United States, and feel at home here, both for his sake and for ours. . . . Contact with these yellow children of the Celestial Empire would convince us that the points of human difference, great as they, upon first sight, seem, are as nothing compared with the points of human agreement. Such contact would remove mountains of prejudice."[20] The temptation to assert common ground and like-mindedness in these renderings of Asia—including their exoticizing undertones—is, however, undermined by further observations by Marx. Chinese war with another country, he observed in 1857, would be a popular war "for the maintenance of Chinese nationality, with all its overbearing prejudice, stupidity, learned ignorance, and pedantic barbarism."[21]

Marx's characterization of what he called elsewhere "the rotting semi-civilization of the oldest State in the world" iterates one of his favorite words to describe not just China but Asia generally: *barbaric.* He used it elsewhere to describe Persia—"Asiatic barbarity,"[22] consistent with his characterization of other feudalisms: "It is almost needless to observe that, in the same measure in which opium has obtained the sovereignty over the Chinese, the Emperor and his staff of pedantic mandarins have become dispossessed of their own sovereignty. It would seem as though history had first to make this whole people drunk before it could rouse them out of their hereditary stupidity."[23] Asia, in Marx and Engels's enlightened view, was the unhappy inheritor of absence. Just as Hegel, their dialectical master, declared that Africa had "no history," so Marx and Engels perceived that only when European capitalism had created the conditions for proletarian revolution in Asia could it enter the evolutionary narrative of history. This teleological view substantiates allegations by Hélène Cixous and Robert Young that, in Young's words, "Marxism's standing Hegel on his head may have reversed his idealism, but it did not change the mode of operation of a conceptual system which remains collectively Eurocentric. It is thus entirely appropriate that Hegelian Marxism has become generally known as 'Western Marxism.'"[24]

Yet is calling a system of thought Eurocentric the same as calling it, as Said does, Orientalist? Is it true to argue, as does Young, that "for orthodox Marxism there can be only one 'other,' that of the working class, into which all other oppressed groups, so-called 'minorities,' must in the last instance be subsumed?"[25] Making such allegations stick, it seems to me, depends on what Dirlik calls Orientalism's own tendency to rely on culturalist rather than materialist paradigms for defining categories of race, nation, and class. For example, as Sanjay Seth has observed in his nuanced study of Marx and Engels's writings on Asia, Marx and Engels's characterization of Indian "barbarism," or more famously its "Oriental despotism"—a much-seized-upon phrase by critics of Marxism—specifically described conditions of production under primitive accumulation, including state control of irrigation and the virtual absences of social classes. What they are describing are national characteristics under primitive capitalism, that is to say, primitive nationalism, something that they cannot support as Marxists. This prejudice did lead Marx and Engels to look askance on primarily racial, tribal, or small-nation rebellions, a view later revised by Lenin. Yet this dilemma became a fruitful field of engagement for later generations of black, African, Asian, and Asian American radicals in their own engagements with Marxism as a theory of national or international liberation. Sanjay Seth, again, in his analysis of Nehruvian socialism in India, observes that Indian appropriation of Marxist method and ideology raised the difficult specter of using a discourse emblematic of the West for the liberation of the East. Nehru, Seth shows, was ambivalent not only about using a European-centered method of analysis but about entering into a teleology of Western industrial rationality that had produced, among other products, colonialism. Marxism ultimately appealed to Nehru as this rationality purged of its own racism: "Marxism," writes Seth, "became and presented itself, often explicitly, as the fulfillment and true heir to the Enlightenment, a knowledge expunged of its 'bourgeoise' limitations and mistakes, and thus constituted as a true science."[26] The manifestation of this purging was Lenin's support of national liberation struggles. "Rationalism and nationalism were reconciled with the aid of historicism, for Western science and industry could now be praised and emulated by a militant nationalism— precisely by postulating their socio-historical origins, rather than their origins in a specific spirit or culture."[27] Vis-à-vis my earlier discussions of diasporic hybridity, Nehru's dilemma was negotiating between materialist and culturalist/raciological epistemologies for thinking East and West, and of the possibilities for their mutual liberation. Seth elaborates: "It was this combination of Marxism's endorsement of nationalism, and its development into the most consistent form of Enlightenment rationalism, which facilitated its appropriation by nationalism of the Nehruvian variety, one which was also committed to modernisation, and also wedded to notions of science and progress."[28]

We will find a remarkably similar revisionist logic at work in the writings of other twentieth-century African American and Asian American radicals who, like Nehru, struggled to apply Marxian theory not just to Asian liberation struggles but to struggles in Africa and African America. In the process, as has often been noted, numerous features of Marxian analysis would be radically revised and reformed. Most famously, colored people themselves, particularly peoples of African and Asian descent, would often come to supplant the international (i.e., European) working class. From the early-century work of Marcus Garvey, to the anti-imperialist political organizations of the U.S. 1960s like the Revolutionary Action Movement, African American political writers like Robert F. Williams, Max Stanford, and James Boggs would come to use "black" to describe not just all peoples of color across Africa, Latin America, and Asia but the vanguard class of world revolution. This logic of equivalence, or relationality, derived from intellectual linkages between racial (or national) and class-based theories of analysis that necessarily bridged the hemispheres of struggle. This reconciliation became its own dialectical movement within Western Enlightenment discourse—not identity or hybridity movements, though they have been transformed at times into such, but a movement to reimagine black and Asian people as handholding grave diggers of Western capitalist modernity. It also mirrored the theoretical advances of anticolonial writers, among them M. N. Roy, Robert Williams, and Mao Tse-tung. Later, I will examine how in particular key figures and locations, like Detroit, played a seminal role in the translation of Maoist theory into a practice of local and international struggle. The centripetal and central force driving this struggle, I will argue, was a materialist analysis meant to distinguish itself from its culturalist variant as practiced by black and Asian radicals elsewhere in the United States. Detroit's own political and cultural development during the Black Power era, I will argue, was a culminating moment of revolutionary engagement with the principles of what is often referred to as the Bandung era of anticolonial struggle. At the same time, Detroit's Black Arts movement (BAM) reflected the struggle to delineate definitions of the "cultural" as an argument for political work that might consecrate Afro-Asian exchange. Mao's seminal "Talks on the Forum at Yenan," a touchstone for many BAM artists and theorists, raised these issues in regard to national (and ethnic) definitions of cultural practice.

The international circulation of 1960s Afro-Asian liberation discourses is thus a logical extension of questions urgent to efforts to define transnational affiliations. *Afro-Orientalism*'s title points to the at times unresolved contradictions and intentions that have haunted (and inspired) answers to these questions. Indeed, many of the debates within contemporary academic discourse about race, hybridity, and the nation are forecast by the tradition of Afro-Asian exchange that this book attempts to describe.

Afro-Orientalism and Hybridity:
Disciplinary Routes and Roots

Postcolonial studies and African American studies have grown up with some degree of historical and intellectual parallelism while remaining, professionally and methodologically, discrete. The importation to, and influence in, the United States for the past fifteen years of a Birmingham-influenced model of black cultural studies, particularly hybridity theory itself, has been an effort to mend, if not tear down, these fences. Its critiques of racial essentialism and insistence on blackness as a global phenomena have helped U.S. scholars in particular recognize the limits of both nationalist and racially essentialist views of black and other subaltern experience. Yet as Tiffany Ruby Patterson and Robin D. G. Kelley have noted, the rush to embrace diasporic paradigms has also contributed to a tendency to view all diasporic moments as equal and thus to eradicate the local conditions of their making, on one hand, and to forget that diaspora is itself a process and condition mirroring the history of imperialism and Western racism. Patterson and Kelley theorize diaspora, diaspora studies, and by implication Africana studies in ways that alert us to their relationship to the discursive practice with which this study is also concerned, Orientalism.

> Along with the African diaspora's long history is the equally broad-based impact of its conceptualization. Scholars' efforts to understand the black world beyond the boundaries of nation-state have profoundly affected the way we write the history of the modern world. The making of a "black

Atlantic" culture and identity, in general, and pan-Africanism, in particular, was as much the product of "the West" as it was of internal developments in Africa. Racial capitalism, imperialism, and colonialism—the processes that created the current African diaspora—shaped African culture(s) while transforming Western culture itself. In saying this, we are not speaking of the "black Atlantic" as merely "countercultural," but as an integral part of the formation of the modern world as we know it. One reason that New World black cultures appear "counter" to European narratives of history is that Europe exorcized blackness in order to create its own invented traditions, empires, and fictions of superiority and racial purity.[29]

One way of interpreting Patterson and Kelley's argument is as a warning that both the making of black diaspora and the attempts to claim it as a paradigm can be suffused with the same reifying tendencies that produced Western racism itself. Recognizing "blackness" as, like Orientalism's Asia, an "exorcism" whose process included creating and sustaining the traditions of racial supremacy and superiority of Western culture should give us pause to proceed carefully before rushing to embrace blackness, or diaspora, as its countercultural Other. This tendency is responsible for what I have already described as the culturalist fundamentalism that is part of the Afro-Orientalist tradition. It is precisely thinking about blackness as a corrective to Eurocentrism that has led to the profoundly ahistoricist (and even racist) readings of both black and Asian culture that began, as we shall see momentarily, early in the history of black experience in the United States and play on today, particularly in the arenas of American popular culture. From Martin Delany to Du Bois to Malcolm X to Wu Tang Klan, the temptation to privilege diaspora and diaspora culture has produced a paradigm that veers dangerously close to the celebratory multiculturalism about which Prashad also warns us. Paul Gilroy's important book *The Black Atlantic: Modernity and Double Consciousness* offers a nuanced but extremely influential example. Near the end of the chapter titled "The Black Atlantic as Counterculture of Modernity," Gilroy writes:

I have already implied that there is a degree of convergence here with other projects towards a critical theory of society, particularly Marxism. However, where lived crisis and systemic crisis come together, Marxism allocates priority to the latter while the memory of slavery insists on the priority of the former. Their convergence is also undercut by the simple fact that in the critical thought of blacks in the West, social self-creation through labour is not the centre-piece of emancipatory hopes. For the descendants of slaves, work signifies only servitude, misery, and subordination. Artistic expression, expanded beyond recognition from the grudging gifts offered by the masters as a token substitute for freedom from bondage, therefore becomes the means towards both self-fashioning and communal liberation. Poiesis and poetics begin to coexist in novel forms—autobiographical writing, special and uniquely creative ways of manipulating spoken language, and, above all, the music. All three have overflowed from the containers that the modern nation-state provides for them.[30]

Gilroy identifies the cultural as the sphere that organically realizes diasporic form, overflowing the boundaries of the nation-state. The realm of materiality—including work, economic process, and the Marxism that would be heir to its study—is by implication static, reified, nation bound, a kind of dead white history from which black culture seeks to awaken us. There are numerous obvious complications to this formula: as Kelley, Patterson, and Prashad note, capital's movement directed diaspora at nearly every turn, including the movement of black labor *and* culture, and particularly in our notorious age of globalization, the two remain constantly interdependent. Indeed, one is tempted to find evidence here of Dirlik's (and Aijaz Ahmad's) contention that postcolonial theory at times constructs itself as the means of avoiding or allegorizing the consequences of global capitalism by whatever name we want to give it. At the least, Gilroy's idealist formulation has much in common with the Enlightenment logic he seeks to critique, namely, a fetishization of subjectivity as transcendental universal sign, albeit here as a sign of blackness. Diaspora and hybridity are, in his words, the basis of a new "planetary humanity."[31] Its ideological base is the privileging of lived over systemic experience, a move that depends on a tactical essentialism (or humanism) that our contemporary moment of scholarship has troubled in ways too numerous to list here. Indeed, the universalizing tendency within Gilroy's discourse—"in the critical thought of Blacks in the West . . . for the descendants of slaves"—depends on essentializing geographies that are likewise fundamental to the premise of a black Atlantic (as Marcus Rediker and Peter Linebaugh have shown in *The Many-Headed Hydra*, to take one example, that same Atlantic was often motley)[32] and, I would argue, vaguely Orientalist.

Likewise, Gilroy's narrow attention to a decidedly Westernized triangle of influence—Europe/Africa/North America—occludes significant areas of the diasporic world and black experience. Most recently, for example, Kate Baldwin has assessed the travelings to Soviet Russia of Claude McKay, Langston Hughes, W. E. B. Du Bois, and Paul Robeson. Baldwin argues that the Soviet Union, and Soviet Communism, were crucial components for each of these thinkers in imagining the place of black people in the modern world. Each similarly perceived affiliations among populations of Africans, Slavs, and other ethnic minorities in Soviet Russia living on the margins of Western capitalism, feudalism, and colonialism.[33] Stalin's and Lenin's writings on the national question had drawn black American intellectuals like Du Bois to a conception of Soviet Communism as an alternative not just to capitalism but to white supremacy. The Soviet Union's geographic affiliation with the East likewise complicated early-century hemispheric definitions of race. The occlusion of these moments in preceding paradigms of diaspora speaks, as Baldwin notes, not just to a rather narrow and Westernized epistemology ruling American (and, I would add, African American) studies but to the deep-seated influence of anti-Communism, one fairly clearly marked in Gilroy's own paradigmatic work. My own study of Afro-Orientalism might then be seen as complementary to Baldwin's, shifting the critical gaze to African American engagement with Asia proper. It also complements her efforts to read Communism and Marxist thought back into an organic history of African American intellectual work. Where my study deviates from hers is in locating the scene of Afro-Orientalism most often on U.S. soil, and measuring the companion contributions of Asian Americans to the rich discursive mix of thought on race, nation, and internationalism.

In so doing, *Afro-Orientalism* hopes to challenge other limitations evolving from the casual consensus at times dominating celebrations of hybridity theory. Gilroy is one of several critics who assert the hybrid as an alternative to cultural nationalism and racial essentialism: "Against this choice stands another, more difficult option: the theorisation of creolisation, metissage, mestizaje, and hybridity."[34] This metaphor for cultural exchange, as many other critics have noted, often cannot help but reiterate the more nefarious features of cultural or biological essentialism it intends to undermine. Indeed, with its emphasis on ethnic crossing or mixing, as critics like Marcial Gonzalez have shown, hybridity/mestizaje theory tends to reinforce the empirical, geographical, and biological fact of boundaries and borders, resuscitating the imperatives it had hoped to overturn.[35] Gilroy unconsciously redraws these borders the further we travel his diasporic roots and routes. His attack on what he calls the "New Racism" of the postbiological period culminating in the biopolitics of World War II appears to offer to critique both nationalism and racial essentialism by assaulting "bioculturalism," the synthesis of old opposites of racial thinking, primarily nature and culture, biology and history. Against this, and against race, Gilroy posits diaspora and diasporic consciousness as a way of surpassing "the idea of natural difference by the claims of mutually exclusive, national cultures."[36] Gilroy appears, that is, to premise his argument on an attack against culturalist fundamentalism. Yet Gilroy's own definitions of diaspora appear to resuscitate fundamentalist thinking about diaspora's capacity to represent the black world.

> As an alternative to the metaphysics of "race," nation and bounded culture coded into the body, diaspora is a concept that problematizes the cultural and historical mechanics of belonging. It disrupts the fundamental power of territory to determine identity by breaking the simple sequence of explanatory links between place, location, and consciousness. It destroys the naive invocation of common memory as the basis of particularity in a

similar fashion by drawing attention to the contingent political dynamics of commemoration. . . .

. . . Consciousness of diaspora affiliation stands opposed to the distinctively modern structures and modes of power orchestrated by the institutional complexity of nation-state. Diaspora identification exists outside of and sometimes in opposition to the political forms and codes of modern citizenship.[37]

The self that, like culture, overflows the boundaries of the nation-state escapes both nationalist and raciological ways of thinking. Yet "consciousness of diaspora affiliation" itself constitutes a consciousness based on the *state* (or lack thereof) of identity, rather than challenging the "mechanism" of the nation-state that still produces that consciousness—Gilroy says it "stands opposed" to the state without in any way showing how. As Brent Edwards has noted of Gilroy's diasporic trope, "One is left uncertain about what 'the African diaspora's consciousness of itself' might refer to—where that self-awareness might be located."[38] Thus the "institutional complexity" of nation-states that perforce enforce crucial "mechanics of belonging" such as living standards, education, housing, voting, political organizing, religion, and even work—these so-called "political forms and codes of modern citizenship"—is largely unexamined as specific locations or practices in his work. At best, it seems to me, Gilroy offers identity politics without the politics, positing diaspora consciousness as a new form of "common memory" while mystifying the public sphere where identity will live. To again invoke Evelyn Hu-DeHart: "Diasporic notions of culture, if employed without due regard to the social and political complexities of so-called diasporic populations, may issue in reifications of their own, opening the way to new forms of cultural dominations, manipulations, and commodification."[39] Gilroy wends his way through an internal dialectical debate between biological and culturalist ways of thinking about race and reinvents the latter as relief from the former. This is another way of understanding the intellectual and moral frisson in Gilroy's advocacy of what he calls "anti-essentialist essentialism." Afro-Orientalism prefers, in its place, strategic antiessentialism: an insistence on what Prashad calls a dialectical view of race and culture that seeks to leave vestiges of debate over authenticity, purity, and its opposites by the side of the road.

Disciplining Race:
Afro-Orientalism and Some Roads Not Taken

In addition to bringing a new critical framework to bear on diaspora and hybridity theory, seeing Afro-Orientalism as a continuing thematic in U.S. intellectual thought also helps to underscore formations of racial and ethnic studies in the American university. The road to the current moment in African American studies, ethnic studies, and postcolonial studies passes through and incorporates many of the tendencies, questions, and resolutions to be identified in this historical study. National liberation and race theory, for example, is the bridge from twentieth- to nineteenth-century Afro-Orientalism as it developed in the United States, a bridge that again triangulates African America, Asia, and Europe. In his 1998 book *Afrotopia: The Roots of African American Popular History*, Wilson Moses delineates the varieties of African American philosophical idealism that have deployed Asia as a trope for political and intellectual aims, most of them nationalist in outlook. Primary among them were black Egyptocentrists, who were among the first to claim ancient Egyptian ancestry for black Americans. Egypt's place in the hemispheres of the nineteenth century was, as scholars from J. A. Rogers to Martin Bernal have shown, and as Malcolm X discovered in prison, no innocent matter. In a debate that can only be understood as a tributary in the stream of an idea like Afro-Orientalism, claims for Egypt as either fundamentally white and Hellenic (and thus Western) or black, African, or Asiatic undergirded both racist and antiracist discourses applied vigorously to the lives of African Americans. Black Egyptocentrists, Moses argues, attempted to "prove that black people were something more than semi-humans, cultural parasites who could do nothing more than crudely imitate the achievements of the white race."[40] Doing so required "the attempt to reconstruct the peoples of ancient Egypt in terms of traditional American racial perceptions" (6). Whether these efforts were oppressive or liberatory, in the manner of Chinese Occidentalism, is a subject for another book. However, the effort and strategy were reiterated across a range of other nineteenth-century African American political programs: Ethiopianism, a teleological approach to black history based on Psalms 68:31, prophesying that "princes shall come out of Egypt; Ethiopia shall soon stretch forth her hands unto God"; redemptionism, which, in Moses's words, "attempted to reconcile the slogan African for the Africans with the modernizing formulas of the so-called three C's, Christianity, Commerce, and Civilization" (26); and early Afrocentrism, which attracted the broadest spectrum of prominent black intellectuals of the nineteenth century and the early twentieth. These included Frances Ellen Watkins Harper, Martin Delany, Alexander Crummell, Edward Wilmot Blyden, Pauline Hopkins, and later W. E. B. Du Bois and Marcus Garvey. In 1859, Delany left on an exploratory venture to West Africa with the goal of creating "Africa for the African race and black men to rule them" (25). The dominant methodology of early Afrocentrists, according to Moses, was to describe black experience in the Western world as a "historiography of decline" necessitating a counterdiscourse, Afrocentrism, to restore the ancient greatness of the race. The objective for Afrocentrists, writes Wilson, was the future creation of a nation-state where black Americans could establish and control once and for all their historical destiny.

Yet just as nineteenth-century Marxist theory could not develop outside of—and was entirely dependent on—Europe's attempted mastery of Africa and Asia, so did nineteenth-century African Americans find themselves working within and against dominant European discourses of race. Afrocentrists, in particular, found themselves adopting aspects of profoundly racist European discourse as a means of defining their own nationalism. Central to this influence was the nineteenth-century racial theorist Count Arthur d'Gobineau, whose work stands at something like the crossroads of many of the themes and ideas in this book. In 1856 Gobineau published his widely influential book *Essai sur le inequalité de les races* (Essay on the Inequality of the Races). Heavily influenced by nineteenth-century biology, particularly classificatory science, the book identified three primary racial species or types: Aryan, Asiatic, and Semitic. Into the last category were folded most dark-skinned peoples, including blacks. Gobineau, concerned about racial intermixing, described the Aryan and Semitic races as naturally "repulsive" to one another. He also gendered the races, as if for breeding purposes, assigning a feminine quality to the African race and a masculine quality to the European (77). Yet Gobineau also speculated that Negro blood held special properties, particularly regarding passion and the aesthetics, that, once infused, could foster creativity in other races. Further, he argued that the special creativities of ancient Egyptians, Assyrians, Grecians, and Etruscans owed to the presence of black blood. Such knowledge, received by Afrocentric American nationalists, was the scientific vindication they were looking for, and an important contribution to the emerging cultural mythology of Afrocentrism as a counterdiscourse to white racism. Frederick Douglass's "The Claims of the Negro" parroted Gobineau's "creativity" thesis regarding black blood (124). Martin Delany followed Gobineau's lead by accepting that the biblical Ham—the prototypical sinner on which elaborate pro-slavery treatises were based—was, as the masters had declared, a Negro. Following from this premise, Delany argued that Ham and Cush had settled a colony in Asia, "contiguous to Egypt," according to Moses, from which they entered through Isthmus into Africa. Ham was thus an original settler of Egypt, the person on whom the Egyptians based their god Ammon, and for whom the pyramid of Cheops was constructed (84). Conversely, George Wells Parker adopted Gobineau's early "hybridity" theory to argue that Egyptians, Assyrians, Grecians, and Etruscans were "nothing but half-breeds, mulattoes" (77). Gobineau's pioneering scientific racism also endeared him, as Said notes, to the fellow scientists, biologists, and adventurers in his wake who formalized the political and racial discourse of Orientalism. Beyond that, his work was a seminal influence on German fascism.

Gobineau's critical influence on African American conceptions of race and nationalism would also become a linchpin in the famous critical divide between Marcus Garvey and W. E. B. Du Bois. The celebrated Garvey–Du Bois debate in the years during and after World War I may be understood as a divide over the two strands of Afro-Orientalist thinking I have been describing thus far, one primarily Marxian socialist in outlook, the other a form of culturalist fundamentalism. Before World War I, Du Bois and Garvey shared a roughly contiguous Egyptocentric outlook commemorating Nilotic cultures as the sources of world civilization and offering a form of what Moses calls "anthropological Afrocentrism" to project an image of a monumental African past linked to ancient Asiatic culture. Both, likewise, reiterated features of nineteenth-century racial romanticism that had more in common than is generally acknowledged by scholars of their work. Blackness, for each, was a flexible metaphor able to include not only mulattoes but Asians, Africans, and Jews (194). Each was early on drawn to Asia via the influence of nineteenth-century Egyptocentrism and Afrocentrism, particularly in their early writings on race and culture. Du Bois, for example, wrote that citizens of India and Egypt were "ancient friends, cousins, blood-brothers, in the hoary ages of antiquity" (284). In his poem "The Riddle of the Sphinx," Du Bois described "black men of Egypt and India, / Ethiopia's sons of the evening / Indians and yellow Chinese, / Arabian children of morning, / And mongrels of Rome and Greece." In 1913, Garvey worked as a messenger and handyman in the Fleet Street office of the *African Times and Orient Review*, a monthly magazine under the direction of Duse Mohamed Ali. The magazine began publishing in 1912 with the self-stated goal of creating a "Pan-Oriental Pan-African journal at the seat of the British Empire" (26). Nearly simultaneous with Du Bois, Garvey in 1915 published the poem "The Tragedy of White Injustice," which proposes, "Millenniums ago, when the white man slept / The great torch of light Asia kept" (195).

The Indian nationalist movement of the early century presented both Du Bois and Garvey with what might be called a secular challenge to this hoary romance. The movement began in response to the 1905 British partition of Bengal. By 1913, the Ghadr (Revolution) Party had been formed in the United States, comprised mainly of Indian nationals in exile. In 1915, Mahatma Gandhi, an early hero of Du Bois, returned to India from South Africa, where his war on apartheid was simultaneously beginning. In the same year, Lala Lajpat Rai, a founding member of the Hindu reformist movement, arrived in the United States, helping to found in 1917 the Indian Home Rule League of the United States and the important journal *Young India*. By 1920 both Garvey and Du Bois were speaking and writing regularly on behalf of Indian nationalism. On August 1, 1920, at a UNIA meeting at Madison Square Garden, Garvey noted that Ireland, Egypt, and India were simultaneously, in his words, "striking out for freedom."[41] He sent a message of solidarity to leaders of the Indian nationalist movement, asking them to "please accept best wishes of 400,000,000 Negroes through their representative."[42] Du Bois, meanwhile, wrote recurringly in columns for the *Crisis* in praise of Gandhi and Indian home rule. He became intimate friends with Lala Lajpat Rai. Between 1917 and 1928, when he published his novel *Dark Princess*, Du Bois predicted over and over in print that the Indian anticolonial movement held the key to the liberation of Africa, and by extension of people of color the world over.

Yet by 1925 their views of Asia were becoming a fundamental marker of difference in Garvey's and Du Bois's views of race and the place of people of color in the international world. The difference may best be measured by their responses to Japan's emergent twentieth-century imperial power. Garvey had confidently looked to Japan's leadership for black Americans in the immediate aftermath of World War I. The country was fast becoming what Prashad calls the "Ethiopia of Asia" in the minds of African Americans beset by the desires for an outlying beacon of racial hope.[43] Indeed, former followers of Garvey, including Robert O. Jordan, would in the 1930s cousin with Japanese nationalist Hikida Yasuichi to form the Ethiopia Pacific League, in effect an Afro-Asian alliance forged in protest of European assault on Ethiopia. The league's politics were racialist and nationalist in the extreme; Jordan famously earned the epithet "the Harlem Hitler."[44] Other crypto-nationalist groups forged from black-Japanese alliances like the Black Dragon Society appeared simultaneously. These movements were largely dissipated by the time of Japan's most egregious acts of imperialism like the rape of Nanking, but their popular hold on the political imaginations of small but earnest bands of mostly black urban working-class citizens testified to the appeal of Afro-Orientalism's right wing.

Meanwhile between the wars Du Bois underwent a chastening though dramatically conflictual struggle of his own with Japan's imperial extension of power. I will provide some details of that conflict in chapter 1, but its larger outline is instructive here as a culminating point to Afro-Orientalism's discursive place in this century. Du Bois's enthusiasm for Japanese world ascent after its 1904 conquest of Russia was nurtured by several streams: the imperialist venturings of World War I by the European powers; the continuing subordination of Asian colonies; the spread of Orientalist phobia in the United States; and the craving for a colored national model of autonomy. It was also fostered by selective support for Japanese nationalists in the United States. One example was Hikida Yasuichi, an agent of Japanese expansionism who arrived in the United States after Japan's failed proposal for a racial equality amendment to the League of Nations Covenant. According to David Levering Lewis, Hikida attempted to capitalize on African American sympathy for the proposal by speaking at historically black colleges.[45] Du Bois later recalled meeting Hikida around 1930. In 1935, Hikida expressed enthusiasm for Du Bois's plans to return to the United States from his scheduled European trip via Russia, China, Japan, and Hawaii, and helped to plan in careful detail Du Bois's trips to Manchukuo (Japanese-occupied Manchuria) and Japan in 1936. Levering Lewis writes that, on his subsequent trip, Du Bois met with the president of Manchukuo State Railways, observed separate elementary schools for Manchurians and Japanese, and noted "no racial superiority on the part of the occupiers."[46] He next visited Tientsin, China's second-largest port city recently incorporated into the Japanese sphere of influence, and then Shanghai. The latter's population of 3 million was at the time subject to Japanese, British, Russian, and U.S. colonial presence. In a remarkable report in the *Pittsburgh Courier*, one of many dispatches from his trip, Du Bois compared the streets of Shanghai to those of Mississippi. At a luncheon in his honor at the Chinese Bankers' Club, Du Bois also challenged members of the city's elite to answer the questions, "How do you propose to escape from the domination of European capital? How are your working classes progressing?"[47] Whatever the response, Du Bois was not pleased. He left China persuaded that its compliance with colonial rule was a form of complicity akin to Uncle Tomism. Japanese force, he concluded, was preferable to Chinese obeisance. The transference of one image of black benignity to an Asian counterpart highlights the gravitas of Afro-Orientalism's infectious hold. It carried for the moment the massive weight of containing and resolving the contradictions of white empire. Levering Lewis notes:

> In the winter of 1936–1937, the political map of the world looked almost unchanged from how it had appeared to Du Bois at the turn of the century. Defeated Hohenzollern Germany and Ottoman Turkey had been deprived of extensive African and Middle Eastern real estate under various League of Nations fictions of benefit to Great Britain and France: Iraq and Palestine as British mandates; Syria and Lebanon as French mandates; Libya to Italy. Egypt and India were still British whatever mainly formalistic concessions had been enacted or were promised by Westminster. South Africa belonged to Great Britain. Central Africa was Belgian. North Africa belonged to France. Indo-China belonged to France. Indonesia belonged to Holland. China, like much of Latin America under the protection of the Monroe Doctrine, existed in the iron vise of informal imperialism. The political map of the world, then, colored British red, French green, and even Portuguese yellow, was, in Du Bois's eyes, simply everlastingly white, and the whitest sector of the map was in black Africa. Certain that he had found an answer to Africa's subjugation in the rise of Japan, he would accept with chilling equanimity the Japanese rampage in China and its voracious appetite in the Pacific.[48]

Yet as I will demonstrate in detail in chapter 1, Du Bois's critical reflections on Asia did not end there. Indeed, it was later reflection and rumination on his Japanese "mistake" that moved Du Bois ultimately and decidedly in the firm direction of a materialist analysis of imperialism, race, and capitalism. Garvey meanwhile delved further into blood and soil notions of culture, anticipating Senghor's and Césaire's adoption and revival of Gobineau's pseudoscience for the construction of the negritude movement. Offered competing and complementary views of Pan-Africanism by the growing Pan-Asian movement of the early twentieth century, Garvey and Du Bois came to ultimately conflicting and irreconcilable views of diaspora: the former delineating a nativist politics of return, the latter struggling, not always successfully, to wed antiracist politics to a materialist internationalism. This negotiation drew Du Bois steadily and magnetically in the twin directions of Asia and Marxist theory, ultimately reconciled in his 1958 visit to the Soviet Union and his 1959 visit to Maoist China, and Garvey into a détente with the Ku Klux Klan over shared convictions about racial essence and miscegenation— the U.S. end zone and endgame for Gobineauian Orientalism.

So understanding the role of Asia in the Du Bois–Garvey debate can also help us understand several other trajectories and roads taken and *not* taken in contemporary critical discourse within African American and postcolonial studies. I have already suggested, for example, that Afro-Orientalism, as its own intellectual lifeline, offers a like but different way of reading diaspora and hybridity. In recent years, Orientalism's place in more contemporary formations of African American studies has also been alluded to in ways that bear further thought. For example, in the spring 2000 issue of the *Black Scholar*, Ali A. Mazrui attacked Henry Louis Gates Jr.'s PBS video documentary *Wonders of the African World*, accusing the author of "Black Orientalism." "The question which has been raised by Skip Gates' television series is whether it signifies the birth of Black Orientalism," wrote Mazrui. "Are we witnessing the birth of a new Black paradigm which combines cultural condescension with paternalistic possessiveness and ulterior selectivity?"[49] Mazrui's attacks on Gates underscored the touristic, voyeuristic, and reductive aspects of its representation of African history. It perceived the show, rightly, as a patronized and subsidized colonial excursion into Africa, bringing with it the distortive baggage of middlebrow America. Yet Mazrui's apt attack on a very bad piece of television should not stand in isolation. *Wonders of the African World* symbolized what might be called an imperial moment in Africana studies. African American studies' general emergence out of a turbulent period of political and intellectual strife in 1960s America included numerous paradigmatic struggles over the course of "black" studies in the university. The shapes of those contesting paradigms have been discussed elsewhere: they include, but are not limited to, models of diaspora, Afrocentrism, cultural studies, black nationalism. None of the dominant models or paradigms that emerged and were instituted in the 1970s and afterward took the form that many black, Chicano, and Asian activists of that period were calling for, namely, a Third World or internationalist studies. The rejection of these models resulted in a more essentialist conception of Africana studies, and the deferral—and ultimately separate development—of postcolonial studies as something outside and different from its more aggressively politicized alternatives. The moment of dialectical linkage between black Americans and other national groups in disciplinary formation in the academy was likewise delayed and ultimately morphed into a model more compatible with a multicultural conception of race and ethnicity, one that helped give birth to the paradigms of hybridity and diaspora discussed earlier in this introduction.

What this earlier moment of disciplinary identity formation also replicated was a distinctively Western epistemological leap of faith. As with Martin Delany's African voyage of the nineteenth century to establish a black nation-state, so the arrival of black studies programs in American universities announced a reversal of the historiography of decline for African Americans in the West. Black studies would now do the important and much-needed work of identifying the black subject as a subject of study, thus making visible the historical erasures of blackness in the West. Black studies, that is, was imagined fundamentally as a counter-discourse to modernity.

Yet despite the significant inroads of alternative models and methods like diaspora studies, and the impress of globalization and postcolonialism and vital academic discourses, black studies has too often complacently accepted itself, as Tiffany Patterson and Robin Kelley have playfully noted, as how the West was won/one.[50] I have already made a case, for example, that the general scholarly ignorance of the vast body of writing by Du Bois on Asia represents a significant diminishing of understanding of many of his essential ideas, including that of the color line. It has sacrificed analysis of his Pan-Asianism to his interest in Pan-Africanism, and ultimately Du Bois's complication of both. Likewise, it has prevented scholars in postcolonial studies from identifying a canon of writing on Asia by African Americans dating to the mid-nineteenth century and has discouraged scholars in African American studies from thinking of their work as global. In short, the absence of attention to Asia in Africana studies, and to African American writing on Asia in postcolonial studies, has been an Orientalist albatross for both fields.

The hyphen in Afro-Orientalism, then, hopes to function as a speculative bridge over and across these disciplinary and political divides. It represents the dialectical relationship that writers of African and Asian descent have long created *for themselves* as intellectual and political wiggle room between and among traditional Westernized disciplinary understandings (or knowledges, in the Foucauldian sense) of race, nation, ethnicity, and empire. Indeed, one of the common stories told by the writers and activists to be discussed here is of their positive alienation from most of the West's own racial, political, and even academic classifications. They include, in addition to Du Bois, the novelist Richard Wright, the civil rights advocate and later exile-to-China Robert F. Williams, activist authors James and Grace Lee Boggs, and the contemporary cultural worker Fred Ho. The first four are African American, the last two Asian American. The fourth and fifth were married. Excepting Wright and Du Bois, none has been studied carefully in relationship to each other, despite the singular intellectual trajectory of thought on Afro-Asia their work represents. Placing them together, rather than a display of mestizaje practice, is meant to suggest the ideological kinship and dialectical sharing generated by their endeavors to move outside conventional understandings of culturalism and identity and to forge new political movements. Indeed, I will demonstrate how for each, an intellectual engagement with Afro-Orientalism facilitated or was produced out of a recognition of learned activist crisis in their own lives and work that produced a variation on what Wright calls "negative loyalty" to the West. That is, for each of these writers, recognizing the need to build a better world coincided with the recognition of their own positive alienation not just from the West's capitalism and racism but from existing political and cultural movements that could not easily accommodate their revolutionary conceptions of Afro-Asian exchange, affiliation, and activism. *Afro-Orientalism* thus aspires to stand side by side with, and on the shoulders of, these pioneering thinkers. It does so in hopes of finding its own counternarrative to tales of the diasporic West that have placed so many of us interested in a better world in the same boat.

Chapter Summary

Chapter 1 of *Afro-Orientalism* retells the evolution of the political and cultural thought of W. E. B. Du Bois through examination of his lifelong body of work on Asia. Du Bois viewed the relationship between the modern and ancient worlds of Asia and Africa as a dialectical site of struggle for the future of the races of men. It was also the testing ground for most of his internal struggles with concepts of culture, nationalism, racial authenticity, and, toward the end of his life, Marxism. The evolution of Du Bois's ideas regarding Africa and its role in the Western world is also incomprehensible, this chapter argues, without careful attention to his analysis of Asia as its fraternal twin in global struggle. Particularly in his 1928 novel *Dark Princess*, long out of print but now rightfully restored to prominence by the University Press of Mississippi, Du Bois provided a map of Afro-Asian relations predictive of much of the twentieth century that followed.

Chapter 2 examines in tandem Richard Wright's exiled writings on Asia and Africa. The chapter argues that Wright's fraught and shifting analyses of race, and Marxism, reflect his conception of himself as "Outsider," a figure transcending the entirety of his career but most clearly understandable in his writings on colonialism. This same figure can be described as a figure for the Orientalist. Wright's unresolved relationship to Western modernity and a Western epistemology superseded his early commitment to historical materialism. As he moved further from the citadel of Western empire, he was ironically drawn back to its telos and epistemology as a way to assess the non-Western world. This led Wright into essentialist judgments and hostile conceptions of both race and historical materialism. It also eliminated the possibility of a dialectical resolution of themes in his writing. The chapter contends that Wright's exiled writings of the 1950s thus constitute a key chapter not only in his career but in the career of Afro-Asian thought and exchange, particularly on the question of colonialism.

Chapter 3 documents forms of political and cultural correspondence practiced among Afro-Asian radicals during the so-called Bandung era from 1955 to 1973. Black American radicals and cultural workers in Detroit constructed imaginative forms of solidarity with Third World struggles in Asian countries by forging internationalist links through intertextual strategies of exchange. A crucial conduit for this process was the fugitive NAACP organizer Robert F. Williams. During his exile to Cuba and China from 1961 to 1969, Williams became a literal and figurative correspondent for sympathetic internationalists in Asia and black America. Much of the cultural work produced under the Black Arts movement rubric in Detroit also found direct inspiration in Mao's famous Yenan Forum address on the arts, and more generally in the example of China's Cultural Revolution. This chapter will explore the strategy of transnational correspondence as a means of building a dialectical Afro-Asian exchange across continents, and redefining notions of East and West by rethinking the political geography of cities like Detroit.

Chapter 4 makes a careful examination of the evolution in political thought of the most significant Afro-Asian collaboration in U.S. radical history, the marriage of James and Grace Lee Boggs. Architects of and participants in some of the most vital grassroots political organizing of the twentieth century, the Boggses' work stands at the crossroads of important Marxist and anticolonial writings attempting to synthesize in particular the struggles of Afro-Asians as "people of color" and representatives of the world proletariat. Beginning with their work with the Trinidadian Marxist C. L. R. James, up through their serious study and use of Maoist theory during the Black Power movement, the Boggses consistently used a dialectical comprehension of race and class—and, toward the latter stages of their careers, gender—to fashion a fundamentally Marxian theory of liberation. Even in moments of contention and disavowal, their durable theory of "dialectical humanism" has remained faithful to the premises of Marx and Engels's assessment of colonialism and racism as the brute forces underpinning the exploitation of the majority of the world's citizens. This chapter will delineate the growth and movement with Boggsism to bridge seminal moments of transformation in the century that comprises the story of Afro-Orientalism. It will also identify the independent trajectory of Grace's own body of thought after the death of her partner and comrade in 1993.

Chapter 5 will take up the work of the important Asian American jazz musician and composer Fred Ho. The creator and leader of the Afro-Asian Music Ensemble, and a veteran of both early Black Arts and Asian Pacific American movements, Ho has devised an Afro-Asian cultural politics based in what he describes as "new Afro-Asian multicultural music." Borrowing liberally from Marxist, anticolonialist, and feminist theory, Ho's work puts the props back in agitprop. His performances, operas, recordings, and martial arts ballets are dialectical revisions of signal moments in the intertwined history of African and Asian descendants. Each is revised to accord with a parallel or continuous stream of cultural and political struggle emerging from its twin tradition. Ho describes his own radical hybridity as guerrilla theater, or what I call trickster jazz. It summons up linguistic, musical, and political touchstones of subversion and liberation from Afro-Asian culture and deploys them in the service of a revolutionary vanguardism beyond the boundaries of mainstream taste and consumer culture. Ho is indeed liberal multiculturalism's worst nightmare: a serious class antagonist who refuses to release the dream of a Third World internationalist aesthetic. As such he looks backward at the Afro-Asian century and forward into a future where Afro-Orientalism may yet do the work of changing the world.

CHAPTER 1

W. E. B. Du Bois's Afro-Asian Fantasia

> Last night I sat in Utopia and saw Egypt and India, Africa and the
> South Seas parade in the sleek sweet splendor of Parisian finery made
> and planned in High Harlem. It was a lovely sight—such a poem as
> only colored New York can do, and do it carelessly, laughingly,
> perfectly, bathed in light and music.
>
> —W. E. B. Du Bois, *Crisis*, June 1922

> At last India is rising again to that great and fateful moral leadership
> of the world which she exhibited so often in the past in the lives of
> Buddha, Mohammed, and Jesus Christ, and now again in the life of
> Gandhi. . . . This mighty experiment, together with the effort of
> Russia to organize work and distribute income according to some
> rule of reason, are the great events of the modern world. The black
> folk of America should look upon the present birth-pains of the
> Indian nation with reverence, hope and applause.
>
> —W. E. B. Du Bois, *Crisis*, 1930

W. E. B. Du Bois dedicated more writing to the subject of Asia than
any African American public intellectual before or after him. He visited
Asia twice, first in 1936 and again in 1959. The book he described as his
"favorite," *Dark Princess*, featured an Indian protagonist, Princess Kautilya. His columns, newspaper articles, and essays on Japan, China, and
India in the *Crisis*, the *Pittsburgh Courier*, the *Chicago Defender*, the *Aryan
Path*, and other periodicals number more than one hundred. In 1906,
only three years after he published *The Souls of Black Folk*, events in Asia
forced Du Bois to refine his prescription for the twentieth century.
About the recently completed war between Japan and Russia, Du Bois
wrote, "For the first time in a thousand years a great white nation has
measured arms with a colored nation and has been found wanting. The

Russo-Japanese war has marked an epoch. The magic of the word 'white' is already broken, and the Color Line in civilization has been crossed in modern times as it was in the great past. The awakening of the yellow races is certain. That the awakening of the brown and black races will follow in time, no unprejudiced student of history can doubt."[1]

In 1914, Du Bois again reconfigured his color line trope to predict "a great coming war of Races." In "The World Problem of the Color Line," he wrote, "If . . . men would look carefully around them . . . they would see that the Problem of the Color Line in America instead of being the closing chapter of past history is the opening page of a new era. All over the world the diversified races of the world are coming into close and closer contact as never before. We are nearer China today than we were to San Francisco yesterday."[2]

That his famous color line conception always included Asia is perhaps the most overlooked aspect of Du Bois's most hallowed formulation. Recovering this aspect is significant. Seeing the color line as both racial and hemispheric allows us to see all the things that Du Bois saw in his corpus of Asian writings: the history to antiquity of Afro-Asian exchange; global geographic border crossings; ongoing multiracial diasporas; emerging black Atlantics *and* Pacifics; infinite horizons of political possibility. Indeed, as the epigraphs to this chapter begin to make clear, across the span of his life, Du Bois tended to invest Asia and the Asiatic with his most far-flung hopes and desires as they pertained to a range of issues that preoccupied him: the political and biological relationships between colored peoples and nations; the role of culture in the definition and preservation of racial attributes; the fate of national, anticolonial, and other revolutionary struggles; the temporal and geographic parameters of ideas.

Yet the interpretive burden of these ambitions, suggested by the fantastical language with which he often expressed them, was also a recurring theme of much of Du Bois's Asian writings. On February 20, 1937, after his initial visit to China in the midst of its civil war and battle with imperialist Japan, Du Bois sketched this dilemma in his *Pittsburgh Courier* column in ways central to an understanding not only of his own lifelong body of thought but of the larger discourse I am calling Afro-Orientalism:

China is inconceivable. I have been here four days, and I am literally dazed. Never before has a land so affected me. For Africa I had more emotion—a greater wave of understanding and recognition. But China is to the wayfarer of a little week, and I suspect of a little year, incomprehensible. I have of course a theory, an explanation which brings some vague meaning to the mass of things I have seen and heard. But I know, as I have never known before, that in the face of a people and a human history, I have missed the whole meaning; perhaps even I have missed any significant part. But this I know: any attempt to explain the world, without giving a place of extraordinary prominence to China, is futile. Perhaps the riddle of the universe will be settled in China; and if not, in no part of the world that ignores China.[3]

Du Bois's conception of Asia as the solution to "the riddle of the universe" proposed Afro-Asian mutuality and recognition as a cornerstone of global liberation. Closing the geographic and knowledge divide between African Americans and Asian Americans was thus for Du Bois a task not peripheral but central to his lifework. Influenced by a wide range of views of race, culture, and empire, and particularly by the writings of Marx and Engels, Du Bois developed a dialectical brand of thought positing affiliation between blacks and Asians against white Western racism and capitalism as the central struggle bridging and binding the ancient and contemporary colored worlds. As in his earlier quotation on the Russo-Japanese War, Du Bois throughout his career welded quasi-mythic renderings of colored empires in antiquity to a secular, though idealized, socialist comprehension of the major political movements of the twentieth century. This synthetic and syncretic fusion has led Wilson Moses to describe Du Bois's resulting worldview as "Afrocentric Marxism."[4] I will both build on and revise Moses's view by demonstrating how both of these features of his thought depended heavily on his analysis of Asian countries and people. Indeed, I will argue that Du Bois's view of Asia informed many of his major theoretical formulas on race, including his central trope of "double consciousness," while determining more strongly than any other factor his turn to dialectical materialism after World War II. As with Marx and Engels, this task entailed a revisionist struggle against Enlightenment discourses of race and culture. At the same time, Du Bois's writings on Asia disclose an epistemological rupture in his intellectual development reflected in the sometimes-egregious breaches of judgment that accrued there. In his writings on Asian culture, his essays and poetry, and especially his 1928 novel *Dark Princess*, aptly subtitled *A Romance*, Du Bois both knowingly and unconsciously deployed Orientalist ideas and tropes that dramatize the peculiar and unique contradictions in his position as a black Western intellectual crisscrossing the hemispheric color line. These breaches were the subject of some of Du Bois's most revealing and significant self-criticism and self-revision, not always on display in his work and rarely attended to by critics. In all these aspects of his thought, Du Bois was typically capacious and prophetic, synthesizing the major tendencies underwriting African American writing on Asia dating to the nineteenth century, and predicting the byways, successes, and adjustments of later generations seeking to create Afro-Asian affiliation.

Wilson Moses has argued persuasively that Du Bois held a "unilinear conception of progress" predicated on the popular Afrocentric nineteenth-century notion that "the great civilizations of the past were Hamitic and therefore creations of the black Afro-Asiatic race."[5] Evidence that Du Bois shared some version of this idea exists in writings like his seldom-discussed "The Star of Ethiopia," a pageant of black history first written in 1911 and performed several times afterward until 1925. A four-page folder published with a 1915 production of the pageant described it as "the story of the history and development of the black race from the prehistoric times down to the present."[6] The pageant is presented in six episodes of "Argument." In episode 1, 50,000 years BC, African "Savages" flee from beast and storm, pray to Shango (the thunder god), and receive from his daughter Ethiopia the "Start of the Fire of Freedom." In episode 2, 5000 BC, "Asia mingles with the Egyptians. The Savage Shepherd Kings attack them. Ethiopia rescues them. The pharaohs of New Kingdom are crowned." In subsequent episodes from 1000 BC to 1750, Ethiopia triumphs, Christ is born, and war threatens between three world religions: Christianity, Mohammedanism, and Fetich. Ethiopia escapes, and in episode 5, "her children march." In the final episode, "Colored America appears," and the heralds "call the five rivers of Ethiopia, the Congo, the Nile, the Niger, the Mississippi and the Orinoco."[7]

In broad outline, the pageant follows the contributionist logic of nineteenth-century Egyptocentrism and Afrocentrism. In other writings on Egypt, Du Bois anticipated Bernal's *Black Athena* thesis, arguing that Egyptian and especially Ethiopian cultures were the Afro-Asiatic source of Greek and Roman culture in antiquity. In *The World and Africa*, for example, Du Bois argued strenuously that Egypt's mixture of black Africans and Mongoloids produced antiquity's most vital culture. "The Greeks," he wrote, "inspired by Asia, turned toward Africa for learning, and the Romans in turn learned of Greece and Egypt."[8] Elsewhere anticipating the work of scholars like Prashad, Du Bois described the precolonial ocean spheres as an Afro-Asian paradise lost to the incursion of Western imperialism. "The people of Malaya," he argued, "are yellow Mongolians grafted on Negroes; Negroes who were the greatest sailors of the ancient world and Mongolians who represented the great empires of China. In the 16th century, the castigation and degradation of the Malayan people began when the Portuguese occupied Malacca and began to seek cloves and nutmegs."[9] "This interpretation of Negro history," Du Bois added, "contradicts the theory of the natural and eternal inferiority of black folk, which rendered them natural slaves and a cheap labor force for nineteenth-century industry."[10] Recurringly looking backward to figures like Jupiter Hammon, and forward to Afrocentrists of every stripe, Du Bois argued that, beginning with the Renaissance and up through the end of the nineteenth century, Western modernity constructed itself on the bases and erasure of its Afro-Asiatic roots. The Renaissance was a "stolen legacy," to use J. A. Rogers's term, of "that new light with which Asia and Africa illumined the Dark Ages of Europe" (18). "Without the winking of an eye, printing, gunpowder, the smelting of iron, the beginnings of social organizations, not to mention political life and democracy, were attributed exclusively to the white race and to Nordic Europe" (20). Colonialism and the slave trade, meanwhile, were the motive forces and engines of Enlightenment telos meant to shackle the contributions of Afro-Asia: "Africa saw the stars of god; Asia saw the soul of man; Europe saw and sees only man's body, which it feeds and polishes until it is fat, gross, and cruel" (149).

Du Bois's juxtaposition of an acculturated Afro-Asia with a vulgar, bourgeoisified Europe in *The World and Africa* at once reveals the tensions implicit in what Moses calls his Afrocentric Marxism. Both Eric Williams's *Capitalism and Slavery* and George Padmore's *How Britain Rules Africa* were sources for Du Bois's book, which includes citation of the "rosy dawn of capitalist production" passage from *Capital* cited and discussed earlier. Indeed, *The World and Africa* was virtually a Marxist historiography of Du Bois's Afrocentrism, predicated on the linkage of the fate of peoples of African and Asian descent under capital. The cultural epoch from Renaissance to French Revolution that had eradicated the Afro-Asiatic roots of Western civilization was the cultural work of capitalism meant to separate white workers from "the degraded yellow and black peoples" (21). "His [the European worker's] aim and ideal was distorted. He did not wish to become efficient but rich. He began to want not comfort for all men, but power over other men for himself. He did not love humanity and he hated 'niggers'" (21). Thus *The World and Africa* called for a war on two fronts, separate but equal, bridging the fecund glory of Afro-Asian antiquity with the rosy future of a multiracial workers' paradise:

> Despite the crude and cruel motives behind her shame and exposure, her degradation and enchaining, the fire and freedom of black Africa, with the uncurbed might of her consort Asia, are indispensable to the fertilizing of the universal soil of mankind, which Europe alone would nor could give this aching earth. (260)

> On the other hand, if a world of ultimate democracy, reaching across the color line and abolishing race discrimination, can only be accomplished by method laid down by Karl Marx, then that method deserves to be triumphant no matter what we think or do. (258)

The story of Du Bois's Afro-Orientalism is the story of his long and contentious journey to these political and philosophical resolutions. It is also the story of his vision of an alternative modernity rooted in and routed through the African and Asian worlds. The joint time line of this diaspora tale begins in 1885. In that year the Indian National Congress was established, and Africa was partitioned at the Berlin Conference. The INC initiated stirrings of Pan-Asianism, which Du Bois perceived and wrote about frequently in his columns for *Crisis* and other publications. They included the 1900 Boxer Rebellion in China, the victory of Japan over Russia, and the 1906 Arab conference in Morocco. The Pan-Asian movement accelerated when Sun Yat-sen established the Pan-Asian Front in China after World War I. The front was a creation of the Black Dragon secret society, an organization that spread rapidly into Japan and into the teachings and preaching of both Japanese and African American nationalist militants in the United States. A second crucial moment for Du Bois's support of Pan-Asianism was the establishment of the Ghadr (Revolution) Party in San Franciso in 1913. Ghadr was formed by Indian national émigrés to the United States. In 1915, Lala Lajpat Rai, a founding member of the Hindu reformist movement, Arya Samaj, arrived in the United States to begin a five-year visit. In 1917, Rai helped to found the Indian Home Rule League of the United States and formed the journal *Young India*. Rai became Du Bois's fast friend and mentor to Indian nationalism. His influence manifests itself in Du Bois's promotion of *Young India* and his attention to the role of Gandhi both in his work in South Africa and upon his return to India in 1915. In 1921, Du Bois reported positively in *Crisis* on the national convention of the Friends of Freedom for India in New York City.[11] In 1922, Du Bois wrote a long article in support of swaraj, comparing Gandhi to Lenin. In the same year, the Soviet Comintern hosted numerous Indian nationals, among them the brilliant Bengali Brahman M. N. Roy, at a Congress of Eastern Peoples at Baku and held vigorous open debate on the "Eastern question" at the Comintern. Du Bois's collective attention to these events became transparent, as I will argue later, in *Dark Princess*, which is in part an allegory of the rise of Pan-Asianism.

Much better recorded in this same general interim between 1885 and 1915 are Du Bois's conception of, and support for, Pan-Africanism. The first Pan-African conference occurred the same year as the Boxer Rebellion, 1900. The simultaneous rise of Pan-Asia and Pan-Africa informed Du Bois's 1906 and 1914 essays cited earlier and was the basis of his "world color line" conception. Two key phenomena after 1910 also helped to motivate their dependency in Du Bois's mind: the rise and importation into the United States of scientific racism, particularly eugenics, and the outbreak of World War I. An example of Du Bois's efforts to conjoin these issues came in 1915. In that year Du Bois published "The African Roots of the War" in the *Atlantic Monthly* (later reprinted as "The Hands of Ethiopia" in his 1919 book *Darkwater*). There Du Bois again revised his 1903 color line thesis, viewing the war as an exaggeration of the divide between white Western Europe and the colored world. European countries supportive of colonialism drew Du Bois's condemnation and a call for "the trained man of darker blood" to organize against Europe.[12] The revised essay of 1919 also invoked biblical and nineteenth-century images of Ethiopia, with "hands of helplessness for an agonized God!" (74). The resurrection of Africa was symbolized by the ascent to the throne of Queen Nefertiti, who "redeemed the world and her people" (74). In "The Damnation of Women," published for the first time in *Darkwater* in 1919, Du Bois returned to the image of defiant black womanhood in antiquity: "the primal black All-Mother of men down through the ghostly throng of mighty womanhood, who walked in the mysterious dawn of Asia and Africa" (165). The black All-Mother is the progenitor of dark and dusky heroines of history—Cleopatra, Candace, Sojourner Truth. Du Bois names this mother figure as "Isis . . . the titular goddess," whose spell still pervades the land of Africa. Du Bois's final formulation is a global family tree descending from the primal moment of Afro-Asian commingling: "The father and his worship is Asia; Europe is the precocious, self-centered, forward-striving child; but the land of the mother is and was Africa" (166).

Du Bois's transhistorical rendition of an ancient Afro-Asian culture "siring" Europe miscegenated and inverted the biopolitics of an emerging eugenics discourse given urgent play in the United States in part by the outbreak of war. Its first significant book-length articulation was Madison Grant's 1916 *The Passing of the White Race, or The Racial Basis of European History*. That book deployed nineteenth- and early twentieth-century eugenics theory to argue that World War I constituted a thinning of the global Aryan blood supply. It included a foreword by Henry Fairfield Osborn, professor of anatomy at Princeton, calling for Anglo-Saxon superiority, the "elimination of defective infants," and sterilization of adults of "no value." The book's more general significance was in helping to initiate the widespread popularity of scientific racism in the United States, recruiting Anglo-Saxon mothers to the cause of racial reproduction, and framing World War I as a race war to stabilize white world supremacy. The book resonated with and deepened established U.S. national narratives of reproduction, genealogy, and citizenship (the "one drop" rule, for example) while codifying "race suicide" as a fate likely to befall Anglo-America in the face of increasing migration and population shifts. In a perceptive essay, Alys Eve Weinbaum argues that the recurring appearance of the "primal black All-Mother" in Du Bois's World War I–era writings bespeaks a lifelong effort to write within and against these sexual and reproductive politics. Weinbaum argues that the black All-Mother figure signals Du Bois's effort to create an image of "black belonging in the world" via the productive and reproductive power of black women. Resisting a "national genealogy" that would exclude them, Du Bois attempted to create instead a countergenealogy of black womanhood. Weinbaum's "globality" trope suggests in another register the pan-internationalism I have been describing, conceptually wedded to the historical relationships between Africa and Asia, or even perceived as its apotheosis.[13]

Yet an equally urgent eugenics debate with which Du Bois was likewise engaged during and after the war concerned the position of Indian women under colonialism. In 1916, the same year as publication of Grant's book, American Katherine Mayo published the book *Mother India*. The book drew on Mayo's experience in 1915 and 1916 traveling in India to study the lives of women and children. Mayo offered a statistical and argumentative indictment of reproductive risks, overpopulation, child-bride customs, and paternalism in Indian society. The book was also patently racist and Orientalist in its methodology, taking no account of British colonial rule as a factor in its study, and representing a monological account of atrocity. The sharpest direct and indirect retort to Mayo's representative Orientalism for U.S. readers was provided by Lajpat Rai. In 1916, the same year as Mayo's book appeared, Rai published *Young India: An Interpretation and a History of the Nationalist Movement from Within*. The book was the first strong anticolonial critique published in the United States by an Indian national. Inspired generally by Rai's work, Du Bois in 1921 devoted attention in the *Crisis* to the illiteracy and exploitation of women in India, tying it directly to the near breakdown and disappearance of its industrial system.[14] Rai in turn disclosed his reciprocal intellectual and ideological affiliations with Du Bois, and his own conceptual matrix of Pan-Asianism and Pan-Africanism, in his subsequent 1928 book *Unhappy India*. The book was an attack on Mayo's *Mother India* mediated by Du Bois's 1917 reports in the *Crisis* on the notorious East St. Louis race riots.[15] Rai compared *white* bloodlust against blacks in the United States to Mayo's racist report on India:

> There you have the American love of slogans and lust for excitement. The jaded senses of the American rioters were athirst for something striking. They wanted to revel in their grim sport. The extreme mechanization of life in America creates an abnormal craving for crazes, students, sensation-mongering, and produces yellow journals and shilling-shockers like *Mother India*. Such orgies have always a peculiar fascination for American crowds. But for utter joy let it be white *versus* black.[16]

Rai's analogization of American lynch lust to the orgy of Mayo's Orientalism redrew from the Asian side Du Bois's world color line thesis. In fact Rai's rebuttal of Mayo was an immediate echo of an ideological storm in the United States inaugurated by Du Bois's 1919 publication of *Darkwater*. The book's critical confluence of eugenics, World War I, imperialism, race, and matriarchy had triggered a momentous firefight between Du Bois and the most vociferous raciologues of his era. The debate was to last nearly a decade and disclosed Du Bois's attempts to merge his color line thesis with a new, related passion, Bolshevism. It is to this crucial but underexplored chapter in the history of Du Boisian thought, and Afro-Orientalism, that I will now turn.

In 1920, one year after the end of World War I and three years after the Bolshevik revolution, the American historian Lothrop Stoddard published *The Rising Tide of Color against White World Supremacy*. Stoddard's book openly owed two debts: the first was to Count Arthur de Gobineau, the nineteenth-century eugenics theorist cited by Edward Said as a pioneer of European Orientalism. De Gobineau's 1853 *Essai sur l'inegalite des races humaines* (Essay on the Inequality of the Races) described a stark racial hierarchy of Aryan supremacy and Asian and Negro inferiority. In *Rising Tide*, Stoddard evoked Gobineau to interpret the decimation of western Europe in World War I as a tragic white holocaust. Ideologically, Stoddard's book was a sequel to Grant's aforementioned *The Passing of the Great Race*. Stoddard's book deviated from Grant primarily by fixing its scientific-racism hypothesis to events of 1917. "Now that Asia," he wrote in his introduction, "in the guise of Bolshevism with Semitic leadership and Chinese executioners, is organizing an assault upon western Europe, the new states—Slavic Alpine, with little Nordic blood—may prove to be not frontier guards of western Europe but vanguards of Asia in central Europe."[17] "Bolshevism is the renegade," he wrote, "the traitor within the gates, who would betray the citadel, degrade the very fibre of our being, and ultimately hurl a rebarbarized, racially impoverished world into the most debased and hopeless of mongrelizations."[18]

Stoddard's second debt was in complement to the first, and of even more direct significance to this essay: *The Rising Tide of Color* included an attack on Du Bois's 1915 *Atlantic Monthly* essay "The African Roots of the War," which had appeared one year earlier, in revised form, as "The Hands of Ethiopia" in *Darkwater*. In addition to his aquatic title, Grant's fusion of red scare and yellow peril had been fueled by Du Bois's provocative revision of his 1903 color line thesis in *Darkwater* as "the color problem of the world." Du Bois's allegory of Afro-Asian coupling and images of the black All-Mother had ignited strong reactions from others besides Stoddard: the *Times Literary Supplement* of London said that *Darkwater* revealed "the dark depths of a passionate and fanatical mind." The Paris edition of the *New York Herald* devoted an editorial to the book titled "Black Bolshevism": in *Darkwater*, the paper wrote, Du Bois is "intoxicated" by colonial self-determination, which "partakes of frenzy" and "represents the spread of the Bolshevist madness."[19]

In fact Du Bois's writings in *Darkwater* were by far his most militant to date. The just-concluded world war, he wrote in "The Souls of White Folk,"

> was primarily the jealous and avaricious struggle for the largest share in exploiting darker races. As such it is and must be but the prelude to the armed and indignant protest of these despised and raped peoples. Today Japan is hammering on the door of justice, China is raising her half-manacled hands to knock next, India is waiting for the freedom to knock, Egypt is suddenly muttering, the Negroes of South and West Africa, of the West Indies, and of the United States are just awakening to their shameful slavery.[20]

Typical of his color line formulations after 1903, Du Bois positioned Asian liberation struggles as leverage onto black emancipation. Yet *Darkwater* also featured a new characterization of U.S. blackness that was to take pride of place in Du Bois's long-term assessment of hemispheric struggle. In the essay "Of Work and Wealth," Du Bois described the ongoing black migration to the North and the horrific events of racist attacks in 1917 and 1919 as "the old world horror come to life again: all that Jews suffered in Spain and Poland; all that peasants [are] suffering in France, and Indians in Calcutta."[21] Du Bois's new conception of American blackness invoked a stagist view of history that had deposited American Negroes in the vanguard of international workers' struggles:

There is not only the industrial unrest of war and revolutionized work, but there is the call for workers, the coming of black folk, and the deliberate effort to divert the thoughts of men, and particularly of workingmen, into channels of race hatred against blacks. . . . The American Negroes stand today as the greatest strategic group in the world. Their services are indispensable, their temper and character are fine, and their souls have seen a vision more beautiful than any other mass of workers. They may win black culture to the world if their strength can be used with the forces of the world that make for justice and not against the hidden hates that fight for barbarism.[22]

Du Bois's conception of the souls of black folk as a touchstone of internationalist race and labor consciousness and his characterization of black workers as "the greatest strategic group in the world" would find an echo in Soviet policy on the Negro question, itself much influenced by theorizing on American race by rebel expatriates to the Soviet Union like Otto Huiswood and Claude McKay (Du Bois would visit the Soviet Union for the first time in 1926).[23] "Of Work and Wealth," in positing a black workers' culture as African America's most seductive offering to the world, was also a significant internal revision in his own thought, a downward mobilizing of the "kingdom of culture" pronounced in his more famous 1903 formulation. In addition, the culture of black labor thesis carried with it in "Of Work and Wealth" the blood message of ancient wounds suffered across the colored world, the stigmata of economic exploitation from Israel to Calcutta. Du Bois's pan-internationalism in *Darkwater*, that is, assumed an economist rhetoric absent from his prewar writings. The causes for this transformation of tropes and ideas in his work are best apprehended through close reading of his 1928 novel *Dark Princess*, a book that encapsulates and dramatizes the events between 1917 and 1928 that reconfigured his views on Afro-Asia and the color line, as well as the color of his own political ideas.

Subtitled *A Romance, Dark Princess*'s story line is both simple and complex. Matthew Towns, a twenty-five-year-old black American medical student, exiles himself from the United States in 1923 after being excluded by race from registering for obstetrics at the University of Manhattan in New York. He arrives in Berlin—where Du Bois attended university in 1892—and one day intervenes on behalf of a striking young Indian woman after a white American accosts her with a racist expletive. The woman is the twenty-three-year-old Kautilya, princess of Bwodpur, daughter of the maharaja, "the last of a line that had lived and ruled a thousand years"[24]—the first of several indices of *Dark Princess*'s orientalist undertow. Fresh from solidarity visits to China's Sun Yat-sen, India's Gandhi, Japan, and Egypt, the princess invites Matthew to meet with a circle of international radicals coordinating the "darker" races against white world power. They include a Japanese, two Indians, two Chinese, an Egyptian and his wife, and a "cold and rather stiff Arab." The group represents "all the darker world except the darkest," the black American. One thrust of the group's deliberation is to unite "Pan-Africa . . . with Pan-Asia" as a response to "dominating Europe which has flung this challenge of the color line."[25] Another is to decide how to act on their recent collective education in the Soviet Union, sketchily referenced in the text, where the theater of Meyerhold and "reports on the American Negro" have left equally deep marks. "Their [the Negroes'] education, their work, their property" and the "odds, the terrible, crushing odds against which, inch by inch, they have fought" have led some in the group, including the princess, to consider it essential to draw the Negro into the darker global sphere. For others, like the Egyptian, Moscow is "dangerous company" and like "leaning on broken reeds," while for the Japanese, "there is a deeper question—that of the ability, qualifications, and real possibilities of the black race in Africa or elsewhere." This remark elicits in Matthew one of a number of political epiphanies in the text, this one that "there loomed plain and clear the shadow of a color line within a color line, a prejudice within prejudice, and he and his again the sacrifice."[26]

The princess then solicits Matthew to act as an agent of information on black Americans in hopes of orchestrating a U.S. uprising. Back home Matthew follows instructions and falls in with a man named Perigua, a West Indian (something like a Garveyite) who seeks to explode the "lynching belt" in the United States by persuading Matthew to assist in the bombing of a passenger train carrying Ku Klux Klan members to Chicago. Matthew agrees, and the scheme is averted by happenstance when the princess ends up a passenger on the same train. When the plot and Matthew's part in it are exposed, he is sentenced to prison. He is released through the hard work of an ambitious black Chicago ward politician, Sammy Scott, who is persuaded by his mulatto assistant Sara Andrews to use the case as political bait in his next election. Matthew works for Sammy's office upon his release and enters a chilly political marriage with Sara. The princess meanwhile is promised several times in marriage, including once to a British soldier, but her love for Matthew and a fear that the marriages will abrogate the royal line and Indian home rule persuade her to evade them all. Instead the partners descend together into the American working class, the princess incognito as a house servant and union organizer, Matthew as a laborer and organizer among subway workers in Chicago. After consummating their affair, Kautilya travels to Prince County, Virginia, to meet Matthew's mother, a onetime sharecropper "who sold her forty acres" to pay for Matthew's education. The book ends at Matthew's Virginia homestead with a miraculous rendering of their marriage and Kautilya's surprise presentation of their newborn child, "Messenger and Messiah to all the Darker Races." The climactic scene takes place at sunrise, May 1, 1927.

Despite its 1923 dateline, the epigraph to *Dark Princess*, like its finale, suggests a more sweeping political, narrative, and biological cycle. "Earth is pregnant," writes Du Bois. "Life is big with pain and evil and hope. Summer in blue New York; summer in gray Berlin; summer in the red heart of the world!"[27] Du Bois's color imagery and geography playfully evoke the "red summer" of 1919, the year of antiblack racial rioting in the United States resulting from the violent conflict of southern black migration and white northern labor, and the year, we are told, that Matthew Towns leaves Prince County, Virginia, for New York City. That year also marked a split in the world socialist movement and the formation of the Third Communist International, events with immediate consequences for Du Bois's fictional political constituents. In the United States the split occasioned a break in the New York New Negro movement between opponents of the Bolshevik revolution and its supporters—a schism to which I will return momentarily. The Third International was also noteworthy for its description of India as one of the "slaves" of colonialism following a 1919 visit to Moscow by Mahendra Pratep, a prominent émigré leader of the Berlin "Provisional Government of India" established by the Indian Revolutionary Committee during World War I. Pratep was no communist, but he did present Lenin with a tract entitled the "Religion of Love," a nonmaterialist bid to force the Soviet leader to use the so-called provisional government to establish links with revolutionary centers in Bengal and Punjab.[28] His example may well have given Du Bois the idea to use Matthew and Kautilya's erotic romance as the test case of Afro-Asian solidarity.

Despite these suggestive historical roots, however, 1922 was most likely the year that crystallized the idea for *Dark Princess* in Du Bois's mind. The Fourth Congress of the Comintern in Moscow in that year featured its first black representatives from America: the Dutch Guianan Otto Huiswood, and the Jamaican poet and resident Claude McKay, pro-Bolshevik survivors of the 1919 New Negro split. Also present and a key player in the debate was the brilliant Bengali Brahman M. N. Roy, another veteran of the Berlin Committee and cofounder of the Mexican Communist Party. McKay and Roy in particular left both the Comintern and the triangular relations of the Soviet Union, American blacks and Asia depicted in *Dark Princess* deeply changed. McKay presented a "Report on the Negro Question" that argued that the great migration, World War I, northern industrialization, and American racism, particularly in the trade union movement, had made "the Negro question . . . at bottom a question of the working class."[29] By insisting that "the International bourgeoisie would use the Negro race as their trump card in their fight against world revolution," McKay's report helped give impetus to the congress's "Theses on the Negro Question," exhorting the Communist International to "use every instrument within its control to compel the trade unions to admit Negro workers to membership."[30] (McKay's subsequent essay on his Soviet visit, "Soviet Russia and the Negro," was published by Du Bois in the *Crisis* in 1924.) Indeed, Cedric Robinson, Harry Haywood, and most recently Bill Maxwell have demonstrated how McKay's and Huiswood's reports and influence at the 1922 Comintern helped lead to the articulations of Lenin, Zinoviev, and Stalin on the "National Question" and helped to formulate the "black belt thesis" of African Americans as a special "nation within a nation" debated hotly throughout the 1920s. In his autobiography *Black Bolshevik*, Haywood summarized this shift in the party line as follows: "As the theory was put into practice, we learned that national cultures could be expressed with a proletarian (socialist) content and that there was no antagonistic contradiction, under socialism, between national cultures and proletarian internationalism. . . . Thus the Bolsheviks upheld the principle of 'proletarian in content, national in form.'"[31]

Du Bois registers the impact of these events in *Dark Princess* in several ways. In the book's opening pages, the princess speaks of her recent study of the Negro Question in Moscow as the impetus for inviting Matthew to join her colored circle of anticolonialists in Berlin. It is, she says, "a report I read there from America that astounded me and gave me great pleasure—for I almost alone have insisted that your group was worthy of cooperation."[32] Elsewhere in the opening section of *Dark Princess*, Kautilya insists to Matthew that "you American Negroes are not a mere amorphous handful. You are a nation!"(16). Still other events in the novel suggest contemporary real-world black internationalists as models: it was while working as a Pullman porter, for example, that the young Claude McKay wrote the notorious 1919 sonnet "If We Must Die" urging black compatriots to "nobly die" fighting antiblack, antilabor rioters in cities like Chicago. In Part 2 of *Dark Princess*, "The Pullman Porter," Matthew joins the first all-black American trade union and commits to a plan of violent retaliation against the Ku Klux Klan after a failed strike. He justifies his participation by explaining to himself, "He was dying for Death. The world would know that black men dared to die" (85). The Pullman job also allows Matthew to see the Ku Klux Klan and white American labor as parallel organizations, using the threat of Filipino workers to break black strikes and trying to "pit the dark peoples against each other" (78). Du Bois thus presents both violent retaliation and all-black organizing as strategic local responses to attempts to divide the international proletariat by making "colored labor . . . the wage-hammering adjunct of white capital" (58). Indeed, parts 2 and 3 of *Dark Princess*, including a description of Chicago machine-style politics, are rendered as locus classicus reiterations of World War I's imperialist dimensions: "There was war in Chicago—silent, bitter war. It was part of the war throughout the whole nation; it was part of the World War. Money was bursting the coffers of the banks—poor people's savings, rich people's dividends. . . . So there was war in Chicago,—World War, and the Republican machine of Cook County was fighting in the van. And in the machine Sammy and Sara and Matthew were little cogs" (168).

Meanwhile, at the same 1922 Comintern that formulated the New Negro thesis, the Eastern Commission of the Fourth Congress, in direct response to Roy's pressuring of Lenin, drafted its "Theses on the Eastern Question" defining the goal of the Communist International to organize working and peasant masses and to "fight for the most radical possible solution of the tasks of bourgeois-democratic revolution."[33] John Haithcox has written that the Roy-Lenin debates in the 1922 Comintern were its first attempt to "formulate a policy which would successfully merge the revolutionary aspirations of nationalist anticolonialism and communist anticapitalism."[34] In his long 1922 *Crisis* essay titled "Gandhi and India," Du Bois favorably cited the observation by a British Labour Party representative at the 1920 Indian National Congress that Gandhi was India's equivalent to Lenin.[35] Indeed, Du Bois's 1922 support of the efforts of the Indian National Congress toward self-determination anticipate his epigraph to this essay supporting India as an example for African Americans to follow. In an effort to fuse and sustain his evolving Marxist and anti-Orientalist agenda, then, Du Bois sought to literally make analogous what he called, in a phrase that resonated especially with Stoddard, the "rising tide of new and popular thought" in all corners of the colored world.[36]

It is this complex moment of theoretical and geographic rapprochement that *Dark Princess* astutely allegorizes. As Cedric Robinson has noted, Du Bois's hostility to narrow nationalism and Garveyism and his Fabian socialism were romanced and wedded by the 1920s turn in the line of international Communism. In 1925, Du Bois gave one clear indication of this turn. His December column in the *Crisis* noted that "two significant moments have recently taken place among us," the organization of a Pullman porters' union and a meeting of "colored Communists" in Chicago.[37] The short-lived American Negro Labor Congress held in Chicago that year was a direct response by the American Communist Party to the new Soviet position on black labor and was so registered by Du Bois: "If black men wish to meet and learn what laborers are doing in England or in Russia and sympathize with their movements they have a perfect right to do so. . . . *The Crisis* . . . asserts the right of any set of American Negroes to investigate and sympathize with any industrial reform whether it springs from Russia, China or the South Seas."[38] Matthew Towns's engagement with the Pullman porters and the Chicago setting thus provided Du Bois a symbolic landscape and platform for Towns's blatant transformation to revolutionary consciousness: "If then in Chicago we can kill the thing that America stands for, we emancipate the world," writes Matthew to Kautilya. "There must be developed here that world-tyranny which will impose by brute force a new heaven on this old and rotten earth."[39] Reciprocally, Matthew's new theses on black labor find a parallel in the princess's work with the New York Box Makers Union, a fictitious rendering of the Paper Box Union in New York that Du Bois had also singled out for praise in the *Crisis* for accepting colored workers. Indeed, at every turn of *Dark Princess*, Du Bois sought to analogize the proletarian content of his protagonists' respective racial and national experiences: Kautilya suffers sexual harassment from a white overlord while working as an American domestic; Matthew's work as train car servant and subway digger not only evokes the important role of the All India Railway Federation in the organization of Indian trade unions after 1919 but mirrors the extracurricular labor undertaken by Harry Haywood and his Egyptian, Chinese, and Indian colleagues at the Moscow University of Toilers of the East, a comrade training school opened with the support and instruction of M. N. Roy. Haywood in fact arrived for training at the university in 1926, the same year of Du Bois's first extensive six-week tour of the Soviet Union, undertaken while writing *Dark Princess*. Du Bois's awareness of, and support for, such training was not so subtly referenced in the novel via Towns's experience of racism from an Italian worker aboard his steamship home: "They hated and despised most of their fellows, and they fell like a pack of wolves on the weakest. Yet they all had the common bond of toil; their sweat and the sweat of toilers like them made one vast ocean around the world."[40]

Du Bois's image here of darkwater as the amniotic fluid of proletarian internationalism also points to the complex configuration of the feminine in *Dark Princess*, particularly in light of hysterical Orientalist readings of global politics by his contemporaries. Du Bois's representation of an essential maternal African nation in *Darkwater*, for example, was consistent with his early Pan-Africanist identification of the female as repository of national—and nationalist—culture. Yet Princess Kautilya's is a lethal "mongrel" blackness. Her colored allies believe that the princess's visit to Russia has "inoculated her with Bolshevism of a mild but dangerous type."[41] Du Bois's playful troping on the one-drop rule is deepened by the semantic wedding of the princess and Matthew: both are called, at various points in the text, "Bolshevik" and "nigger," the equation of terms suggesting what is most logical and dangerous about their union. Through the résumés and pedigrees of his protagonists, Du Bois creates quite literally a "mongrel" and matrilineal genealogy of the revolutionary colored world. Like Matthew and his mother, the princess describes her family as emerging from the "black South in ancient days";[42] India is described as the "birthplace" and "black womb" of the ancient world;[43] the princess's and Matthew's disparate lineages are fused by the image of Matthew's mother as "Kali, the Black One; wife of Siva, Mother of the World."[44] Kautilya's Bolshevik tough love not only evokes Kali's double aspect of destruction and compassion but mirrors Du Bois's invocation of the black spirituals as cultural touchstones of Matthew's relationship to black earth, including his mother's experience of forty acres and a mule.

This complex and overdetermined doubling motif, as Paul Gilroy

has noted, shows Du Bois struggling after "not the fusion of two puri-
fied essences but rather a meeting of two heterogeneous multiplicities that
in yielding themselves up to each other create something durable and
entirely appropriate to anti-colonial times."[45] More concretely, Du Bois
is straining to release his own famous figure of "one dark body" in *The
Souls of Black Folk* from the "unreconciled strivings" of a single (and singular) double consciousness. In *The Souls of Black Folk*, Du Bois famously
cast the Seventh Son as he who is "longing to attain self-conscious man-
hood, to merge his double self into a better and truer self." This proto-
messianic figure is an heir to a cosmopolitan line of descent, "after the
Egyptian and the Indian, the Greek and the Roman, the Teuton and
Mongolian."[46] In *Dark Princess*, Kautilya trades her political inheritance
as Indian royalty for an internationalist pedigree that includes collaboration with national revolutionary movements in China, Japan, and Egypt.
Her and Matthew's commitment to the international proletariat also
adds the specter of class consciousness to double racial consciousness.
"Can we accomplish this double end in one movement?" asks the princess of their joint efforts to liberate black workers and achieve Indian
home rule. "Brain and Brawn must unite in one body. But where shall
the work begin?" asks Matthew. The answer is in the physical and theoretical potential of their coupling: "Workers unite, men cry, while in
truth always thinkers who do not work have tried to unite workers who
do not think," writes the princess. "Only working thinkers can unite thinking workers."[47] Du Bois's conception is indeed immaculate: his recipe for
the newborn messiah of *Dark Princess* must by necessity be "proletarian
in content, international in form!"

Dark Princess was completed in 1927 and published in 1928. In February
1927, the Association of Oppressed Peoples (AOP) met in Brussels. The
group had been founded in 1924 as the Anti-imperialist League. According to David Kimche, the AOP had "strong Communist leanings," but also
the support of many nationalists and radical non-Communists "centered
mainly in Berlin."[48] Representation at the AOP included 175 delegates
from thirty-seven countries and territories, including Nehru, Ho Chi

Minh, Muhammad Hatta, Madame Sun Yat-sen, and Léopold Senghor. Kimche has described the 1927 meeting as "the father of Afro-Asian solidarity, the forerunner of the conference at Bandung," in reference to the famous Indonesian summit meeting of that year, to be discussed in detail later.[49] In 1928 the Sixth Congress in Moscow formalized the Comintern's "Black Belt" thesis. The congress consummated the hybrid work of Roy, Lenin, McKay, Huiswood, and others before and after the 1922 Comintern. *Dark Princess* prophetically merged these contemporary historical plotlines. The book ends with the princess declaring that "the colored world goes free in 1952," and Kautilya's closing description to Matthew of the need to center their global revolutionary work in the womb of his own world-historical experience: "Here in Virginia you are at the edge of a black world. The black belt of the Congo, the Nile, and the Ganges reaches up by way of Guiana, Haiti, and Jamaica, like a red arrow, up into the heart of white America. Thus I see a mighty synthesis: you can work in Africa and Asia right here in America if you work in the Black Belt."[50]

This culminating image of black penetration into the heart of whiteness is, to return to my introduction, more than a celebration of diaspora consciousness or multiple essences. Du Bois had found in historical events between 1917 and 1928 a tentative political formula for his Afro-Asian fantasia. *Dark Princess* was his most pronounced, if veiled, statement of his interest in what he called in 1933 the "Russian experiment," while providing incontrovertible support for national liberation struggles motivated by the self-determinationist rhetoric of the World War I era, ranging from Woodrow Wilson to Lajpat Rai to the Comintern. The foreshadowing and fallout of these themes in Du Bois's illustrious career work on Asia are likewise readily apparent for the careful observer. In his report in the *Crisis* on the 1927 Pan-African Congress, the last of four held between 1919 and that year, Du Bois concluded with an appeal for "real national independence" of Egypt, India, and China.[51] In his "As the Crow Flies" column of February 1932, in a series of itemized observations on the world situation, Du Bois surmised, "If the white race is really wise it will let the yellow race commit suicide without interference.

Then only the blacks will remain for exploitation and empire."[52] Du Bois's satirical impatience targeted internecine conflict between Japan and China, yet to become military. By 1933, Du Bois was writing of this conflict in the *Crisis* both as a key to the fate of colored nations in their struggles with white Western colonialism and as a metonymy for the need of black Americans to find their own internal unity:

> Colossi of Asia and leaders of all colored mankind: for God's sake stop fighting and get together. . . . Unite in self-defense and assume that leadership of distracted mankind to which your four hundred millions of people entitle you. . . .
>
> . . . The real rulers of the world today, who stand back of Stimson, Macdonald and Herriot, are blood-sucking, imperial tyrants who see only one thing in the quarrel of China and Japan and that is a chance to crush and exploit them both. Nothing has given them more ghoulish glee than the blood and smoke of Shanghai and Manchuria or led them to rub hands with more solemn unction and practiced hypocrisy.
>
> Unmask them, Asia; tear apart their double faces and double tongues and unite in peace. Remember, Japan, that white America despises and fears you. Remember, China, that England covets your land and labor. Unite! Beckon to the three hundred million Indians; drive Europe out of Asia and let her get her own raped and distracted house in order. Let the yellow and brown race, nine hundred million strong take their rightful leadership of mankind. . . . Get together and wire word to Asia. Get together China and Japan, cease quarrelling and fighting! Arise and lead! The world needs Asia.[53]

Du Bois's rendering of nationalist struggle as domestic (or familial) dispute and his deep aspiration for easy ethnic affiliation across Pan-Asia bespoke remnants of the romantic racialism lingering from nineteenth-century Afrocentric influences. This residual and persistent raciology in fact led to the most egregious, if temporary, political misjudgment of Du Bois's career. In 1937, as the national conflict between Japan and China deepened, Du Bois weighed Japanese ambitions in the global scales and resisted the logic of his own conclusions. I quote this passage at length to convey the tonal and discursive tensions endemic to the tradition of Afro-Asian discourse I am describing in this book:

> What Japan has done is to take the European imperialism and use it in Asia against Europe. This is of course contrary to all the rules of the game. Imperialism is great and benevolent only when it is conducted by Great Britain or France or the United States of America. In the hands of Japan, it becomes an awful and menacing thing, and yet we can only believe in the sincerity of the white nations who criticize Japan when they themselves disgourge the colonial loot on which they are today continuing to fatten. If Great Britain does not like the advance of Japan into Manchuria and Mongolia, she might show her change of heart by giving up her grip on Nigeria and Kenya. If the virtual exclusion of European and American merchants from large areas of China does not please them, they might show their conversion by opening up empty Australia and New Zealand to colored immigration. Of course this failure of white imperialism to change its attitude does not at all excuse Japan for extending Colonial imperialism, if that is what she intends to do. Personally, I do not believe it. In the first place, the Chinese and the Japanese are cousins and there cannot be anything of the bitter race hatred that exists between the black and white subjects of the British Empire. There is in Japan today a leven of economic reform which must in time bankrupt and change the older imperialism learned from the West. In the meantime, the thing that must impress us as colored people is that the chance for economic reform under Japanese imperialism is infinitely greater than any chances which colored people would have under the most advanced white leaders of Western reform, except in Russia.[54]

Du Bois's zero-sum race game and the underlying impulse to perceive Japan as the colored world's gentle (if sleeping) giant recalls the complex forms of identification with Japan enacted by African Americans of the 1930s documented by Ernest Allen and others.[55] The appeal of

Japanese Black Dragon societies particularly to working-class urban blacks in cities like Chicago and New York reflected their massive disenfranchisement and a desire to hitch themselves to an external force that would throw off the yoke of U.S. racism. Indeed, Du Bois anchored his own favorable assessment of Japan in the early to mid-1930s in its modest but symbolically important assistance for Ethiopia. News of an economic treaty between the two countries in 1933 motivated Du Bois to declare "a rapprochement between Asia and Africa which foreshadows closer union between yellow and black people."[56] Even while acknowledging the blind profiteering motive of Japan, Du Bois found the treaty favorable in the global scale, since "the treatment of Ethiopia by England and Italy and France has been so selfish and outrageous that nothing Japan can do can possibly be worse."[57]

Yet as the global depression deepened, so too did Du Bois's analysis of events in Asia. A series of columns for the *Pittsburgh Courier* of 1937 reveals how the conflict between Japan and China became the litmus test for resolving the culturalist/economist tensions in his writing on Asia and moved him decidedly in the direction of Marxism. His travels within China in late 1936 had given him firsthand evidence to document the ravaging effects of both Japanese and western European intervention and investment. In Shanghai and Hangchow, he wrote in the *Courier* for February 1937, foreign investment, the presence of foreign troops and workers, and the disempowerment of the Chinese working class had created a kind of Jim Crow martial law: "I saw last night a little white boy of perhaps four years order three Chinese out of his imperial way on the sidewalk of the Bund, and they meekly obeyed: it looked quite like Mississippi."[58] The results, for Du Bois, were disheartening and baffling: "Japan and China herself has invested in Chinese cheap labor and called this Progress."[59] Seven months later, in the September 25, 1937, pages of the newspaper, Du Bois stepped cautiously back into an assessment of the conflict. "I talked so long and said so much about China and Japan a few months ago that I have hesitated to return to the subject."[60] Yet "events have moved swiftly in the East, and we see the forerunners

of that great change in the world's center which is going eventually—
not, of course, this decade or this century—but eventually, to make Asia
the center of the world again which is its natural place" (ibid.). Referring
to the escalation of Japanese attack in Manchuria and its annexation, Du
Bois now located Japan's motives in an effort to combat European intervention and profiteering in China following the loss of her "great and
far-sighted leader Sun Yatsen" (ibid.). Rather than arguing for Japan as
the lesser of two imperialist evils, as he had done earlier, Du Bois interpreted Japanese intervention as itself anti-imperialist: "As I have said
several times before, Europe was set to dominate Asia, to enslave its
coolies and exploit its natural resources in exactly the same way that they
are treating Africa and the South Seas. The rise of Japan frustrated this"
(ibid.). Japanese economic survival also depended on extracting cheap
and efficient raw materials from China now that Europe and the United
States had cut them off as trade partners. "There was only one place
where Japan could get these things on her own territory, and that was by
the annexation of North China, and these she proceeded to accomplish"
(ibid.). At the same time, Du Bois mourned the road not taken, symbolized by the Japanese incursion: Russian "aggression" against China had
also been forestalled, though at the price of something grand: "It would
have been magnificent providence of God if Russia and China could have
made common round for the emancipation of the working classes of the
world. The salvation of China then would not have rested upon Japan,
and two-thirds of the world would have been arrayed against the industrial imperialism of Europe." Du Bois offered a darkly prophetic sum-
mation of the Japan-China conflict in closing:

> The only excuse for war is war. It is to escape annihilation and subjection
> of the nameless slavery of Western Europe that Japan has gone into a hor-
> rible and bloody carnage with her own cousin; but the cause and the blame
> of this war lies on England, and France, and America. . . . It was a terri-
> ble effort. It is one of the great deciding wars of the world. And the future
> of colored people is bound up with it.

... I know now, that the present war in Asia has as its effective cause the African slave trade and the Industrial Revolution in Europe. (ibid.)

The shadow of this final resolution would fall heavily over the remainder of Du Bois's intellectual life. Nineteen thirty-seven disclosed to him a categorical imperative to couple Afro-Asia at the center of a theory of political modernity. The Japan-China war motivated the deepest and most daring structuralist analysis of global imperialism he had ever offered. The stark alternative—white world imperialism and intraracial suicide among colored nations—was history's bankrupt bookend. At the same time, Japan's role in World War II presented Du Bois an object lesson in the direction Afro-Asia must take in the postwar period.

> To me, the tragedy of this epoch was that Japan learned Western ways too soon and too well, and turned from Asia to Europe. She had a fine culture, an exquisite art, and an industrial technique miraculous in worksmanship and adaptability. The Japanese clan was an effective social organ and her art of expression was unsurpassed. She might have led Asia and the world into a new era. But her headstrong leaders chose to apply Western imperialism to her domination of the East, and Western profit-making replaced Eastern idealism. If she had succeeded, it might have happened that she would indeed have spread her culture and achieved a co-prosperity sphere with freedom of soul. Perhaps![61]

Du Bois returns here to the racially romantic language of *The Souls of Black Folk* only to evoke the failure of the "kingdom of culture" as a bulwark against Western hegemony and capitalism. Japan ultimately presented Du Bois with a mirror of his own contradictions regarding culturalist and materialist analysis of Orientalism, imperialism, and race. At the same time, the Japan-China conflict underscored two lasting points: that Asia must remain central, not secondary, to his analysis of the world color line, and that a solution to the problem of imperialism would need to address the structural limitations of racialist and nationalist thinking.

After 1945, with the assistance of a single great leap forward in China, Du Bois would find means of reconciling these objectives.

In his 1945 *Chicago Defender* column "The Winds of Time," under the headline "Negro's War Gains and Losses," Du Bois wrote, "The defeat and humiliation of Japan marks the tragedy of the greatest colored nation which has risen to leadership in modern times."[62] Yet the column also included predictions of independence for India, the Dutch Netherlands (Indonesia) and French Indo-China (Vietnam). Du Bois largely rooted his confidence in Asian liberation in the new demands on the world's newest self-proclaimed global policeman, the United States. Having become "one of the three colonial powers" along with Britain and France, Du Bois wrote in June 1945, "she faces the task of not only holding Asia in subjection . . . [but] helping in the continued oppression of India and Africa."[63] In 1947, in *The World and Africa*, Africa and Asia assumed the lead in the refiguration of the postwar world. The book paid homage to the resurrection of the Pan-African Congress in Manchester in 1945, which Du Bois attended, where representation now came from six Asiatic nations, one Arab state, the African National Congress, and the South African Indian Congress, and socialism was a unifying conception for most of the leaders present. At the same time, Du Bois saw emerging in China a resolute alternative to diplomatic rapprochement. In the December 29, 1945, *Defender*, mere months after war's end, Du Bois rhapsodized, "This is a morning when the sunlight is streaming from the East, and I mean the East: China and India and Indonesia."[64] The sunlight to which Du Bois referred was red. His firsthand assessment of the three things that had drawn imperial Japan and Europe to China in 1936—"cheap labor; cheap men, cheap women"—also drew him irrevocably into sympathy with China's Communist Party, the decisive sympathy of the last years of his life. Indeed, as early as 1930, Du Bois had written, "only an upheaval from below, not a compromise from above, will save and restore China."[65] In 1939, he wrote: "The proletariat of the world consists not simply of white European and American workers but overwhelmingly of the dark workers of Asia, Africa, the islands of the sea, and South and Central America. These are the ones who are supporting a super-structure of wealth, luxury, and extravagance. It is the rise of these people that is the rise of the world. The problem of the twentieth century is the problem of the color line."[66]

Maoism and the example of China's peasant revolution suited Du Bois's worldview after 1945 in several important ways. First, it honored the commitment made by China during and immediately after its revolution to a policy of constructive engagement with African nations. China offered the model and the means for the merger at the level of statehood of Pan-Asia and Pan-Africa. Second, China's 1949 revolution placed the country and Asia at the center of colored revolutionary struggle. Third, China's colored Marxist revolution alleviated Du Bois's deep-seated mistrust of Anglo modernity; it was for Du Bois the political and ideological counter to the West's experiment not only with capitalism but Marxism to that point. Fourth, Maoism's mass or peasant-based theory of revolution displaced the (white) industrial proletariat as the center of Marxian revolution, while recalling and respecting the historical pride of place of China's illustrious antiquity. China's successful rural rebellions gave Du Bois confidence and enthusiasm in the possibility of building an African socialism "founded on old African communal life, rejecting the exaggerated private initiative of the West, and seeking to ally itself with the social program of the Progressive nations."[67] Du Bois's romantic reconciliation with precapitalism was in fact a means past the binaristic conception of the relationship of Pan-Africa and Communism influentially articulated by his close friend George Padmore. Padmore, a former delegate to the Comintern, attendee at the 1945 Pan-African Congress, and adviser to Ghanaian president Kwame Nkrumah in his bid to build African socialism there, opined in his influential book *Pan-Africanism or Communism* that "in our struggle for national freedom, human dignity and social redemption Pan-Africanism offers an ideological alternative to Communism on one side and Tribalism on the other."[68] Maoism's theory of a peasant-based revolution resolved this antimony; its practice placed it in the vanguard of postwar models for global liberation.

Indeed, Du Bois's last two major statements on Afro-Asia written before his death demonstrate its dramatic centrality to his lifework, as he understood quite well, but which, for reasons I have already discussed, most critics and readers of Du Bois have willfully or unintentionally ignored. Du Bois made two culminating decisions in his final years: to publicly join the Communist Party of the United States, and to live in exile in Ghana. Critics have tended to view these decisions, somewhat like Richard Wright's decision to leave the United States in 1946, as desperate acts of self-involvement or self-deception brought on by frustration and cynicism with the prospects of a lasting African American radicalism. While there is some measure of truth to the latter in particular, Du Bois's climactic and dramatic personal decisions should instead be read as the fulfillment of an Afro-Asian dream deferred. As many other critics have noted, Ghana had by the time of Du Bois's exile become the black world's symbolic center of political hope. Nkrumah's successful revolution and the installation of the Convention People's Party and his construction of a sustainable African socialism attracted en masse African and African American radicals. Shirley Graham Du Bois, who preceded Du Bois in his conversion to Communism, wrote glowingly of Ghana's revolution and influenced W. E. B.'s decision to move there. Richard Wright, the novelist John Killens, James and Grace Lee Boggs, Robert Williams, and members of the Black Panther Party all visited Ghana during the 1950s or 1960s. Not coincidentally, each also expressed strong support for Asian revolution.

Du Bois's final trip to China in 1959 and his Ghana exile should thus be seen as part of a tendency in the anticolonial period that he nearly single-handedly among African American intellectuals predicted. At the end of his life, Du Bois reflected retrospectively on what might be called the Afro-Asian future past. "China and Africa" was presented at Peking University as a speech on the occasion of Du Bois's ninety-first birthday. Du Bois celebrated his ninety-first birthday in China at the invitation of Mao, this after the lifting of his passport ban. The speech was later published in the March 3, 1959, *Peking Review*. Du Bois begins by declaiming that "China after long centuries has risen to her feet and leapt forward. Africa arise, and stand straight, speak and think! Act! Turn from the West and your slavery and humiliation for the last 500 years and face the rising sun."[69] As was by now a familiar stratagem, Du Bois cast China in the role of mentor and teacher to Africa, debunking the "ancient lie spread by church and state" of colonial dependence. Technological, political, and intellectual rapprochement between the two would not only rebuild their infrastructures but retell the relationship between the two largest continents in the colored world. "Let Chinese visit Africa, send their scientists there and their artists and writers. Let Africa send its students to China and its seekers after knowledge. It will not find on earth a richer goal, a more promising mine of information."[70] The epistemology of liberation and interracial identification Du Bois had described in language of fantastic longing some fifty years earlier is now resolved via a dialectical view of national economic self-determination:

> First, understand! Realize that the great mass of mankind is freeing itself from wage slavery while private capital in Britain, France, and now in America, is still trying to maintain civilization and comfort for a few on the toil, disease and ignorance of the mass of men. Understand this, and understanding comes from direct knowledge. You know America and France and Britain to your sorrow. Now know the Soviet Union and its allied nations, but particularly know China.
>
> China is flesh of your flesh and blood of your blood. China is coloured and knows to what a coloured skin in this modern world subjects its owner. But China knows more, much more than this; she knows what to do about it.[71]

Asia and Africa will move out of Orientalism's mutually made darkness only when each recognizes its mass revolutionary potential. Neither race nor the kingdom of culture alone can expedite this revolution. It must be firmly grounded in the objective conditions undergirding each:

> The object of industry is the welfare of the workers and not the wealth of the owners. The object of civilization is the cultural progress of the mass of workers and not merely of an intellectual elite. And in return for all this

communist lands believe that the cultivation of the mass of people will discover more talent and genius to serve the state than any closed aristocracy
ever furnished. . . .

. . . Africa, here is a real danger which you must avoid or return to
the slavery from which you are emerging. All I ask from you is the courage
to know; to look about you and see what is happening in this old and tired
world; to realize the extent and depth of its rebirth and the promise which
glows on yonder hills. . . .

. . . Stand together in this new world and let the old world perish in
its greed or be born again in new hope and promise. Listen to the Hebrew
prophet of communism:

Ho! every one that thirsteth; come ye to the waters; come, buy and
eat, without money and without price![72]

Du Bois's "new-time" religion can be judged for its idealistic fervor and messianic zeal, but it cannot be dismissed as an aberration or
deathbed conversion. Du Bois in fact achieved what might be called the
revolutionary sublime in his final writings on Afro-Asia. It elicited an
ecstatic mode of thought and writing congruent with the leap of intellectual faith that Afro-Asia had always represented in his life's work. Fit-
tingly, the most grandiloquent and important testimony to this is a poem,
"I Sing to China." Composed for and dedicated to Kuo Mo-jo, chairman of the China Peace Committee, with whom Du Bois spent much
time on his final 1959 visit, "I Sing to China" is best read against *Dark
Princess* as a literary performance of his favorite intellectual obsession:
the flash of light connecting the Afro-Asian worlds. Indeed, the poem's
May 1, 1959, dedication dateline gestures backward to the birth date for
Princess Kautilya and Matthew Towns's Dark Prince, "messiah to all the
darker races," the seventh son of a portentous colored people's revolution that in "I Sing to China" finds its love object and consummation.
The poem is also both epitaph and resurrection for the aging "I," the
author himself, who sees in the extinguishing of his own intellectual
flame the phoenix rising of a life's prophecy realized. Rather than expli-
cate the poem—by far the longest of Du Bois's life—I will reproduce it

here as a figural unearthing of what I take to be the central text or corpus of Du Bois's life as an internationalist: the revolutionary dream work
of America's most capacious intellectual, absorbing and refracting through
the veil of millennial vision the "Chinaman's chance" of a different world
that the remainder of this book will set out to explore.

> Hail, dark brethren of mine,
> Hail and farewell! I die,
> As you are born again, bursting with new life.
> Kith you are of mine, and kin.
> That Sun which burned by fathers ebony,
> Rolled your limbs in gold,
> And made us both, cousins to the stars!
>
> Farewell and Hail!
> Now I turn West, where kindly Death
> Opens its arms of endless sleep
> Crying as I die: be born, New China,
> Celestial Kingdom, Golden Realm!
>
> Hail, China!
> I go, I leave, I hasten home
> Where Dulles' brink can punish a nigger,
> For greeting a chink!
> My country, 'tis of thee,
> Rich land of slavery, of thee
> I cannot sing.
>
> But I can bring greetings
> From six hundred eight million souls—
> Marching, pushing, pulling;
> Singing, weeping, crawling to conquer
> Themselves and the world.
> Bursting pale bonds of poverty

Dull ignorance, dread Disease!
Hand held in hand
Of that strong elder brother
Great Soviet Russia, Northern Light,

Emperor of all Snow and ice;
Who wounded and scarred from fighting half the
    World,
Stands today, wise, strong and proud;
Exulting and exalted.

She who once felt Pain blasting Pain,
Blood bleeding Blood
Hope eating up Despair
But now sits aloft, unconquered and unconquerable;

Not perfect but with her eyes firm-fixed
On perfection!
Beckoning all her brethren: south, east and west
White and black, yellow and brown
All colors, all men!
All knowledge, all good!
Eternal China!
Live again, unending Life of Death!
Hear not the howling of the Hounds of Hell,
Old China Hands who kicked their servants,
Raped their daughters
And Prostituted their wives;
Sent priests, with opium in their right hands, guns
    in their left;
Crosses on their foreheads and gin in their flasks,
To baptize the heathen!

Torment yourselves, O Chinese people,
Flagellate your souls, my brothers,
Do bitter penance for those awful years
And centuries of yielding
To self-murder, degradation and despair;
To faithfulness to China and mankind.

Cowering as you did before the sons of bitches
Bastards of lords and millionaires;
Beneath the roaring guns of murderers
And hiss of whoring serpents
And prayers of snivelling hypocrites.

Work now and struggle; sacrifice with joy,
In just requital for the cruelty and neglect,
You, yourselves, meted out to
Your mothers, wives, and children
And yourselves.

Count sweat and toil today;
Hunger and cold;
Nakedness and suffering, as just pay
For centuries of surrender.

Be proud that with no whimper, no whisper of
        complaint,
You now transform the Lowest into the Highest,
The Poor into the Rich, the People into the Rulers;
Tears into smiles, prayer into praise.

Forget the little shrimp that stinks and stews on
        Taiwan
Forget his gods, Rhee and Diem.

Remember alone their ravaged peoples, the helpless
    pawns
Of blood-stained paws, of bloody jaws.
Be calm: their end is written in the stars;
Even their fellow-thieves in America
Cower in defeat.

You have faced the Dragon, China,
That fearsome Beast who ruled a thousand years:
A writhing coil of sin, a poison fang, a slimy horror!
Who frightened you to submission
And bound your feet and bowed your backs.

Hearken to the drums, listen to the feet:
The March, the Long, Long March from Ming to
    Mao, led by the Ghost
Of Sun Yat-sen!
With the song of Tu Fu, the memory of Confucius
    and Tao!

Sing, Liu, to the starving; starve with the song, Chou!
And Chu The, fight, fight, fight!
Through the snows and over the mountains,
You carry treasure;
You carry Gold, but not the Gold
Of banks and war-lords

But the fine Gold of human hearts
Whose price can never fall!
Which is scarce only as it is not used
Spend your Gold, China, scatter it and throw it
    abroad

Buy all mankind as you have bought me
Bought me and bound me and made me
Forever and forever yours!

Down then, Religion and Church, Temple and Pagoda
Away Myth and Miracle, Creed and Dogma;
Up Science, Truth, Right and Reason
Come, Little England, dying France,
Live on your own toil and no longer on the stolen
     land and labor
Of slaves.

Rejoice, Honesty, God lives again!
But not your God, Europe and America!
Not that, not that;
No Christ to kill, no faith to fan
What China worships is a Man!

A workman, who earns his good
And toils and sweats through day and night;
And tills his land with all his might;
And owns the harvest that he sows,

And winds and pulls,
And hauls and lifts,
And counts his children as his gifts;
And thinks and plans,
And learns and knows;

And plants the tree and sails the seas,
And works for all and all for me;
And they for us and we for them;
Who love their fellows more than self.
And toil for others not for pelf.

And write and dream and dance and sing,
And paint and build, and let the air
With music ring.
Color the world, and be as free, as men can be,
And not let Freedom, prison me.
This is our God—Praise to His name!
To Him be power, Wealth and Fame!

No lofty lineage does China rear—
No lords to strut, no fools to fear
And all its myriad millions sing
Work save the people, God damn the king!
Let Poet, Seer and Thinker rule,
Raise age to honor, child to school.

To school, to school, Golden baby, China doll.
Kowtow, all Sons of Heaven
To the Daughters of Destiny!
Mothers of Men,
To the women of China
Pregnant with the fairest Future
Man ever knew!

Reach down, O mighty People,
With your clenched left fist,
Grip the hands of Black Folk!
Hold fast the men from whom this world was born:

That great-brained Ape
Who stood erect and talked to his fellows
Who planted seed and first boiled Iron
And civilized a World.

Night fell, silent and noisome night, ghost-haunted!
Earthquake tore, flood roared, serpent and insect bit;
Fever raged, starvation reigned; but Africa lived;
Africa lived and grew, fared far and flourished,
Vitalized mankind.

Until the Devil rose and ruled in Europe and America,
Worshipping Greed, proclaiming God, enchaining his
    children;
Preaching freedom, practicing Slavery
Making Africans the Niggers of the World.

To be mocked and spit upon,
To be crucified! Dead and buried!
But Africa is not dead; she never died, she never
    will!
She writes in sleep; this century of her degradation
She struggles to awake.

Help her, China!
Help her, Dark People, who half-shared her slavery;
Who know the depths of her sorrow and humiliation;
Help her, not in Charity,

But in glorious resurrection of that day to be,
When the Black Man lives again
And sings the Songs of the Ages!
Swing low, Sweet Chariot—
Good news! the Chariot's a'coming!
Then again, Peace! Then forward the World,
    forward Mankind!
No more Murder!

Forget today the Past, Great China:
Forget how many would shriek with Joy
If dread disaster, killed China and her friends
Choked Africa again to death
While they drink blood
With the murders of Taiwan and Korea.

Weep China for your Eternal dead
Who died for the Unborn
Sing, Children of the Golden Horde
Sing, birds and blooms.

Ignore the memory of white men who tossed pence
    to paupers
Yoked children to machines
Ate babies in their mills
Waxed fat on profits.

Remember only the Saints of the West
John Brown and Garrison
Lincoln and Douglass
Pray that lost Britain
Lives in truth as once it wanted to live
And bring back the World it murdered.

America, stop lying, stop worshipping liars, stop!
Dare hear the Truth, no matter what it costs
Turn back from falsehood and distortion
Face Fact and birth and not abortion

Commune, Communes, with the Elect of Heaven
With Mother Earth, daughter of Sky and Sun
Born of Democracy, fertilized by Communism
Parents of Revolution, Makers of the World!

Sweet cities of China
With gold-coil roofs and curling eaves
With flaming walls and flowering gardens
And laughing children rolling in the sun,
Thunder your lightnings
From the Great Wall to Himalayas
Where pearls and jewels of Jolma Lungma
Peer down on all the earth

Shout, China!
Roar, Rock, roll River;
Sing, Sun and Moon and Sea!
Move Mountain, Lake and Land,
Exalt Mankind, Inspire!
For out of the East again, comes Salvation!
Leading all prophets of the Dead—
Osiris, Buddha, Christ and Mahmound
Interning their ashes, cherishing their Good;
China save the World! Arise, China![73]

CHAPTER 2

The Limits of Being Outside: Richard Wright's Anticolonial Turn

If Orientalism involves a science of inclusion and incorporation of the East by the West, then that inclusion produces its own disruption: the creation of the Orient, if it does not really represent the East, signifies the West's own dislocation from itself, something inside that is presented, narratized, as being outside.

—Robert Young, *White Mythologies*

My position is a split one. I'm black. I'm a man of the West . . . I see and understand the West; but I also see and understand the non- or anti-Western point of view. . . . This double vision of mine stems from my being a product of Western civilization and from my racial identity, long and deeply conditioned, which is organically born of my being a product of that civilization. Being a negro living in a white Western Christian society, I've never been allowed to blend, in a natural and healthy manner, with the culture and civilization of the West. . . .

Yet I'm not non-Western. I'm no enemy of the West. Neither am I an Easterner. When I look out upon those vast stretches of this earth inhabited by brown, black and yellow men. . . . my reactions and attitudes are those of the West. I see both worlds from another and third point of view.

—Richard Wright, "Tradition and Industrialization," in
White Man, Listen!

Richard Wright was living in New York City when the Fifth Pan-African Congress convened in Manchester, England, in 1945. The congress was the first held since 1927. Its organizing impetus had come from several sources: the approach of the end of World War II and the urgent question of postwar alignments; increasing disillusionment among Pan-Africanists with Soviet Communism and its role in nascent African liberation struggles, particularly on the part of former Comintern member and conference organizer George Padmore; the emergence in the Gold Coast of Kwame Nkrumah, the young, Western-educated socialist revolutionary; the conjoining of labor and national-based liberation struggles in Africa that had given birth to the World Federation of Trade Unions at Country Hall, London, in February 1945. WFTU labor and anticolonial leaders from across West Africa were in fact present in Manchester to hear Nkrumah, acting as *rapporteur*, delineate the possibilities for Gold Coast challenge to English colonial rule, and to propose a number of resolutions, unanimously adapted by the congress, on constitutional, economic, and social problems for the liberation of West Africa. Also present at Manchester was W. E. B. Du Bois, who wrote a report titled "The Race Problem in the United States." Du Bois had militated for a convening of the conference from his home in the United States. In the same year as Manchester, Du Bois published the book *Color and Democracy*, his first full volume dedicated to the anticolonial movement. *The World and Africa* would follow in 1947.

In November 1946, Wright was introduced in Paris to the Pan-African circle at which Du Bois had one year earlier been the center in Manchester. In addition to Padmore and Nkrumah, Wright met the Senegalese poet Léopold Senghor and the West Indian writer Aimé Césaire and renewed his acquaintance with the Trinidadian Trotskyist C. L. R. James. Wright was in an exile mood and mode. In 1944 he had broken publicly with the Communist Party of the United States in his celebrated essay "I Tried to Be a Communist," published in *Atlantic Monthly*. The last piece of fiction Wright wrote and published in the United States was also profoundly predictive: "The Man Who Lived Underground," derived from Dostoyevksy's *Notes from Underground*, depicted a black male fugitive entering into a literal and figurative no-man's-land of retreat. In 1952, Wright would publish his first émigré fiction, *The Outsider*, written in Paris, in which protagonist Cross Damon lived an even more radically alteritized existence beyond the kith and kin of political organizations, family, national boundaries, virtual identities. Wright's deepening conception of what he called "disinheritance" in black experience, tinged with existential influences that accompanied his arrival in Paris, produced a literary enactment in *The Outsider* of a theme that would come to dominate all his writings of the 1950s, namely, the contingency of his own identification with the Western world.

It was reflections on exile while in Paris that had prompted Wright's revision of Du Bois's "double consciousness" trope cited in this chapter's second epigraph. Wright's 1957 declaration "I'm black. I'm a man of the West" reconfigured Du Bois's image of "two warring selves"—a Negro, an American—into a figure of hemispheric division and dislocation. In *The Black Atlantic*, Paul Gilroy seizes upon Wright's variation on Du Bois's theme to move Wright to the center of his conception of black diasporic identity. "Perhaps more than any other writer, he [Wright] showed how modernity was both the period and the region in which black politics grew. His work articulates simultaneously an affirmation and a negation of the western civilisation that formed him. It remains the most powerful expression of the insider-outsider duality which we have drawn down the years from slavery."[1] Gilroy reads religious loss, literally a crisis of faith, as the cornerstone of Wright's disaffiliation with Western civilization. Likewise, he notes that what he calls Wright's "dread objectivity" emerged from both his disillusionment with Soviet Communism and his worry as a man of color about his relationship to the West's imperialist ambitions. Gilroy also valorizes Wright's lifelong intellectual task of rendering the Negro as "America's metaphor," an embodiment of the nation's socially constructed ideas about race. Affirming this metaphor helps Gilroy invest Wright's "outsider" trope with an antiessentialist resiliency that underlies his own diasporic paradigm for describing black experience.

Yet it is precisely the figure of the Outsider that Robert White reminds us is fundamental to the mechanisms, ideological and otherwise, of Orientalism. White extends Said's perceptive description of the Orientalist as always "turning something into something else" to the Orientalist himself/herself. The Orientalist's project of Othering, for White, reveals the "dislocation" of the observer himself or herself from the West. Thus viewed, Wright and White offer a convergent understanding of Orientalist epistemology around the figure of outsider that, in the case of Wright criticism, has more than one pair of legs. Arnold Rampersad, S. Shankar, Ngwarungu Chiwengo, and Yoshinobu Hakutani have all argued that Wright's exiled writings on Africa, Asia, and Spain include regressive and politically reactionary representations of the global Other. Rampersad contends that Wright's fetish of being "outside" contributed to a form of Occidental tourism in books like *Black Power*, *The Color Curtain*, and *Pagan Spain* in which Wright cast himself as estranged interloper in the study of Western empire. Gilroy has vigorously defended Wright from such charges, arguing that Rampersad is missing the transatlantic boat: Wright's exile writings, for Gilroy, embody rather an "intercultural hermeneutics" that sympathetically embodies the numerous contradictions, dislocations, and predicaments of the diasporic intellectual.[2]

I want to suggest in this chapter a boat not taken, one that will reveal in relationship to both Wright's and Gilroy's work what I will call the limitations of being outside. More specifically, I want to suggest that a dialectical reading of Wright's intellectual engagement with diaspora and the anticolonial struggles of the 1940s and 1950s helps to illuminate the weaknesses in the temporal/spatial paradigm for conceiving modernity that both writers ambivalently choose. For Wright this paradigm was expressed most poignantly in his description of what he called the "tragic elites," Western-educated intellectuals of color leading Third World liberation movements. Wright dedicated his 1957 book *White Man, Listen!* to Eric Williams, then chief minister of the government of Trinidad and Tobago and leader of the People's National Movement. Williams was also the author of *Capitalism and Slavery*, a book Wright knew well. His dedication cited Williams as well as "the Westernized and tragic elite of Asia, Africa, and the West Indies"— men described as "lonely outsiders who exist precariously on the clifflike margins of many cultures," who "seek desperately for a home for their hearts."[3] "The more Westernized that native heart became," he wrote of this group, himself included, in *White Man, Listen!* "the more anti-Western it had to be, for that heart was now weighing itself in terms of white Western values that made it feel degraded." Wright's conception of the outsider also borrowed from Nietzsche's "frog perspective" the notion of psychological abjection, "a sense of someone who feels himself lower than others."[4] The limitations of Wright's paradigm, I will argue here, are best understood by reference to his own ambivalent struggle with the discourse of Orientalism. What Amritjit Singh refers to as Wright's "creative use of prevalent binarisms"—the West and the anti-West, the master and the servant, the native and the exiled—also disclosed his special vulnerability to an epistemology that is at the heart of Orientalism's cultural work.[5] In his book *Marx and the End of Orientalism*, Bryan Turner defines the latter as manifesting three distinctive conceptions: that "social development is caused by characteristics which are internal to society"; that "the historical development of a society is either an evolutionary progress or a gradual decline"; and that society is an "expressive totality" in which all institutions express a primary essence.[6] Wright's life under Jim Crow in the American South, his experiences of racism in the Northern United States, his participation in the Communist Party, and finally his exile to Europe contoured in varying ways these features of his anticolonial thought. Especially after his break with Communism, I will argue, Wright evolved an increasingly parallel sense both of displacement from the West, and of the West's fundamental or essential character that fostered this displacement. This inner dialectic infused and informed his subsequent representations of traditionally non-Western cultures, African and Asian in particular, while displacing, in ways that were hardly benign, the Marxian dialectics that had grounded his earlier analysis of these same phenomena. Wright's hybrid and peculiar Orientalism carries these marks, or scars, as the stigmata of his own "negative loyalty" to Communism and Marxism and reiterates both prior debate and subsequent conjecture over their relationship to a wide variety of discourses of liberation. Wright's work, thus considered, provides a unique and important intersection and continuation from the life and work of Du Bois as it engages from a distinctively African American point of view the place and role of Asia as an index to black world fortunes. Making manifest this index is a crucial task for imagining the range of alternative modernities each writer struggled to identify in his respective lifework.

In *Native Son*, Wright's first novel of 1940, Bigger Thomas contrasts his anemic social position and powerlessness in Depression-era Chicago to what he imagines is the efficiency of faraway countries like Italy and Japan, whose autocratic forms of government, he vaguely senses, would add order and purpose to his seemingly abject life. In "How Bigger Was Born," Wright's famous account of the writing of *Native Son*, he acknowledged his source for Bigger's fantasy, claiming that he "even heard Negroes, in moments of anger and bitterness, praise what Japan is doing in China, not because they believed in oppression (being objects of oppression themselves), but because they would suddenly sense how empty their lives were when looking at the dark faces of Japanese generals in the rotogravure supplements of the Sunday newspapers. They would dream of what it would be like to live in a country where they could forget their color and play a responsible role in the vital processes of the nation's life."[7] Ernest Allen's work on the topic cited earlier has described the ways working-class blacks in urban centers like Chicago during the 1930s were targets for pro-Japanese sentiment spread by both Japanese and pro-Japanese black nationalists.[8] The appeals continued a thread of black sympathy for Japan begun in black newspapers after the 1904 war with Russia and sustained during the 1920s by Japan's autonomy in the face of post–World War I European dominance over the colored world. Japan's military emergence in the 1930s gave this autonomy a martial cast and partly explained its temporary appeal to Du Bois. Though the black U.S. pro-Japan movement never swelled, the Depression helped it gain leverage in marginal black cultural or religious groups like Moorish Science Temple and cause alarm among black conservatives and leftists alike who perceived its sympathy as a form of ideology. In 1937, the Communist Party of the United States went so far as to publish a special pamphlet on the topic, "Is Japan the Champion of the Colored Races?" discouraging black support for Japan in its war with China. The pamphlet was consistent with the Comintern's Popular Front antifascism and retained an anti-imperialist understanding of Japan's role in Asia.[9]

Wright, still a member of the CPUSA when he wrote *Native Son*, likewise understood the appeal of Japan as structural rather than skin deep: it announced profound economic distress that, Wright argued in "How Bigger Was Born," was likewise motivating the German proletariat to ally itself with Hitler's regime and had fueled the Russian peasantry toward revolution. Wright perceived each of these as latent impulses in Bigger Thomas. "Nationalism" was the term Wright used to describe these tendencies in "How Bigger Was Born," though the novel more aptly represents them as a form of false consciousness. Bigger's Asian fantasy is understood by the reader as misguided desperation. Bigger's Communist lawyer Max also finds chilling irony in Bigger's protofascism, while Wright freights Bigger's incarceration, isolation, and eventual execution with the undertones of a proletarian racial tragedy. Bigger's blackness is understood by readers as existentialized essence precisely because it embodies the essentialist mechanisms of racist capitalism that condemn him in *Native Son*. That is, Bigger is a victim of American fascism. The novel's "dread objectivity" toward this condition is ameliorated only by the possibility that Max's vision of an alternative modernity that is fundamentally Marxian may emerge phoenixlike from the funeral pyre of Bigger's fear, flight, and fate.

Native Son also introduced an evolving temporal/spatial paradigm for black experience that would become increasingly dominant in Wright's subsequent work. Chicago was represented in the novel as both the center and margin (or, as Gilroy suggests, the inside and outside) of Western modernity. In "How Bigger Was Born," Wright described the city as

old as the mountains and seas, of dramas as abiding as the soul of man itself! A city which has become the pivot of the Eastern, Western, Northern, and Southern poles of the country. But a city whose black smoke clouds shut out the fine balmy May morning, one can sniff the stench of stockyards: a city where people have grown so used to gangs and murders and graft that they have honestly forgotten that government can have a pretense of decency![10]

Wright's predilection for creative binarisms in this description—the pastoral and the urban, the primitive and the modern, the refined and the fallen—reveals a conceptual topography reflecting the very Western logocentrism that allowed Wright to imagine Chicago as its center. During the 1930s Wright was drawn to the Soviet and CPUSA Black Belt thesis in part because it seemed to both confirm and offer a way out of this epistemological and political iron cage. *Native Son* included the following description by the Communist attorney Max: "Multiply Bigger Thomas twelve million times, allowing for environmental and temperamental variations, and for those Negroes who are completely under the influence of the church, and you have the psychology of the Negro people. But once you see them as a whole, once your eyes leave the individual and encompass the mass, a new quality comes into the picture. Taken collectively, they are not simply twelve million people; in reality they constitute a separate nation, stunted, stripped, and held captive within this nation, devoid of political, social, economic, and property rights."[11] The Black Belt thesis was intended by Stalin and Lenin to describe, dialectically, the creation via colonialism and the slave trade of a revolutionary class at the heart of America that was African. The Negro is indeed "America's metaphor" in *12 Million Black Voices*, but it is also a metaphor for this feature of Wright's Black Belt analysis of America:

> Imagine European history from the days of Christ to the present telescoped into three hundred years and you can comprehend the drama which our consciousness has experienced! Brutal, bloody, crowded with suffering and abrupt transitions, the lives of us black folk represent the most magical and meaningful picture of human experience in the western world. Hurled from our native African homes into the very center of the most complex and highly industrialized civilization the world has ever known, we stand today with a consciousness and memory such as few people possess.

We black folk, our history and our present being, are a mirror of all the manifold experiences of America. If we black folk perish, America will perish.[12]

Temporal and spatial dislocations under modernity are made meaningful by the integration of the black subject into history. History, in *12 Million Black Voices*, also retains a fundamentally dialectical character: slavery and the Enlightenment as historical processes substantiate the historical materialist premise of Wright's study: the Lords of the Land who rule the South are succeeded by the Bosses of the Buildings. This matrix of exploitation gives coherence to racial trauma: "The seasons of the plantation no longer dictate the lives of many of us; hundreds of thousands of us are moving into the sphere of conscious history."[13] Wright's dialectical method thus attempts to resolve past/present, insider/outsider binaries that racism and capitalist history pose as otherwise unresolvable contradictions.

Twelve Million Black Voices was the last book Wright wrote as a member of the Communist Party and under open identification with its interpretation of black history. Between 1942 and 1944, Wright began his slow march away from public (and private) affiliation with the CPUSA. During these years Wright began serious work on *Black Boy*, the autobiography published in 1945. There Wright returned to his theme of black subjectivity and Western historical processes, but with a markedly different inflection. In one of the most famous passages of the book, Wright intones:

Whenever I thought of the essential bleakness of black life in America, I knew that Negroes had never been allowed to catch the full spirit of Western civilization, that they lived somehow in it but not of it. And when I brooded upon the cultural barrenness of black life, I wondered if clean, positive tenderness, love, honor, loyalty, and the capacity to remember were native with man. I asked myself if these qualities were not fostered, won, struggled and suffered for, preserved in ritual from one generation to another.[14]

Wright's language and tone suggest a cognitive shift in his conception of the black outsider. Wright's litany is essentialist; his catalog of black life is a series of deficient characteristics or absences defined in relationship to the cultural presence of the West. It is not until part 2 of *Black Boy*, however, that Wright discloses the relationship between this culturalist estrangement and his traumatic break with Marxism. Near the end of *American Hunger*, Wright plays witness to the party trial of Ross, his friend and comrade, when he is accused, as Wright will eventually be, of Trotskyism. Because of the antiracist affiliation he still feels for these "fair-minded men," Wright is at first astonished that the trial will take place. "Jews, Germans, Russians, Spaniards, all races and nationalities were represented without any distinctions whatever."[15] Wright perceives racial harmony as a corrective to the racial hate that "had been the bane of my life."[16] The trial redirects this: "A new hate had come to take the place of the rankling racial hate," he writes in this deliberative passage, which I quote in full:

> It was irrational that Communists should hate what they called "intellectuals," or anybody who tried to think for himself. I had fled men who did not like the color of my skin, and now I was among men who did not like the tone of my thoughts. In trying to grasp why Communists hated intellectuals, my mind was led back again to the accounts I had read of the Russian Revolution. There had existed in Old Russia millions of poor, ignorant people who were exploited by a few, educated, arrogant noblemen, and it became natural for the Russian Communists to associate betrayal with intellectualism. But there existed in the Western world an element that baffled and frightened the Communist party: the prevalence of self-achieved literacy. Even a Negro, entrapped by ignorance and exploitation—as I had been —could, if he had the will and the love for it, learn to read and understand the world in which he lived. And it was these people that the Communists could not understand. The American Communists, enjoying legality, were using the methods forged by the underground Russian Bolshevik fire, and therefore had to have their followers willing to accept all explanations of reality, even when the actual situation did not call for it.

The heritage of free thought—which no man could escape if he read at all,—the spirit of the Protestant ethic which one suckled, figuratively, with one's mother's milk, that self-generating energy that made a man feel, whether he realized it or not, that he had to work and redeem himself through his own acts, all this was forbidden, taboo. And yet this was the essence of that cultural heritage which the Communist party had sworn to carry forward, whole and intact, into the future. But the Communist party did not recognize the values that it had sworn to save when it saw them; the slightest sign of any independence of thought or feeling, even if it aided the party in its work, was enough to make one suspect, to brand one as a dangerous traitor.[17]

Vis-à-vis the epigraphs to this chapter, Wright limns the process of encrypting his own displacement from the West. He imagines fixed binary ideological geographies of West and East, into neither of which he fits. Wright's brief historical tour of the Russian peasantry as the pagan antithesis of the West's free inquiry, his insinuation of a covert Russian presence in the heart of American liberty, and the echoes of Asiatic despotism in his caricature of the Soviet face all bespeak Wright's newfound desire to renarrate his own position as double outsider. This representation hinges on Wright's projection of "free thought" as the creed betrayed by American Communism. Wright's fragile alignment of himself, and black intellectual life, with this principle ironically marks his sudden inclusion in the Western Enlightenment project at the very moment he denounces what had been his vehicle for escaping its most deleterious consequences—Communism. Marxism in this new formulation is instead a mirror of Western Jim Crow exclusion responsible for his prior miseducation. It is on this new binary, rather than dialectical politics, that Wright's representation of his outsider self stands, one that no longer has *any* perceivable resolution. In the remainder of this chapter, I will examine how this epistemological process, the process of being outside, was both deepened and challenged by Wright's exile and encounters with the anticolonial movement and the non-Western subject. Wright's attempts in his exile writings to demonstrate that the condition of the colored nations or Third

World were "symbolically prefigured" by black experience in the United States threw into relief not only emerging tendencies I have been describing thus far but other contradictions of the anticolonial period sometimes known as the Bandung era.

Wright was visiting his friends George and Dorothy Padmore on Easter Sunday 1954 when he was moved, as it were, by the spirit of Africa. Wright had already been living in Europe for seven years. Beginning in 1950, he had lectured across Europe on topics related to anticolonial struggles in Asia and Africa. Wright had become Padmore's friend in part on the strength of their shared commitment to Pan-Africanism, and their recent disavowals of Communism. Padmore's disillusionment had begun with Soviet supplying of oil and other products to Italy during its campaign against Ethiopia, and evolved into a harsh criticism of what he perceived as Soviet opportunism in Africa. This critique was articulated broadly in his 1954 book *Pan-Africanism or Communism*, for which Wright wrote an admiring preface. The book shared with Wright's 1945 autobiography an experiential dismay with organizational Communism productive of a strong commitment to new forms of black political self-determination. In his introduction to *Black Power*, Wright described this transformation in graphic detail that also echoed the political contingency in the title of Padmore's tract. From 1932 to 1944, Wright admitted, "I held consciously in my hands Marxist Communism as an instrumentality to effect . . . political and social changes."[18] When historical events "disclosed that international Communism was mainly an instrument of Russian foreign policy," Wright says, he dropped it. "Yet, as an American Negro whose life is governed by racial codes written into law, I state clearly that my abandonment of Communism does not automatically place me in a position of endorsing and supporting all the policies, political and economic, of the non-Communist world. . . . The Western world, of which I am an uneasy member, has not materially altered many of its attitudes toward the aspirations of hundreds of millions of minority people caught by chance, time and culture within its wide sway of power" (xxxvi).

Wright's uneasy relationship to a brokering Western hegemony on the one hand and a demonized Soviet sphere on the other reiterated the conditions surrounding *Black Power*'s publication. Before publishing the book, Harper and Brothers' president Frank McGregor insisted that readers know that "although Wright is anti-Western in certain respects, he is not by the same token pro-Russian" (xxxi). Elsewhere in his introduction Wright took pains to formalize a methodology and intention that would satisfy his publisher, and by implication his reader, if not his own mood of ambivalence:

> This book seeks to provide Western readers with some insight into what is going to happen in Africa, so that, when it does happen, they will be able to understand it, so that they will not entertain the kind of illusions that held forth about China; my point is that if Africa today is in turmoil, it is not merely the omniscient hand of Moscow that is fomenting all the trouble; but that, given the harsh background of Africa and the numbing impact of the West that it has suffered, what is happening was bound to happen. (xxxviii)

Wright's analogizing of black Africa to his self-description in "I Tried to Be a Communist" and *Black Boy* as Cold War martyr/Cold War exile reflects the durability and flexibility of his outsider vision during his period away from the United States. Indeed, from the beginning of his African narrative, it is the outsider who is rendered as Occidental interloper. Wright maps out his voyage in the book's opening pages to an Africa "that was conjuring up in my mind notions of the fabulous and remote: heat, jungle, rain, strange place names like Cape Coast, Elmina, Accra, Kumasi . . ." (6). Yet as Ngwarsungu Chiwengo has argued, Wright's sojourn to Africa also begins as a profoundly ironic revision of the trajectory of the western travel narrative itself. "Wright's initial European departure," Chiwengo writes, is "already a problematized space—epistemologically, socially, and historically constructed as the land of exile while Africa is his point of origin."[19] Wright's outsider trope is in a way redundant in *Black Power*. Wright seeks in Africa not his black identity but what

Chiwengo calls "an odyssey to confirm the African American's racial and cultural difference."[20] *Black Power* is thus an allegory of displacement in which the African subaltern is subordinated, in an unintended sequel to colonialism, to the subaltern American. The book is also a self-conscious but self-regulating fantasy of Wright's own power to cajole, protect, nurture, and counsel the African as a means of healing and revising his own experiences of Jim Crow America. It is dedicated to what Wright calls the "Unknown African" who "because of his primal and poetic humanity, was regarded by white men as a 'thing' to be bought, sold, and used as an instrument of production; and who, alone in the forests of West Africa, created a vision of life so simple as to be terrifying, yet a vision that was irreducibly human"[21] Wright's trope of the poetic African will, we will see, rekindle in his description of Indonesia. Yet *Black Power* is significant for beginning the figuration of race and culture that became Wright's epistemological method after his break with Marxism. Wright's self-consciousness about this break is plain in the text of *Black Power*. After describing the difference between the "tempo of progress . . . between the Western and non-Western world" as "almost absolute," and the African as "tribal man" against the modernity of the West, Wright struggles to escape the implications of his own logocentrism:

> A Westerner must make an effort to banish the feeling that what he is observing in Africa is irrational, and, unless he is able to understand the underlying assumptions of the African's beliefs, the African will always seem a "savage." . . . The Western assumption of the inferiority of the African compels the Westerner to constrict the African environment; so, in time, African psychological attitudes and conditions of life come to reflect the West's assumptions. And the African, anchored amidst such degrading conditions, cannot help but reinforce them by accepting them; and what was, in the beginning, merely a false assumption, becomes a reality. Men create the world in which they live by the methods they use to interpret it. (130)

Wright's final sentence is a self-conscious remnant of his discarded Marxian *epistēmē*: "Men are the makers of the world in which they live."

The shift from a dialectical view of racial and class struggle as history's motive force—apparent in *12 Million Black Voices*—to a psychoexistential complex of subject/object perception binds Wright to the same Western paradigm of analysis he seeks to cast off. It is only a matter of time in *Black Power* before Wright makes explicit the consequences of this process. Wright describes the "vitality of primal attitudes" in the West African as paramount emblems of "outsiderness" to the cognate rationality of the Western mind that he has tried and failed to deconstruct. "What are the basic promptings of artists, poets, and actors but primal attitudes consciously held?" he writes in describing the Ashanti, whose mystery he compares to "a big, shiny-eyed cat [that] might leap out of the rainy black jungle, just as an impulse toward impiety might leap compulsively out of the unconscious of a deeply devout Christian" (283). Having established Africa as what Said calls in *Orientalism* the nation as "surrogate or underground self," Wright makes concrete and decisive his own Western map of this perception: Ashanti is vaguely Oriental; there is something hidden here, a soul that shrinks from revealing itself. The Ashanti are polite, but aloof, willing to do business with you, but when business is over, they turn away from you. They will learn the codes of the Western world and will practice them; but when day is done they go back to their own" (304).

Wright's racial melancholy blithely manifests the spiritual state of his own Afro-Orientalism. The Ashanti are an irretrievable part of the Othered world that is Wright's best symbol for his own disconnection, as an African American, with the West. Wright's ambivalent seduction by the heart of Western darkness discloses his construction of a world rising not from the ashes of the old but from the failure to imagine outside the temporal and spatial limits of the West's own narrative of black displacement. It is also, to return to his preface to *Black Power*, a mirror of the Cold War's particular Orientalist logic. Essentialist binarisms to describe Africa—the tribal and the modern, the passionate and the cognate, the poetic and the pragmatic—are key elements of Wright's culturalist allegory. Nkrumah's Convention People's Party is described as neither nationalist nor socialist (it was, ideologically, both) but as a "new kind of religion. They were politics plus!" (61). Elsewhere Wright describes the Gold Coast challenge to colonial rule as "a mixture of religious fanaticism and anti-European sentiment" (46). "These men," he writes, "were not being so much guided as they were being provoked by elements deep in their own personalities, elements which they could not have ignored even if they had tried" (100). The African personality, according to Wright, supersedes even social organization as a target for reform: "Until there is an inner reorganization of that personality, there can be no question of marching from the tribal order to the twentieth century. . . . At the moment, this subjective mask is more important than economics!" (386).

In the final pages of *Black Power*, Wright assesses the African future as a complex of Cold War binaries. He advises Nkrumah against Soviet assistance—"why should you change one set of white masters for another?" (389). He cautions against Western aid, "for tied to Western money is Western control, Western ideas" (380). Wright then lays out a surefire plan for African self-determination:

> There is but one honorable course that assumes and answers the ideological, traditional, organizational, emotional, political and productive needs of Africa at this time:
>
> AFRICAN LIFE MUST BE MILITARIZED!
>
> A military form of African society will atomize the fetish-ridden past, abolish the mystical and nonsensical family relations that freeze the African in his static degradation; it will render impossible the continued existence of those parasitic chiefs who have too long bled and misled a naive people. . . .
>
> Over and above being a means of production, a militarized social structure can replace, for a time, the political; and it contains its own forms of idealistic and emotional sustenance. A military form of life, of social relations, used as a deliberate bridge to span tribal and industrial ways of life, will free you, to a large extent, from begging for money from the West, and from the degrading conditions attached to such money. (391)

Wright's ambivalent prescription echoes and conjoins several discrete keynotes in Afro-Orientalism's peculiar intellectual history: Marx and Engels's prescriptions for static India; Marcus Garvey's martial nationalism; the Nation of Islam's discipline fetish; Bigger Thomas's autocratic Asian fantasy. The most striking feature of Wright's discipline formula, though, is how intellectually and politically undisciplined it is. If militarizing African life is the cross-pollinating "intercultural hermeneutic" (Gilroy) of Wright's diasporic double consciousness, then it is strange fruit. Wright's final solution for Ghana concludes with quotations from Walt Whitman and the stern admonition to "be on top of theory; don't let theory be on top of you" (392). Wright implies Marxism but identifies no theory. Rather, the North/South/East/West logic of Wright's metaphoric politics mimics his strictly spatialized metaphors of political liberation: both replicate the insider/outsider binarism that brought Wright in a search for self to Africa to begin with. Wright's full relationship to anticolonialism, the Cold War and Asia in particular, however, can only be fully gleaned by reviewing the consequences of *Black Power* for his most significant intellectual encounter with the Other world, namely, his follow-up trip one year later to the Bandung Conference in Indonesia.

The 1955 Bandung Conference of decolonizing African and Asian nations in Indonesia has aptly been called the high water mark of twentieth-century anticolonial struggle. As discussed in chapter 1, the conference was anticipated by nearly half a century of Afro-Asian organizing and exchange: the formation of the Anti-imperialist League after World War I; the meeting of the Congress of Oppressed Nationalities in Brussels in 1927; the parallel formation of Pan-African and Pan-Asian societies from 1900 to 1930. In 1945, the same year as the Manchester Pan-African Congress, several Afro-Asian nations achieved formal diplomatic recognition at the first meetings of the new United Nations. On January 20, 1949, fifteen African and Asian states met in New Delhi at the invitation of the Indian government to discuss "police action" in Indonesia by the government of the Netherlands and called for the "restoration of the Indonesia Republic."[22] In 1954 a Geneva conference on Indo-China was held featuring prime ministers of India, Indonesia, Pakistan, Burma, and Ceylon in Colombo. The nations agreed to support independence for

Indo-China, Morocco, and Tunisia, urged the end of nuclear weapons testing, condemned colonialism, and agreed to support the rights of Palestinian refugees in the wake of the recent establishment of the state of Israel.[23] After 1947 an Arab-Asian group began meeting under the leadership of ambassador Asaf Ali of India to discuss the views of various Arab-Asian nations including Libya, Korea, and Tunisia.[24]

In April 1955, twenty-three Asian and six African nations—all of them sovereign—convened in Indonesia for the first-ever Afro-Asian summit meeting of heads of state. The so-called Bandung Conference had been initiated and organized by the state leaders of the 1954 group that had met in Colombo. At opening ceremonies at Bandung on April 18, Indonesian president Sukarno offered the following motive for the meeting: "We are united . . . by a common detestation of colonialism in whatever form it appears. We are united by a common detestation of racialism. And we are united by a common determination to preserve and stabilise peace in the world."[25] For Sukarno, the meeting of Afro-Asia symbolized the destruction of an "intellectual blockade."[26] The image invoked the eradication of a racialized Berlin Wall (an image to which I will return) and the porous intellectual and ideological borders symbolized by the summit between and among colored nations.

Wright was living in Paris after returning from Andalusia for research for his book *Pagan Spain* when he "idly" picked up the evening's newspaper and saw a notice for the Bandung Conference. Using virtually the same language as he used to describe Nkrumah's Convention People's Party, Wright remarked that the meeting "smacked of something new, something beyond Left and Right. . . . There was something extra-political, extra-social, almost extra-human about it; it smacked of tidal waves, of nature forces"[27] As he had in Ghana, Wright settled on a temporal paradigm by which to try to understand the moment's gravitas. "In Asia and Africa the leaders of the newly freed nations were meeting to find ways and means of modernizing their countries to banish fear and superstition."[28] In a characteristic attempt to make autobiographical this nationalist impulse, Wright conceived of his desire to attend Bandung as a reversal and break with the historiography of the West: "I was ready to fly to Bandung, to fly from the old world of Spain to the new world of Asia."[29]

Wright's attempt to renarrate the moment of colonial beginnings at Bandung underscores self-consciously the ironies implicit in his undertaking the task. Wright's outsider persona determined that his encounter with the Orient would serve to both confirm and disrupt his Columbian ambitions. The conference crystallized the ongoing thematic of Wright's life as an exiled citizen of the West. Persistently in his book *The Color Curtain,* his report on the 1955 conference, Wright struggled to theorize the decolonizing process at Bandung as a mirror and index to his own past and future. "I'm an American Negro," he wrote.

> As such, I've had a burden of race consciousness. So have these people. I worked in my youth as a common laborer, and I've a class consciousness. So have these people. I grew up in the Methodist and Seventh Day Adventist churches and I saw and observed religion in my childhood; and these people are religious. I was a member of the Communist Party for twelve years and I know something of the politics and psychology of rebellion. These people have had as their daily existence such politics.[30]

Wright's description threw into sharp relief both the expanding horizons and ideological constraints of the strategies for political and symbolic representation at Bandung. His earlier prediction that the U.S. color line and Jim Crow foreshadowed the world struggle of the color line underscored a larger shift in anticolonial discourse in which questions of national determination, class struggle, and political identity became understood, as Wright understood them, relationally. Aijaz Ahmad has given the term "Three Worlds Theory" to this political formula as it emerged from the Bandung moment. "The *main* contradiction was now said to be not between capital and labour, nor between the capitalist and the socialist systems of *production*, but between the socialist and capitalist systems of *states*. . . . The main point in all this was that the struggle between capitalism and socialism was to be waged (peacefully) between the (capitalist) First World and the (socialist) second World, and the progressive character of any regime in the (nondescript) Third World was to be determined by the character of its foreign policy and external relations."[31] This new internationalism poignantly demonstrates what I have been calling the limits of being outside. Akin to Wright's description of the bleakness of black life under Jim Crow, it posited interstitial absence, or "negative loyalty," as the epistemological platform of something vaguely discerned as Third World politics. Indeed, Wright characterized the new era of "colonial and postcolonial facts" in spectral terms as "a universe of menacing shadows where disparate images coalesce— white turning into black, the dead coming to life, the top becoming the bottom—until you think you are seeing Biblical beasts with seven heads and ten horns rising out of the sea. . . . Imperialism turns out to have been much more morally foul a piece of business than even Marx and Lenin imagined!"[32] The passage enacts Wright's desire to refigure Marxian historiography, as well as a profound historical alienation from that task. More deeply, it offers the Third World as the First World's abject shadow, an epistemological conundrum. This version of the inside/outside dilemma is writ large across *The Color Curtain* and predicts much about the form of Afro-Asian political discourse and struggle in the post-Bandung era.

The outcomes of the Bandung Conference and Wright's perceptions of the event were predictable in the details of its planning. India's Nehru brokered the invitations to the conference, persuading the Colombo countries not to invite the Koreas, South Africa, or Israel and some African countries still seeking independence. He also convinced them that China must be present. One year earlier, five years after its own liberation, and the same year in which Wright declared it permanently gone down a "bloody road," China had announced its "five principles of coexistence," meant primarily to allay fears of neighboring Asian countries that China intended, or desired, further military conflicts like the just-ended war in Korea that had cost it one million lives. The principles, cosigned by India, included mutual respect of each other's territorial integrity and sovereignty, mutual nonaggression, mutual noninterference in each other's internal affairs, equality and mutual benefit, and peaceful coexistence.[33] The document was in tone and intent quite different from Liu Shao Chi's remarks in November 1949 at the World Federation of Trade Unions Conference in Beijing, China's first major policy statement on its international role after liberation:

> The course followed by the Chinese people in defeating imperialism and its lackeys and in founding the People's Republic of China is the course that should be followed by the peoples of the various colonial and semi-colonial countries in their fight for national independence and people's democracy. . . . If the people of a colonial or semi-colonial country have no arms to defend themselves they have nothing at all. The existence and development of proletarian organisations and the existence and development of a national united front are closely linked to the existence and development of an armed struggle. For many colonial and semi-colonial peoples, this is the only way in their struggle for independence and liberation.[34]

At his speech opening the Bandung Conference on April 18, 1955, Sukarno demonstrated how China's very different formulations of Asian and international solidarity between 1949 and 1954 defined the parameters of discussion at the conference. In celebration that "our nations and countries are colonies no more. . . . We are again masters in our own house," Sukarno reminded attendees of the "life-line of imperialism" that had until recently run from the Strait of Gibraltar, through the Suez Canal, the Mediterranean, the Red Sea, the Indian Ocean, the South China Sea, and the Sea of Japan. "Along that life-line," said Sukarno, "that main artery of imperialism, there was pumped the life-blood of colonialism."[35] Among the signs of the new "mastery" at Bandung was a consensual resolution passed on the final day condemning imperialism "in all its manifestations," a resolution generally taken by their enemies at the conference to include criticism of the Soviet Union and China. Yet the conference also ended with near-uniform praise for China, especially Chou En-lai's diplomatic negotiations of the event. Chou had surprised nearly everyone by insisting on China's respect for religious freedoms and diversity, supporting the resolution on imperialism, and even inviting the

United States to a peaceable discussion of the status of Formosa (Taiwan), an issue that was at that moment prompting rumors of nuclear war in Washington.

Yet Wright's diminished faith in Marxian historicism and Occidental anxieties surrounding his interloper status transformed his account of events at Bandung into yet another "surrogate or underground self." Wright primarily uses language of distance and Othering to describe the non-West. In seeking to understand what he called with generic sweep "the Asian personality," Wright resorted to images of primitivism, primalism, and psychic excess: the Asian anticolonialist, according to Wright, undergoes a "torturous 'liberation'" after colonialism "from his irrational customs and traditions, his superstitions and folklore";[36] Asians are "emotionally charged," yet inclined toward superstitious authoritarianism: "There seemed to be in their consciousness a kind of instinct (I can't find a better word!) toward hierarchy, toward social collectives of an organized nature" (73); in contrast to men of the West, deemed by Wright as "political animals," "the men of the East were religious animals" (80). Wright's chauvinism is motivated not by an unreflective or unselfconscious racism but by the shadow threat both of his own political past and of 1950s Asia, namely, Communism. It is Asiatic religiosity that "propelled him [sic], irrespective of ideology, towards those collective visions emanating from Peking and Moscow. . . . And all the fervid adjurations of Washington, London, or Paris to strive for individual glory and achievement left him cold and suspicious" (74). Wright's image of Asian Cold War politics as warm-blooded panic—"that narrow zone where East met West . . . was hot and disturbed" (72) successfully merged Yellow Peril and Red Scare into a racialized Cold War ideology best figured in the title of his account of Bandung: "the color curtain." Its origins lay most obviously in W. E. B. Du Bois's famous turn-of-the-century proclamation of the color line as the fault line of U.S. racism, now conflated with the more-pressing, for Wright, political specter of the Iron Curtain of Communism. Indeed, the line or curtain as trope was a vivid and malleable one for black radicals generally during the Cold War. In his 1947 book *The World and Africa*, Du Bois had emphatically declared, "The iron curtain was not invented by Russia; it hung between Europe and Africa half a thousand years."[37] Du Bois's book mediated a Pan-Africanist and Communist political solution for Africa to conclude: "If a world of ultimate democracy, reaching across the color line and abolishing race discrimination, can only be accomplished by the method laid down by Karl Marx, then that method deserves to be triumphant no matter what we think or do."[38] At Bandung, Sukarno's image of a "life-line of imperialism," dutifully reported by Wright in his book, likewise pointed to a political boundary that international racial solidarity must tear down to throw off the onerous burden of colonialism and economic poverty for Africa and Asia.

Wright's curtain, however, was a Trojan horse of a different color. Ultimately it offered an image of Asia (and Africa) as separated, partitioned, or "lost" in the Cold War lexicon of the Dulles-led West, to both the "irrational" nature of racialist politics and the madness of Communist appeal. Thus despite his call for a day in which "Asian and African raw materials are processed in Asia and Africa" as a means toward the "de-Occidentalization" of the globe, Wright's book refashioned and re-hung its own color curtain, appropriately woven from classic imperialist/Orientalist cloth:

> Is this secular, rational base of thought and feeling in the Western world broad and secure enough to warrant the West's assuming the moral right to interfere sans narrow, selfish political motives? My answer is, Yes. And not only do I believe that this is true, but I feel that such a secular and rational base of thought and feeling, shaky and delicate as yet, exists also in the elite of Asia and Africa! After all, the elite of Asia and Africa, for the most part educated in the West, is Western, more Western than the West in most cases. . . . And those two bases of Eastern and Western rationalism must become one! And quickly, or else the tenuous Asian-African secular, rational attitudes will become flooded, drowned in irrational tides of racial and religious passions.[39]

Wright's appeal to the Western-educated elites (and emerging bourgeoisies) of Asia and Africa to choose Western aid, technology, and support was the final nail in his Cold War construction of Bandung. His characterization of the Asian and African populations at Bandung as a "gummy mass" dissolved images of class solidarity or collective militancy into the nondescript figure of a helpless horde discursively invisible behind the color curtain.[40] Wright's means of giving shape to this mass through a continued course of Western rationalization constituted an attempt to bleach it of its red, yellow, or even black excesses in order to reconfigure Asia itself in the image, and imagination, of the ambivalent Western interpreter. Wright, in short, accomplished his goal at Bandung of narrativizing his own displacement from the West.

Richard Wright's trip to Bandung was financed in part by financial support from the American Congress for Cultural Freedom. In 1967, the congress was revealed to have been a front for the CIA and State Department, themselves surveillants of wartime and Cold War radicals like Wright. Despite his rhetorical nods to de-Occidentalization, the congress must ultimately have been pleased by Wright's report. It both reflected and dovetailed with a fervid black anti-Communism and confusing racialized discourse on Bandung also present in the congress's domestic sphere of surveillance, black America. New York City representative Adam Clayton Powell, who self-financed his trip to Bandung after the Eisenhower administration refused his request to send a delegation, sent reports on the conference to the *Pittsburgh Courier*, which offered less-blatant though still-mystifying constructions of the Orient while cautioning black readers, "From here on in Asia and Africa can be our friends if we institute a bold new foreign policy based not only on fighting communism, but on the ancient problems of the East—disease, hunger, illiteracy and colonialism."[41] Other writers for the black press, like former National Negro Congress president Max Yergan, *Black Metropolis* author Horace Cayton, and CIO veteran leader Willard S. Townsend, all sounded the same note of support for racial progress at home and anticolonialism abroad while attacking Communism, especially China. Townsend, the presiding black veteran leader of the CIO, even reported in his "Labor Front" column that a recent press release by the International Confederation of

Free Trade Unions reported that workers in China were routinely punished for workplace accidents, since "as in other totalitarian states, they are more concerned with the material losses suffered by state-owned industry than with damage inflicted on the health and life of the workers."[42] Like Wright, Townsend effectively posited working Communism as a surrogate for Asian nationhood and identity, thus destabilizing coherent analysis of both color-based politics and the practical potentiality of Afro-Asian solidarity.

This manufacture of an Orientalist anti-Communism and an anti-Communist Orientalism also defined and contained American domestic racial radicals in 1955. The AFL-CIO merger of that year was characterized, as Manning Marable has shown, by simultaneous attacks and purges of Communists and increasing refusal to criticize racially segregated unions.[43] Indeed, the American labor merger had been foreshadowed by an eight-year campaign against Communists and radicals in the trade union movement, the dissolution of the militant National Negro Congress and National Negro Labor Council, and the formation of the aforementioned International Federation of Free Trade Unions in 1948 in order to separate "free" workers from its predecessor, the Communist-supported World Federation of Trade Unions, formed in 1945.[44] This national and international Cold War hairsplitting was reflected at the microlevel in the United States of 1955 as southern politicians and California legislators came under pressure to review or uphold state laws forbidding interracial marriages of whites to blacks and "Mongolians," a trend exacerbated by the movement of U.S. troops in Asia during and after World War II.

Wright's global dramatization of this Cold War miscegenation hysteria was thus symptomatic of a larger, more-prescient Orientalism that in retrospect has the force of a blood feud. "The Western world must make up its mind as to whether it hates colored people more than it hates Communists or does it hate Communists more than it hates colored people," he wrote after his break with Communism. "It cannot, without being foolish, act as though it hated both equally."[45] The tautological and apocalyptic logic of Wright's formulation is the political subtext of

The Color Curtain as Cold War text and Cold War trope. In spite of it, Afro-Asian solidarity persisted after Bandung in the form of continuous Chinese support for African development, the first gathering of the Afro-Asian Youth Movement in Cairo in February 1959, the formation of the Afro-Asian Writers' Movement in 1958, and the establishment of both the Afro-Asian Trades Union and Chambers of Commerce and the Afro-Asian Solidarity Fund in 1960. Still, largely because of American influence of black anti-Communists like Wright, most African Americans, with the notable exceptions of W. E. B. Du Bois and Paul Robeson, remained sheltered from, or hostile to, these Cold War developments until the very-public reassertion of Afro-Asian politics in the 1960s through the work of Robert F. Williams, Jimmy and Grace Lee Boggs, and the Revolutionary Action Movement, to be discussed in subsequent chapters.

Wright's tortured struggle to straddle the color line and color curtain may also be found replayed with widely varying conclusions in his final book of exile, *White Man, Listen!* Originally published in 1957, the book comprises a series of essays drawn from lectures on anticolonialism that Wright delivered in Italy, Amsterdam, Hamburg, Paris, and Sweden. The lectures were sponsored by European and American cultural organizations, including the U.S. Congress for Cultural Freedom. Two of Wright's lectures in Paris were delivered for the journal *Presence Africaine*. The lectures differ in one marked way from Wright's other anticolonial texts: because, as Cedric Robinson has noted, "their audiences are . . . (silently) implicated in their analytical development,"[46] Wright is less circumspect about Marxist influences on anticolonial politics.[47] In the essay "The Miracle of Nationalism in the African Gold Coast," for example, Wright talks openly about the formation of the Secret Circle, an indigenous African political cell of which Kwame Nkrumah was a member. In a footnote to the American edition of the book, Wright noted that he had "deliberately withheld" mention of the Circle in *Black Power* "for fear that the politically reactionary or ideologically immature would confuse it with Russian Communism and call for the suppression of the African's first modern bid for freedom."[48] Wright also asserts repeatedly in the essays the importance of exposure to Marxism for most of the

Afro-Asian world's revolutionary elite class. Though refusing to give it a name, he asserts that the "ideology does solve something. It lowers the social and racial barriers and allows the trapped elite of Asia and Africa and black America the opportunity to climb out of its ghetto":

> What other road is there out of his Black Belt? His captured homeland? His racial prison? . . . In Asia almost all the national revolutionaries I met had received aid from the hands of Marxists in their youth. The same was true of the black politicians of the Gold Coast, even though Marxism did not even remotely pertain to their non-industrial society. (20)

Wright's engagement with the problem of the Afro-Asian "proletariat" in relationship to Marxist theory is less interesting and ultimately less important than the geographic cast of his thought here. Wright's deployment of Black Belt rhetoric (which moments later he dismisses as an "absurd" Soviet-influenced idea) with Third World liberation nationalisms discloses just how unstable his critical, political, and racial vocabulary had become. Wright was still attempting to translate his initiatory experiences into American Communism—he joined during the party's so-called Third Period or Black Belt thesis period—on to national liberation struggles in the Third World. This effort to map his ideological past to the anticolonial present ironically is a mirror to what he sees as the colonial ailment in *White Man, Listen!* Drawing on Frantz Fanon's and Domingue Mannoni's psychoexistential paradigm for discussing colonialism, Wright describes Asia and Africa as a "neurotic habit that Europeans could forgo only at the cost of a powerfully psychic wound" (5), while white Europe "has become a traditional, a psychological reality in the minds of Asians and Africans" (8). Thus when an American black is lynched, "to an Asian or an African it was not a Mississippi white man who did the lynchings; it was just a Western white man. . . . Europe is indeed one world, small, compact, white, apart" (9). Wright describes the ultimate effect of his own inside/outside paradigm as a negative loyalty to Western modernity, a trope Gilroy seizes on as central and centripetal to understanding diaspora consciousness. "The stance of negative loyalty,"

Wright states, "leads to a whole variety of ironic attitudes. I shall describe this reality briefly under the heading of *acting*" (17; italics mine). Wright's example is, appropriately, a play. "The Miracle of Nationalism in the African Gold Coast" is a story in which a group of six black men representing the Gold Coast revolution discuss the strategies for, and chances of, success. The year is 1948, and the setting the jungle. The historical model for the drama is the 1948 United Gold Coast Convention. The literary model is Thucydides' *History of the Peloponnesian War*. The actors in the play are performing ideas, performing history: "These six black men knew their Marxism, but it is important to remember that they were not really Marxists. They handled Marxist thought self-consciously, standing outside of it, so to speak; they used it as an instrumentality to analyze reality, to make it meaningful, manageable" (24). Their externality to Marxism is paralleled by their externality to the world:

> When they desired to see reality in terms of its external and objective aspects, they thought and felt Western; when they had to deal with their own emotions, they felt and thought African. They lived in two worlds. BUT THEY DIDN'T REALLY AND DEEPLY BELIEVE IN EITHER OF THESE WORLDS. THE WORLD THAT THEY REALLY WANTED, THE WORLD THAT WOULD BE THE HOME OF THEIR HEARTS, HAD NOT YET COME INTO BEING. So, while standing outside of both worlds, so to speak, they were manipulating aspects of both worlds to create the one and single world that they really wanted. (126)

Rather than a negative dialectics, Wright offers a dialectics of negativity. History and historical process are here reduced to an endgame dramaturgy with *no inside*. Echoes of Wright's old world of ideas thus appropriately enter from offstage as minor, illusory characters in the final paragraph of *White Man, Listen!* "We make the world in which we live. So far we've made it a racist world. But surely such a world is not worthy of man as we dream of him and want him to be (142).

Like Du Bois's "Hymn to China," these words form something like Richard Wright's Afro-Asian epitaph. *White Man, Listen!* was his last book on the colonial question and the last book he published before his death in 1960. Cedric Robinson has written of Wright's anticolonial corpus that "whether color or race could be substituted for class in any Marxian paradigm . . . was precisely the issue with which Wright . . . wrestled for three decades."[49] Wright's failure to resolve that question beyond a framework of negative loyalty and metaphysical abjection should caution us against blindly celebratory reclamations of the Bandung era. It should also serve as counterpoint to the final intersection of the lives of Du Bois and Wright, whose deaths three years apart nearly coincided with their interest in Afro-Asia at the terminus of their long careers. Du Bois's embrace of Marxist Communism at the moment of Wright's confused disavowal demonstrates the starkly different paths they chose at the crossroads and end roads of Afro-Orientalism. Yoshinobu Hakutani has argued that Wright's worldview after the influence of Africa and Asia was essentially "primal. . . . His basically poetic apprehension of existence" was a "Zen-like revelation":[50]

> The primal, poetic vision of human existence in nature Wright seized upon in his African journey was reinforced by his view of Asian culture, religion, and philosophy. . . . As an epiphany, it gives the admonition that they must uphold the African and Asian primal philosophy of life and rejects its antithesis of Western materialism.[51]

Hakutani's formula is too neat for the fissures in Wright's anticolonial discourse, yet it does capture the inner dialectic of his writings after his break with the Communist Party. By the time of *White Man, Listen!* Wright was no more or less than the participant observer in his own Orientalist journey to the West. *Black Power, The Color Curtain,* and *White Man, Listen!* are among the most evocative books of negative loyalty written about the subaltern's relationship not only to the West but to the Marxist tradition. That Wright died before the world could become the world he wanted to see, a world without racism, without oppression, without a psychology of abjection, is a tragedy we should not thus excuse or diminish as an ineluctable aspect of diaspora consciousness. It is both a larger ambition and a larger failure than that, one with which few of us, Wright scholars and Afro-Asianists alike, have yet fully reckoned.

CHAPTER 3

Transnational Correspondence: Robert F. Williams, Detroit, and the Bandung Era

Can you imagine New York without police brutality? Can you imagine Chicago without gangsters and Los Angeles without dirilects [*sic*] and winos? Can you imagine Birmingham without racial discrimination and Jackson, Mississippi without terror? . . .

Can you imagine cops and soldiers without firearms in conspicuous evidence of intimidation? Do you think this is a utopian dream? I can understand your disbelief. I believe that such a place exists on this wicked and cruel earth.

—Robert F. Williams, "China: The Good of the Earth," 1963

We learned from Detroit to go to the cities.

—General Vo Nguyen Giap to Robert Williams, 1968

The special issue of *Shijie Wenxue* (World Literature) published in Beijing in September 1963 was dedicated to W. E. B. Du Bois. The lyric poet to China, twice a visitor there, had died in August on the eve of the March on Washington. Working quickly, the editors had compiled an extraordinary gathering of writers and writings in his name. They included Du Bois's poem "Ghana Calls," written to commemorate his final exile; Sie Ping-hsin's "To Mourn for the Death of Dr. W Du Bois"; Margaret Walker's poem "Sorrowful Land"; and a short story, "The Tokolosh," by the South African writer Ronald Segal. Also included were pedagogical texts on black struggle to which 1963 seemed an immediate heir: "Historical Documents of the Struggle for Negroes' Emancipation," including an excerpt from Frederick Douglass's *Narrative*; Han Peh-ping's "Notes on Negroes' Oral Literature in West Africa"; and three articles described as "anecdotes" about Robert F. Williams, the former head of the Monroe, North Carolina, NAACP, now living in exile in Cuba after being charged by the FBI with kidnapping during a 1961 uprising in his hometown. In Cuba, Williams had begun publishing favorable articles and editorials about China in the pages of the *Crusader*, his self-started newspaper. In the fall of 1963, Williams and his wife Mabel made their first visit to China and North Vietnam as invited guests of their respective governments. The trip was precipitated by a letter-writing campaign by Williams to Chairman Mao Tse-tung, urging him to make a statement of support for black Americans. After the racist bombing of the Sixteenth Street Baptist Church in Birmingham in September, killing four African American girls, Mao released his "Support for the American Negroes in Their Struggle against Racial Discrimination and for Freedom and Equal

Robert F. Williams with Mao Tse-tung, Beijing, China, circa 1968. Used with permission of the Bentley Historical Library, University of Michigan.

Rights." Another statement by Mao, titled "Calling upon People of the World to Unite to Oppose Racial Discrimination by U.S. Imperialism and Support the American Negroes' Struggle against America" prefaced the issue of *Shijie Wenxue*.[1]

Mao's statements of support were welcome, if overdue, news to black radicals in the United States, particularly in the city of Detroit, for which Robert Williams was likewise both geographically remote yet symbolically present. Williams had lived briefly in the city in 1942 and 1948. While there, he was an autoworker and member of UAW 600. His commitment to armed self-defense against racist attacks in North Carolina as early as 1957 had brought him to the attention of Detroit activists well before he was charged in the Monroe uprising in 1961. Thus immediately following that charge, supporters in Detroit formed the Robert Williams Defense Committee. In May 1962, the Detroit journal *Correspondence*, edited by Chinese American activist Grace Lee Boggs, published Pamphlet 5, *Monroe, North Carolina . . . Turning Point in American History*. The pamphlet comprised two speeches in Williams's defense by his attorney Conrad J. Lynn and a foreword by James Boggs, a Detroit worker and husband to Grace, comparing Williams's frame-up to the Emmett Till case.[2]

In September 1963, the same month as the special issue of *World Literature*, Detroit poet Dudley Randall wrote his own response to the Birmingham bombing, "Ballad of Birmingham," a haunting lament for the four little girls killed in the blast. At the invitation of the Boggses, the poem was published in the October *Correspondence*. A month earlier, Boggs had published Randall's more polemical "Roses and Revolution," originally written in 1948 and published in 1949, the year of the formation of the People's Republic of China. The poem compared a U.S. lynching victim "lying in the swamp with his face blown / off" to all the war dead, including the victims of the atomic bombs dropped on Hiroshima and Nagasaki.[3] After imagining a "vision of a time when all men walk proudly through the earth / and the bombs and missiles lie at the bottom of the ocean," the poem closes with a political epiphany:

Then washed in the brightness of this vision,
I saw how in its radiance would grow and be nourished and
   suddenly
burst into terrible and splendid bloom
the blood-red flower of revolution.[4]

These synchronous acts of political and cultural translation constitute a singular story of black internationalism in the postwar era. Black
America's call to Asia, and Asia's reciprocal response, reveal the textual
and logistical mechanics of what might be called transnational correspondence. Beginning with the 1955 meeting of decolonizing African
and Asian nations in Bandung, Indonesia, until at least the early 1970s,
African American and Asian radicals imagined themselves as antipodal
partners in cultural revolution, pen pals for world liberation. Motivated
by real and imagined affiliations between race and civil rights struggles
in the United States, anticolonial movements in the Third World, the
Cuban Revolution and the Great Proletarian Cultural Revolution in
China, and a U.S. imperialist war in Vietnam, black and Asian radicals
circulated among themselves a conception of political simultaneity and
indebtedness meant to inform developments on opposite sides of the
world and in so doing to change it. Transnational correspondence refers
specifically to the attempts by black radicals in the United States and liberation leaders in Asia to establish strategic linkages in three areas of
international struggle: military strategizing, including guerrilla tactics;
the role of writers and publishing in building international solidarity;
and the critical relationship between politics and culture. General Vo
Ngyuen Giap's apocryphal quip to Robert Williams ascribing the success of North Vietnamese military operations to the example of Detroit's
urban rebellions of 1967 is but one startling metonymy for these processes. It captures the real and symbolic role that Afro-Asian radicalism
had come to play in the United States as rumors about an "Operation
Giap," an assault by the U.S.-based Revolutionary Action Movement, circulated through black undergrounds and the radical black press of 1966.[5]
It resonated with two oft-circulated declarations by leading exponents of

Afro-Asian revolutionary theory of the 1960s: Robert Williams's "America Is the Black Man's Battleground,"[6] a plaintive insistence that his comrades carry on the war at home during his own Cuban and later Chinese exile; and Detroiters James and Grace Lee Boggs's "The City Is the Black Man's Land."[7] Both slogans figured prominently in the efforts of organizations like the Northern Grassroots Leadership Conference, the Freedom Now Party, the Revolutionary Action Movement, the Republic of New Africa, and the Inner City Organizing Committee to implement Chinese, Vietnamese, and Latin American guerrilla strategies of military and ideological warfare that insisted on a geographic base (be it country or city) for carrying out revolution.

Attempts to link political tactics to relevant forms of black cultural work also followed Asia's example. Especially influential in this effort was Mao's 1942 "Talks at the Yenan Forum on Art and Literature." This seminal essay provided a theoretical template for First World radicals to deploy what Black Arts theoretician Larry Neal called "useable elements of Third World culture."[8] It motivated black artists and writers in particular to incorporate Maoist ideas and an internationalist outlook into publications and activities formative of the Black Arts movement in the United States. Such incorporation is revealed in the torrent of publications, manifestos, books, magazines, newspapers, poems, pamphlets, and journals that circulated from Beijing to Detroit to Havana to Hanoi and beyond. These writings describe Black Arts as an intellectual and textual diaspora of the 1960s. At the same time, the use of literary texts and the printed word as a vehicle for international solidarity underscored political distinctions and differences difficult to overcome. Efforts to analogize such disparate events as the Watts rebellion of 1965 and the Algerian struggle against French colonialism were often unresolved or concluded in makeshift ideologies and temporary or transient positionings. This gave the Bandung era its quixotic revolutionary aura of upstart alliances, improvisatory strategies, and synthetic vocabularies for defining Afro-Asian liberation. One particularly relevant example is the word "black." In their influential writings to be discussed in detail later, groups like the Revolutionary Action Movement came to redefine the term as one of relational *political* (as opposed to racial) meaning. Their call for a "unity of black nationalist[s]" throughout the world defined revolutionary black internationalism as a "philosophy of co-operation. . . . It is the philosophy of a common international cultural heritage and identity among all non-European people, that is African, Asian and South American people all have similar if not the same cultural histories and have a common destiny."[9] RAM's parallel assertion that the "Afro-American revolutionary" is the humanistic "antithesis" of the inhuman West counterposed "counterrevolutionary" white hegemony to its revolutionary Other.[10] This conception of correspondence was a necessary linchpin for bringing Afro-Asian struggles together. It evoked a strategic antiessentialism meant to delink binaries of racial and political separation (African and Asian/First World and Third/Orient and Occident). Seeking correspondence also became a strategy for dialectical understanding of social relations under capitalism and for exposing links in the chain of postwar imperialism and colonialism. Understanding the paradigm of transnational correspondence thus helps to disclose how black and Asian radicals prolonged and remade the so-called Bandung era into a distinctly black formula for liberation.

The momentous 1955 Bandung Conference, intended to foster unity between Africans and Asians, concluded with specific but limited concrete gains for both. Out of the event had come the formation of the Afro-Asian Journalists Association, a network of newspapers and information exchange; the Afro-Asian Writers Bureau, a sister organization; increased economic and political cooperation between China and developing African nations; extended cooperation between African, Asian, and Latin American anticolonial movements; and follow-up conferences like the Havana Tricontinental Conference of 1966, which saw the founding of the Organization of Solidarity of the Peoples of Africa, Asia, and Latin America.[11]

Rewards or consequences for African Americans were more difficult to discern. Limited African American participation in and reporting of the event, including that by Richard Wright and Adam Clayton Powell, had been framed mainly in terms of the benefits Afro-Asian solidarity might accrue to democratic capitalism or Soviet Communism, and the pitfalls of Cold War alliances for African and Asian nations. As Penny Von Eschen and Mary Dudziak have documented, valiant African American efforts to maintain strategic alliances with socialist, Communist, or decolonizing movements in Africa and Asia during the 1950s were generally limited in their success by domestic Cold War restraints and recriminations. In particular, restricting the geographic movement of black radicals by refusing them passports (Paul Robeson and W. E. B. Du Bois, for example) became a crucial way to prevent the construction of anti-colonial bridges.[12]

Robert Williams's example and activities in North Carolina, Cuba, and China came to bear as significant disturbances to this placid framework. As Timothy Tyson has documented, Williams's exposés of the range of acts of white terror against African American citizens in North Carolina in the late 1950s provided timely fodder for both African American activists and U.S. Cold War opponents attempting to destabilize U.S. self-representation of racial democracy. Chinese, Soviet, and other international papers, for example, as well as African American and left newspapers within the United States, raced to tell the story of Hanover Thompson and Fuzzy Simpson, two young boys criminally accused for kissing a white girl in Monroe in 1957. When Williams took the local NAACP lead in protesting the case, he and his attorney Conrad Lynn were publicly accused of being Communist by Chester Davis, a former FBI agent turned journalist.[13] Williams's conspicuous role as a public challenger to NAACP leadership, however, and his public tolerance for support from leftist parties endeared him to white and black radicals alike, particularly those disinclined toward anti-Communism. It also foreshadowed his role in the signal event that revived and described a more prescient internationalism for black radicals in the Bandung era, namely, Williams's much-publicized frame-up, escape, and exile to Cuba after the 1961 uprisings in Monroe.

Williams, along with Julian Mayfield, Amiri Baraka, and others, had through work with Fair Play for Cuba already helped to make the country at least a symbolic outpost of black internationalist hopes. Williams's exile there in 1961 turned Cuba into an even more tangible safe harbor for black militants. It gave increased credibility to the Cuban Revolution and socialism as viable allies for black domestic struggle. Likewise, it renewed interest among black revolutionaries in Latin American political struggles, particularly the figure of Che Guevara. Williams's outspoken support for China from Cuba also began to warm black ears to that country's call. (Du Bois's exile to Ghana after his 1959 visit to China was a preamble to this, as understood by the editors of *World Literature*.) Williams insisted that black Americans side with China in the Cold War Sino-Soviet split of the late 1950s.[14] He argued that China's challenge to Soviet hegemony was tantamount to his own challenge to American racism. The Chinese revolution also captured the Bandung spirit of political self-determination and nonalignment that oddly paralleled his own highly independent relationship to both American left movements like the Socialist Workers Party and more mainstream African American civil rights struggle. In 1965, discouraged by events in Cuba, Williams accepted an invitation from the Chinese government to live in Beijing. From 1965 to 1969, he continued publication of the *Crusader* from Beijing and gave vociferous support to China's revolution. Throughout this period of exile, Williams came to speak to and personify for black radicals what had been important but abstract—and geographically distant— aspects of the anticolonial struggle, giving them domestic relevance and gravitas they had previously lacked.

Equally important to the larger theme of this chapter, Williams recognized his exile, as it was recognized within radical U.S. circles, as an example of political and cultural correspondence. Particularly for radicals with Marxist leanings, his exile came to symbolize the idea of black Americans as colonized or internally exiled figures, an Old Left analysis that would be reconfigured in black nationalist theory of the 1960s. Williams began to circulate his influential views on politics and culture by creating a new information exchange for black internationalists. He began weekly broadcasts of "Radio Free Dixie" on shortwave from Havana, mixing jazz, diatribes about U.S. racism, and inspirational messages drawn from race struggles at home. "Radio Free Dixie" had a circular discursive logic meant to close the gap between himself and America by drawing parallels between his plight in exile and the movement in the United States. Political sermons and editorials by Albert Cleage, pastor at Central United Church in Detroit, for example, resounded back to American listeners who might simultaneously attend a Cleage-sponsored lecture in Detroit on black nationalism in jazz.[15]

From Cuba, Williams also began publishing his own newspaper, the *Crusader*, and sending it back to the United States. The paper derived its name from the newspaper of the African Blood Brotherhood, the post–World War I collective of African American and West Indian Marxists. The ABB drew part of its membership from ex-Garveyites and comprised the first internationalist black publishing collective in U.S. history. Williams's *Crusader*, available by subscription in the United States and distributed with the help of friends in the United States and Canada, initially gave uncritically supportive coverage to the Cuban Revolution and Castro. The early issues of the *Crusader* also insisted, without always supporting its claims, that Cuban support for black struggle was implicit in its socialist revolution and its emancipation from four centuries of Western slavery. The paper was read by civil rights advocates and radicals of a broad stripe—the *Amsterdam News*, John Killens, the Student Non-violent Coordinating Committee (SNCC), Monthly Review Press, and Max Roach were among those listed at one time on Williams's subscription list—and was frequently excerpted in other black and left publications back in the United States.[16]

The impact of Williams's media entrepreneurship as well as his symbolic significance to radicals at home was nowhere more keen than in Detroit. General Baker, later a founder of the League of Revolutionary Black Workers, entered Detroit's black Left through participation in the Detroit Robert Williams Defense Committee in 1962. He recalls reading the *Crusader* and hearing "Radio Free Dixie" while attending Wayne State University, where he helped to form UHURU, one of Detroit's first black nationalist collectives. About those years, recalls Baker, "There was a lot of talk about the 1955 Bandung Conference, you know, the nonaligned nations."[17] In 1963, Baker was one of eighty-four

Michiganders, eleven of them African American, who would travel to Cuba in part motivated by a desire to visit with Williams. Those from Detroit included Luke Tripp, Charles Simmons, Charles Johnson, and John Watson, all to become members of UHURU and the Detroit League. By 1964, Detroiters James and Grace Lee Boggs, Richard and Milton Henry, Albert Cleage Jr., and Dan Georgakas had also either already met with Williams, taken public stands in support of him, read his work, or were basing their own political strategies or thought in part on his ideas or example. In addition, other radicals with Detroit affiliations, including Malcolm X, Max Stanford, and Don Freeman, were developing theories of black nationalism or political liberation heavily influenced by events in Cuba and China, especially after Williams's exile. In a kind of international symbiosis, these radicals made and remade events there, as they did Williams's image, in the name of their own grassroots struggle. Simultaneously, their grassroots struggles became easier to imagine as international events via their real, symbolic, and textual attachment to Williams's exile.

For example, on November 9–10, 1963, the Northern Grass Roots Leadership Conference held its first meeting in King Solomon Baptist Church's sanctuary in Detroit.[18] The conference was occasioned by a split between factions attending the Northern Negro Leadership Conference, arranged by the Detroit Council of Human Rights, in response to events of August and September 1963. Radicals attending the NNLC walked out when the conference refused to discuss two issues: black self-defense and the formation of an all-black political party. The former issue was especially identified with Williams—his self-defense manifesto *Negroes with Guns* had been published in the previous year. Among the dissidents to split with the Council of Human Rights were Albert Cleage, Grace Boggs, James Boggs, Milton Henry, and Richard Henry. The latter, a brilliant young political entrepreneur, and his brother would in 1964 become prominent publishers and organizers of *Now!* the magazine of the all-black Freedom Now Party. As reported in the November 1963 issue of *Correspondence*, under Grace Boggs's editorship at the time, the dissident group from NNLC formed GOAL (Group on Advanced Leadership), a

Cover for the Chinese edition of *Negroes with Guns*. Used with permission of the Bentley Historical Library, University of Michigan.

black nationalist organization.[19] GOAL immediately passed a series of resolutions. They included solidarity with colored people across the world, support for black self-defense, the formation of Freedom Now, support for the newly formed International All-Trade Union of the World, and a demand for political asylum for Mae Mallory and Robert Williams (Mallory had been arrested with Williams during the Monroe uprising and was awaiting trial in Ohio).[20] Boggs, who had written the introduction to the Williams *Correspondence* pamphlet one year earlier, was appointed conference chairman. Malcolm X, who like Williams had given early public support to Castro at speeches in Harlem, spoke in support of both Freedom Now and self-defense resolutions in his well-known speech "Message to the Grass Roots."[21] An intellectual bridge between Malcolm and Williams was provided by GOAL president Richard Henry, whose background paper for the conference was titled "Violence and Non-violence: The Theory of Proportioned Guerilla War."[22] The essay analogized local urban strategies for revolution with guerrilla campaigns in South Asia and Africa, a recurring subject of Williams's writings from Cuba, and Malcolm's speeches in the United States. Another GOAL background paper was prepared by Harold Cruse, then a staff writer for Daniel Watts's New York paper the *Liberator*. Cruse's 1962 essay "Revolutionary Nationalism and the Afro-American" had already established him as a major influence on young black radicals like Max Stanford and Don Freeman. Reflecting his own previous readings of Marxist-Leninist Maoism, and the influence of Fanon, Cruse's essay for the Grassroots Conference attacked the "cultural situation" in the United States and insisted that "no one in America today is able to make culture a political question but the Negro. Hence the Negro's political and economic revolution must be a cultural revolution at the same time."[23]

As these disparate activities suggest, for black radicals seeking to locate local black struggles in an international context, the Detroit Grassroots Conference was a kind of second, domestic Bandung. The conference moved the question of black struggle from one of civil rights to black power and broadened geographic consideration of black liberation from North and South to include hemispheric struggles. It raised more seriously than ever before the question of the relationship between black politics and culture, and the relationship of each to international forms of struggle. For perhaps the first time within the newly emerging black Left, it also clearly demarcated a "reformist" versus "revolutionary" line. At the same time, organizers pledged allegiance to neither the U.S. Communist Party nor Soviet-model socialism, while distancing themselves from black and white reformist struggles or capitalist democracy. The position mirrored in some ways China's (and the Third World's) relationship to conventional Cold War alignments.

Indeed, by the end of 1963, it seemed as if one hundred black flowers were in bloom. Of them, none was more demonstrative of the new transnational correspondence sought by Afro-Asian radicals in Detroit and other northern U.S. cities than the Revolutionary Action Movement. Though Robin D. G. Kelley and Thomas Blair have written more extensively about RAM than any other U.S. scholars, the full history of the organization has yet to be disclosed.[24] The most complete published account of RAM exists as Maxwell C. Stanford's (aka Muhammed Ahmed) 1986 MA thesis "Revolutionary Action Movement (RAM): A Case Study of an Urban Revolutionary Movement in Western Capitalist Society." RAM initially drew together young radicals from SNCC, Marxist organizations, and black student leaders at Central State University in Ohio. According to Stanford, the idea for RAM first began to develop in 1961 when news of Williams's flight into exile reached movement circles. Stanford, Don Freeman, a student at Case Western Reserve College, and several black colleagues organized an off-campus chapter of Students for a Democratic Society called Challenge at Central State. Drawing largely from the writings of Williams and Harold Cruse, Freeman and Stanford decided to organize RAM and to initiate direct-action protest in an effort to create a black working-class nationalist movement.[25] RAM's development was assisted by Mrs. Ethel Johnson, a coworker of Williams's in Monroe who had moved to Philadelphia. Stanford says she helped organize RAM and became a member of its central committees, training young RAM members. She was assisted by Queen Mother Audley Moore, a former Communist who organized the African American Party of National

Liberation in 1963. The party formed a provisional government with Williams elected premier in exile.[26] Stanford also visited Williams in Cuba in 1963, where he intersected briefly with General Baker and the Michigan contingent. By the end of 1963, Stanford had recruited several hundred members into RAM.

In February 1964, four months after the NNLC, Williams published the essay "Revolution without Violence?" in the *Crusader*. The essay criticized nonviolence as a civil rights strategy. It cited the "noble patriots of Concord, Lexington, Valley Forge," and Harpers Ferry as examples of "righteous violence" appropriate to combating attacks on black martyrs like William Moore, Medger Evers, and the slaughtered children of Birmingham. Williams then described a concept of "lightning campaigns conducted in highly sensitive urban communities with the paralysis reaching the small community and spreading to the farm area."[27] The same issue included a report on China and an excerpt from Mao's statement in support of black liberation. Williams's essay inspired Stanford and Freeman to call for an all-black student conference to discuss armed self-defense and black nationalism in the South. Stanford went to Detroit to raise money for the conference, where he met with James and Grace Lee Boggs and discussed Williams's essay. Boggs also asked Stanford to write an essay on RAM that was later printed in *Correspondence*. From there Stanford went south to recruit SNCC fieldworkers to attend the conference, held May 1–4, 1964, at Fisk University. The Afro-American Student Conference on Black Nationalism was, in Stanford's words, "the ideological catalyst that eventually shifted the civil rights movement into the Black Power movement."[28] The conference was titled "The Black Revolution's Relationship to the Bandung World." According to Stanford, the conferees agreed to "translate" nationalist ideology into effective action.[29] Their "strategy of chaos," in the words of Detroit's Cleage, included controlling black neighborhoods, training and disciplining young cadres, and making young black radicals the vanguard of revolution.[30] The conference also adopted thirteen points of implementation, mostly aimed at internationalizing black struggle. It "united" with African, Asian, and Latin American revolutions and sought to gain their financial support; it adopted Williams as leader-in-exile; it described its philosophy as "Pan-African Socialism"; it called for the creation of a national public organ, *Black America;* and finally, as Du Bois, William Patterson, and Paul Robeson had done ten years earlier, RAM charged U.S. imperialism with having committed genocide.[31]

From 1964 to about 1968, RAM existed as groupings of cells primarily in Oakland, Detroit, Philadelphia, Cleveland, and New York. Its circumspectness then and now about the nature and structure of its work, or its degree of cohesion, makes it difficult to make definitive statements about the movement's success or effectiveness. What can be traced is a fairly close symbiotic relationship between Williams's program-in-exile and RAM's internal response to U.S. political events. RAM functioned as a kind of translator, or at times transcriber, of Williams's ideas about race and revolution. For example, in its journal *Black America,* RAM frequently reprinted part or all of essays by Williams first published in the *Crusader*. These included his "U.S.A.: The Potential of a Minority Revolution" and an excerpt from "On Black Self-Defense," published in a compendium of writings titled "Roots of Revolutionary Nationalism" in the fall 1964 issue.[32] The same issue also included "Greetings to Our Militant Vietnamese Brothers," by Max Stanford. Reminiscent of Ho Chi Minh and Frederick Douglass, the essay used the occasion of American independence—July 4—to congratulate the Vietnamese Front of National Liberation for its victories against U.S. imperialism. "We hope that our solidarity will encourage our brothers in South Vietnam and the world over to intensify their revolutionary efforts so that in the near future, all of us will be able to meet and lay the basis for a new world society in which all forms of colonialism and exploitations" will be abolished.[33]

Williams, who received at least some issues of *Black America* in both Cuba and China, embodied RAM's ersatz wish of Afro-Asian solidarity when he appeared months later in Hanoi from November 25 to 29, 1964, at the International Conference for Solidarity with the People of Vietnam against U.S. Imperialist Aggression and for the Defense of Peace. Sixty-four delegations and 169 representatives from fifty countries attended the conference. Also present were representatives from the Association of Afro-Asian Writers, the Japan Afro-Asian Solidarity Committee, the Association of Afro-Asian Journalists, and the Organization of Afro-Asian People's Solidarity, each spawned in the wake of Bandung. Williams identified himself as "chairman-in-exile" of RAM when his turn came to speak, describing the organization as a "united liberation front."[34] He cast support for "the right of all oppressed people to meet violence with violence"[35] and compared U.S. imperialism in Vietnam to the Birmingham church bombings. In symbolic reciprocity, Tran Van Thanh, head of the delegation of the South Vietnam National Front for Liberation, spoke in support of struggles against racial discrimination in South Africa and the United States.[36] The conference ended with statements against U.S. and Belgian aggression in the Congo, and an "Appeal to the American People" to protest U.S. efforts to widen the war in Vietnam.[37]

Ten months later, the Watts rebellion in Los Angeles provided RAM and Williams an uncanny sequel to their political aspirations at Hanoi. The August 1965 issue of *Black America* featured a cover dedicated to the rebellion and reprinted two of Williams's essays: the brief "Urban Guerilla Warfare" and the much-longer "U.S.A.: The Potential of a Minority Revolution." The latter, very influential on RAM thinking, argued that the "lesson of Monroe" teaches that effective self-defense requires massive organization with central coordination. The essay prescribes acts of sabotage that black "freedom fighters" might undertake: deploying gasoline firebombs, using hand grenades, choking gas tanks with sand or sugar, and using long nails driven through boards to slow traffic. Reinforcing his "America Is the Black Man's Battleground" thesis, Williams describes "the complex of cities" like New York, Detroit, and Chicago as "convenient for revolutionary nationalists."[38] It also describes warfare techniques for the Black Belt area of the South— Louisiana, Mississippi, Georgia, and South Carolina. It predicted that "the Southern front would shift quickly from guerilla to mobile warfare."[39] The article was followed by a two-page "Notes on the Philosophy of Self-Defense Warfare," featuring more than a half-dozen quotations from Mao on war and guerrilla warfare. The section ended with a single paragraph titled "RAM Philosophy," which stated:

> RAM philosophy may be described as revolutionary nationalism, black nationalism or just plain blackism. It is that black people of the world (darker races, black, yellow, brown, red, oppressed peoples) are all enslaved by the same forces. RAM's philosophy is one of the world black revolution or world revolution of oppressed peoples rising up against their former slave-masters. Our movement is a movement of black people who are coordinating their efforts to create a "new world" free from exploitation and oppression of man to man.[40]

The challenge of such political bravado, of course, was to delineate between rhetoric and action. Though Williams himself was careful to argue that racial justice, not government overthrow, was the end point of his protestations, the frontline view of Watts inflamed RAM's analysis. "The events in L.A. show we are at war with the United States government," they wrote in *Black America*.

> This shows we are still slaves, i.e. colonial subjects, not citizens denied our rights. . . . As to the international ramifications of this revolt, it further exposes the U.S. as a racist colonialist prison for black people to the Bandung (colored) peoples of the world and shows that the African enslaved in America is not a satisfied "Uncle Tom" waiting to integrate with the racist imperialist beast society, and this shows that we are victims of domestic (internal) colonialism.[41]

RAM also underscored the high percentage of ghetto youth in the Watts uprising:

> We see youth all over the world leading the revolutions of our people. In the Angolan liberation army the soldier's age range is 17–20; in the Congo's

guerilla force called "Youth" the age range is 14–20; in the Viet Cong the
age range is 14–19; in Kenya the Mau Mau was started by roving bands of
youth. In Cuba Castro's forces were very young.[42]

RAM's analysis of events in Watts was consistent with its concep-
tualization of race, revolution, nationalism, propaganda, and paramilitary
planning. The fullest programmatic demonstration of these ideas lies
in the essay "The World Black Revolution," first published in 1965. The
thirty-page pamphlet, with a cover photograph of Mao and Robert
Williams, is perhaps the most complex and synthetic document on black
liberation of the Bandung era. Its primary theoretical and political aim
was to find a new conception of world revolution to replace Marxism,
and a new revolutionary agent in history to replace the industrial proletariat. Methodically, if eclectically, the essay pursues this end. Opening
with an echo of *The Communist Manifesto*—"All over Africa, Asia, South,
Afro, and Central America a revolution is haunting and sweeping"[43]—
the essay proclaims that "the principal contradiction in the world is
between imperialism, particularly U.S. imperialism and the colonies,
between the haves and the have nots" (3). Du Bois's color line thesis and
Lin Piao's writings on imperialism are cited to argue that caste, not class,
is the primary source of this contradiction (4, 6). The Indian Marxist
M. N. Roy is credited with disproving Lenin's imperialism thesis by claiming that the colonies, not the European working class, are the proper
vanguard of world revolution (4). Historical evidence is most compelling
in China's 1949 liberation, the event that, for RAM and most anticolonialists, represented the dawning of the Bandung era. History, then, has
come full circle after Watts: it is now the "black underclass," understood
as the corresponding colored nations across the globe, who must carry
the world black revolution forward (6). The essay's cultural perspective is
Afrocentric—"God is not white but Black, Jesus was a Black African organizing other Black Africans"—reflecting the possible influence of Cleage's
liberation Christianity (7). The essay also recalls Du Bois's writings on
African socialism, suggesting the reorganization of society along "com-
munalist" lines (14). Other influences include Mao, Nkrumah, Fanon,

and Malcolm X's 1963 Grassroots Conference speech, cited directly in the text: "All the revolutions going on in Asia and Africa today are based on Black Nationalism. . . . If you're afraid of Black Nationalism, you're afraid of revolution and if you love revolution, you love Black Nationalism, you love revolution (18).

The last third of RAM's essay proposes to demonstrate the three most significant influences on black struggle for national liberation and "the internationalizing of its intelligentsia and broad masses": Robert Williams, Malcolm X, and Elijah Muhammad (20). Despite this claim, almost all the citations in the essay that follow are to Williams. The essay excerpts lengthy passages from his *Crusader* articles "Revolution without Violence?" "The Potential of a Minority Revolution—Pt 1," and "The Potential of a Minority Revolution—Pt 2." Other citations are to Mao's "Statement in Support of Black America," and two essays by James Boggs, "Black Power: A Scientific Concept Whose Time Has Come" and "Integration and Democracy: Two Myths That Have Failed," the latter originally published in the fall 1964 *Black America*.[44] The essay concludes by calling for a black secretariat (intelligentsia) that can help form the guidelines for all black revolutionary internationalists to be organized in a "central *international* revolutionary action movement."[45] "This movement in order to be successful would have to organize a People's liberation army on a world scale to complete the world black revolution and to thoroughly defeat and annihilate all vestiges of counter-revolution."[46]

It is tempting to dismiss the autodidactic ambitions of RAM, and to an extent Williams, particularly since it is difficult to know how much the latter sanctioned the interpretation of his ideas by the former. Yet their contingent relationship is itself an important indicator of the quest between distant allies to articulate proximity and likeness in what they perceive as revolutionary situations. In coming to understand this challenge for themselves, African American radicals after 1965, in conjunction with select Asian counterparts, began to look for even-greater specificity in the objective conditions underlying their search for political correspondence. In Detroit, the deepening economic problems in the city, the intensification of U.S. war efforts in Vietnam, and the outbreak of

China's Great Proletarian Cultural Revolution in 1966 inspired new organizational approaches to questions of politics and culture. Veterans of the Grassroots Leadership Conference of 1963, for example, founded the Inner City Organizing Committee in the fall of 1966. The ICOC adopted a founding constitution on October 2, which likened the conditions of Detroit residents to the "dispossessed of the earth."[47] The ICOC sought to provide black Detroiters with a "consciousness of . . . history and social identity" and to "encourage cultural activities" intended to carry out the "complete and human reorganization of human life."[48] The echoes of what RAM had called in 1965 "Bandung humanism" were not accidental. James Boggs, a founder of the ICOC, was a key adviser and contributor to RAM in Detroit and, according to Max Stanford, served briefly as "ideological chairman." Bandung humanism was a theory of self- and social transformation borrowing from Mao the notion that "human nature" was a bourgeois fallacy to be dispatched by a total transformation of society: "Genuine love of mankind will be born only when class distinctions have been eliminated throughout the world."[49] In 1965, after its second Afro-American Student Movement Conference, RAM laid out its fullest conception of this idea in the essay "The Relationship of Revolutionary Afro-American Movement to the Bandung Revolution." The essay was a kind of companion piece to "The World Black Revolution." It defined Bandung humanism as a "revolutionary revision of Western or traditional Marxism to relate revolutionary ideology adequately to the unprecedented political, socio-economic, technological, psycho-cultural developments occurring in the post World War II era."[50] The essay described Bandung humanism, or its synonym "revolutionary black internationalism," as the synthesis of the conflict between the "Yanqui" imperialist thesis and the anti-imperialist humanist Bandung antithesis. The precondition for the latter is a "socialist 'classless' world democracy" intent on destroying oppression in all its forms. The prophetic mission of Bandung humanism, the essay argued, was implicit in the modernist music of Bird, Miles, and Coltrane. "The task of the Revolutionary Afro-American Movement," it wrote, "is to express via political action the dynamism embodied in Afro-American music."[51]

The ICOC's call for a cultural reorganization of black life also had roots in both the work of the Facing Reality Group, which had written and published numerous essays on American culture in *Correspondence*, as well as the example of Detroit's evolving black literary culture. The January 1963 issue of *Correspondence*, for example, included a "Special Emancipation Supplement on Black Art."[52] At least twelve of Dudley Randall's early poems were published in *Correspondence*. Many had come out of writers' workshops at Boone House founded by former Chicago poet Margaret Danner. Other participants at Boone House included Naomi Madgett (whom Randall would also later publish with Broadside), Oliver LaGrond, Ed Simplins, Harold Lawrence, James Thompson, and Woodie King.[53] In 1962, Detroit's Rosey E. Pool, a Dutch-born leftist, published the anthology *Beyond the Blues: New Poems by American Negroes* with the Hand and Flower Press in England. *Beyond the Blues* was an exceptional collection of poetry in several ways: it included work by important precursive poets, many with ties to the Old Left or Communist Party, including Margaret Walker, Langston Hughes, Claude McKay, Sterling Brown, Robert Hayden, William Waring Cuney, Countee Cullen, Arna Bontemps, Gwendolyn Brooks, and Owen Dodson. At the same time, the book was the first anthology to gather poets who would become by the end of the 1960s emblematic of the Black Arts movement nationally: Mari Evans, Dudley Randall, Calvin Hernton, Ted Joans, Madgett, Audre Lorde, and LeRoi Jones (aka Amiri Baraka). Poole's anthology preceded and anticipated the explosion of literary anthologies during the Black Arts movement nationally (for example, Langston Hughes's 1964 *New Negro Poets U.S.A.*, John Henrik Clarke's 1964 *Harlem U.S.A.*, Abraham Chapman's 1968 *Black Voices*, Larry Neal and Amiri Baraka's 1970 *Black Fire*, and Toni Cade's 1970 *The Black Woman*). It also signaled the connection between writing as collective enterprise and publishing, something foreshadowed by 1930s organizations like the Communist Party's John Reed Clubs and journals and Richard Wright's South Side Writers' Group.[54]

This communal cultural ethos reached its zenith in Randall's founding of Broadside Press in 1965, a transformative step in Detroit's cultural revolution. Randall described the goal of Broadside as bringing "poetry to the people."[55] His first two broadsides, "Ballad of Birmingham" and "Dressed All in Pink," sold for less than fifty cents and were published with twelve dollars paid out of Randall's own pocket.[56] Randall's first collection of broadsides, *Poems of the Negro Revolt*, included work by Robert Hayden, Margaret Walker, Melvin Tolson, and Gwendolyn Brooks. Though he claimed retrospectively, and even in his time, to eschew verse that sacrificed form for politics, and continuously published formally complex, experimental verse, strong political themes and social protest are the hallmark of most all Broadside poetry published between 1965 and 1970. The most significant contribution of Broadside to Detroit's new cultural politics was its tribute book *For Malcolm: Poems on the Life and the Death of Malcolm X*, coedited by Randall and Margaret Burroughs. Burroughs, a veteran of Chicago's Old Left and founder of the DuSable Museum in Chicago, had persuaded Randall to visit the Soviet Union with her in 1966. It was there that Randall encountered the broadside format he was to imitate. James Patterson, a black Russian they met on their visit, would contribute "Ballada o Neizvestnosti" (Ballad to the Anonymous) to the *Malcolm X* anthology. Still other Detroit contributors included former Chicagoan and Boone House founder Margaret Danner, collaborator with Randall on the book *Poem/Counterpoem*; Robert Hayden; and a score of writers Randall had already published: Etheridge Knight, Mari Evans, Gwendolyn Brooks, and Sonia Sanchez.[57]

The Black Arts movement, as it developed in Detroit and other parts of the United States, also reflected the influence of the writings of Mao Tse-tung on 1960s black radicals. Mao's writings were a staple of Detroit radical study groups as early as 1963. Dan Georgakas, for example, recalls that support for China's revolution and reading of Maoist writings was an article of faith among Detroit radicals, even those who didn't subscribe to Maoist thought.[58] The Boggses frequently cited Mao's essays, particularly "On Contradiction," in their written work and in Detroit study circles. An even more widely studied and debated essay was Mao's "Talks at the Yenan Forum," a speech delivered on May 23, 1942, during the national war with Japan. There Mao raised two questions regarding national cultural struggles directly relevant to participants in the U.S. Black Arts movement. The first, "For whom are our art and literature intended?"[59] was fundamental to efforts of Black Arts entrepreneurs like Amiri Baraka in New Jersey and Woodie King in Detroit to develop independent black theater companies for the staging of black-authored plays, as well as for publishers like Randall aspiring to black-owned publishing ventures. Mao's second question, "How to serve," was fundamentally one of aesthetics: "Should we devote ourselves to elevation or to popularisation?"[60] Mao's Yenan essay argued for both: "What we demand is unity of politics and art," wrote Mao, "of content and form, and of the revolutionary political content and the highest possible degree of perfection in artistic form. . . . We must carry on a two-front struggle in art and literature."[61] Writers and artists, he argued, were to make up a companion cultural "front" to the first-line military front in the war with Japan. Revolutionary art and literature were then to be judged "on the basis of actual life and help the masses to push history forward."[62]

Examples of black translation and interpretation of Mao's Yenan theory for U.S. Black Arts are evident across the spectrum of 1960s black writings and speeches on culture. To begin with one remote example, in 1967, Robert Williams spoke in Beijing to commemorate the twenty-fifth anniversary of Mao's Yenan talk. Williams noted the capacity of the United States to use the "medium of seductive culture" to enact ideological war against black Americans.[63] As would Larry Neal, Sonia Sanchez, Amiri Baraka, and other founders of U.S. Black Arts, Williams attacked denigrating and racist images of blacks in radio and television and argued that black writers must create a "new revolutionary approach to propaganda" (3). He cited as examples "progressive new protest jazz," "bold new works . . . in mushrooming community art galleries," and all-black "People's Theater," such as Frank Greenwood's Los Angeles staging of *If We Must Live*, an adaptation of events of the Monroe rebellion titled after Claude McKay's 1919 sonnet "If We Must Die" (3). Williams also gave a Bandung cast to U.S. Black Arts: he urged black writers in the United States to "work directly with the Afro-Asian writers association" to understand the "mores, customs, traditions and history of the oppressed peoples of the world" (3). The intent of black and Afro-Asian art, Williams wrote, was to "serve to stimulate revolutionary zeal" and to become the "trigger mechanism to detonate the explosion of rebellion" (3).

This same Yenan spirit can be seen in two important Black Arts conferences of 1966 and 1967 held in Detroit. The 1966 Black Arts Conference was organized by the Inner City Organizing Committee, under the direction of Albert Cleage, and Forum 66, a forum on black culture at the Dexter Avenue bookstore hosted by Edward Vaughn.[64] The convention was held on June 25 and 26 at Cleage's Central United Church to coincide with the 1966 Black Writers Conference at Fisk University. It included panel discussions of literature, featuring a presentation by Randall, and a panel on community activism led by Grace Boggs.[65] The conference agenda included an appeal to create new jobs, community control of black schools, the end of a military draft until black service equaled its population proportion, and a training program for youth leaders.[66] James and Grace Boggs, who helped to draft the agenda, attempted to link the political platform for the conference to the creation of "new social values" that might form the basis of a revolutionary national culture:

> A people building a national movement needs the conviction that history is on their side and ultimate victory is certain because as a people they have an inherent dignity which no amount of brutalization and degradation can destroy. It is not oppression which destroys people. It is the acceptance of oppression.
>
> A people building a national movement also needs the conviction that they are creating new social values among themselves. When an individual joins the movement, he must know that he is not doing it just for his own selfish ends but that he has put individualism behind him in order to join a new brotherhood dedicated to changing the world.[67]

The Boggses' dialectical analysis of the relationship between personal values and political practice reflected another theme of Mao's Yenan address, namely, the relationship between the philosophic (ideal) and the mechanical: "Idealists stress motive and ignore effect," wrote Mao, "while mechanical materialists stress effect and ignore motive; in contradistinction from either, we dialectical materialists insist on the unity of motive and effect."[68] In cultural terms, Mao's dialectics insisted that the artist understand his labor as part of national political struggle. Each of these aspects of the "two-front struggle" was sharply in evidence one year later, from June 29 to July 2, when Forum 66 hosted Detroit's 1967 Black Arts Conference, again at Cleage's Central United. The conference featured a literature workshop with Randall, Nikki Giovanni, and John O. Killens. *Liberator* editor Daniel Watts was a featured speaker.[69] Organizers of the conference described it as the nexus of a cultural and political rebirth: "The Black Arts Conference meets in Detroit at a historical crossroads in the development of the black liberation struggle in America. For the first time in the history of this continent the cry of Black Power now echoes nationally from South to North, from East to West and back again."[70]

> At this historical juncture, it is a matter of life and death that we reject the road of black idealism, based on sentiment and self-agitation, and embark resolutely on the road of black realism, projecting a vision of black power and analyzing scientifically where, how and when it can be achieved.
>
> Power means state power or that control of the political apparatus of a given government unit (be it the nation, the state, the county or the city) which guarantees control of economic, military (i.e. army, national guard, police or sheriff) and informational resources. For black people in America the struggle for this power begins at the county level in the South and the big city level in the North, where we have or will soon have a majority, giving us the legitimacy not only of social need and social force but also of historical right.[71]

The 1967 Black Arts Conference called for three things: a vision of a new society initiated by black political rule, mass community organizations, and a cadre organization dedicated to the realization of black political power and conscious of the necessity to defend itself and the community "in these years of the gun."[72] Two significant points merit attention here. First, the conference's numerous direct echoes of Maoism, including Mao's Yenan plea that "man's social life" constitutes the true subject for art, discloses the ways that BAC organizers saw the role of the black artists to "create art and literature that can awaken and arouse the masses and impel them to unite and struggle to change their environment."[73] Second, the agenda confirms the degree to which Detroit's Black Arts movement was perhaps more than in any other American city wedded to questions of political economy and political praxis. Indeed only twenty-one days after the 1967 BAC, the "Year of the Gun" exploded in Detroit: forty-three people were killed and millions of dollars of damage incurred during one of the most extensive urban rebellions in U.S. history. Just as organizers like James and Grace Boggs were falsely accused in Detroit of starting the riots (the Boggses were traveling in California when the riots broke out), so it would be ridiculous to blame the organizers of the 1967 BAC for the Detroit rebellion. Rather, the 1967 BAC, like its predecessor, discloses still another form of transnational correspondence central to Detroit's Bandung era, this one the search for a political aesthetic worthy of capturing and altering the objective conditions of urban crisis.

In fact, the rebellions of July 1967 only deepened the relationship between the political and the cultural in Detroit. In September 1967, John Watson and other members of the black nationalist group UHURU assumed the editorship of the *Inner City Voice*, a new monthly newspaper. According to Dan Georgakas, it was while studying with Facing Reality veteran Marty Glaberman that John Watson and other UHURU member had read Lenin's pamphlets and come to appreciate the importance of a revolutionary press.[74] The paper itself echoed the name of the Inner City Organizing Committee and granted ICOC founding member James Boggs his own column in the paper, "Birth of a Nation." The *Inner City Voice* quickly became paradigmatic of the quest by Detroit radicals to place the African American liberation struggle at the center of an internationalist cultural politics rooted in local conditions. James Boggs's October 20, 1967, column, for example, compared the 1967 rebellion in Detroit to the Santo Domingo revolt in Haiti, and the crackdown of Detroit police to French and British colonial rule.[75] The article "Robert Williams Challenges U.S. Ban" reported on Williams's *Crusader* article written from Beijing protesting the U.S. postal service's recent decision to stop circulating the paper, labeling it subversive (in subsequent issues the *Inner City Voice* frequently printed columns from the *Crusaders* it still received as a service to others whose subscriptions were interrupted).[76] The same issue also included Charles Johnson's review of Frantz Fanon's *Black Skins, White Masks* and reported on the frame-up of sixteen members of RAM charged with plotting to kill Roy Wilkins and Whitney Young. The story was coauthored by Charles Johnson and Dan Georgakas, who had met Baker and other *Inner City Voice* founding members through the Robert Williams Defense Committee in 1962. The next issue of the paper, November 16, featured the first of Stu House's "Third World Report" columns criticizing "radical-turned-Uncle-Tom" Eric Williams, president of Trinidad, for refusing to allow Stokely Carmichael to speak there. In the same issue, the paper reported on Carmichael's recent speech in Algeria, and a rally in Brazzaville, Congo, against U.S. imperialism in Africa and Vietnam; carried an informational article on Che Guevara; and included an inspirational photo of China's Red Guard, meant to support and encourage efforts of RAM to recruit Detroit youth to its "Black Guard," a disciplined cadre of potential revolutionaries.[77]

James Boggs articulated the editorial intent of the *Inner City Voice*'s coverage in a Februrary 29, 1968, column titled "The International." "The new International for the world black revolution," wrote Boggs, "has been in the process of birth ever since the Bandung conference of 1954. . . . But since the vast majority of Bandung nations were more anxious to be neutralists than revolutionists in the conflict between Russia and the United States, they could not be the nucleus of the new International. Instead they became vulnerable to the fragmentation by the counter-revolution in the form of neo-colonialism and foreign aid."[78] Boggs in turn declared the National Liberation Front in Vietnam as the forerunner of a new revolutionary vision and argued for China's proletarian revolution as the center of the new International from which might emerge "the highest development of the colonial peoples in their struggle against colonialism and to build a new society."[79] The *Inner City Voice* also carried ads inviting membership in a new organization, COBRA (Coalition of Black Revolutionary Artists). Given that the March 1968 issue of the *Inner City Voice* reported on plans for a "People's War" in Detroit meant to prepare black readers for the invasion of a white army, the paper left little doubt that it imagined the Motor City as the Western world's corresponding center to Asia's black revolution.

At the same time, the paper became an important outlet for supporting Detroit's national Black Arts profile. It published Newark Black Arts poet LeRoi Jones's seminal poem "Black Art" in its December 15, 1967, issue.[80] Detroit Black Arts poet Gloria House contributed poems to the paper, as did RAM member Rolland Snelling (Askía Touré). The paper also published favorable articles or reviews of novelist John O. Killens (later to live in China); Piri Thomas, author of *Down These Mean Streets;* and the visual artist Glanton Dowell. Even Robert Williams was symbolically adopted by the *Inner City Voice* into Detroit's Black Arts movement. The December 1967 issue of the *Crusader* featured one of Williams's occasional forays into poetry, the acidly witty "The Nationalist Anthem," which opens with this signifying stanza:

> Oh, say can you see by the devil's dim light
> What so proudly he hailed at his twilight's last gleaming?
> Whose blood stripes and deep scars, thru our perilous fight
> O'er the ramparts they watched so arrogantly dreaming.[81]

"The Nationalist Anthem" set to rhyme the prevailing RAM theme that "white" or reactionary nationalism must be stridently opposed by its progressive black opposite or antithesis. The poem was subsequently reprinted, along with Williams's parodic poem "America the Bruteful," in the September 9, 1969, issue of *Sauti,* the single issue of the *Inner City Voice* to appear under this temporary name.[82] The especially long journey of Williams's poetry from Beijing to Detroit was mirrored in the reverse routes taken by African American writing into the Asian radical press overseas. For example, the March 6, 1968, issue of *Red Flag*, the paper of the Ceylon Communist Party, reprinted Williams's December 1967 *Crusader* essay "Why I Propose to Return to Racist America." The March 1968 issue also published the revolutionary poet Sonia Sanchez's protest poem "Slogan (Buy American)." Sanchez had already achieved prominence in the U.S. Black Arts movement by publishing early poems with Randall's Broadside Press. "Buy American" was an acid parody of twentieth-century Americanism:

buy american cars
all you unamerican
looking negroes
buy now and
save yourselves
the frustration of
calling taxis
that never stop
for you men
moving in darkness.
so buy now
and pay later
for the pleasure
of riding to your
own ghettoes
where all white
taximen never go
buy now
and defeat
bigotry
in america.[83]

Like *Shijie Wenxue*'s special Du Bois issue, *Red Flag*'s positioning of African American literature as a companion to liberation struggles helps to disclose how Afro-Asian revolutionaries of the 1960s revisioned not only second Bandungs but second Yenans, where culture could serve the long international march to freedom. Indeed, *Red Flag, World Literature, Correspondence*, the *Crusader,* Broadside Press, *Black America,* and the *Inner City Voice* constituted the informal, discrete, yet global association of Afro-Asian writers that Robert Williams had called for in his 1967 anniversary speech on Yenan. Where African-American writers could not and did not participate in the Afro-Asian writers' associations that emerged in the wake of the 1955 Bandung meeting, these publications nonetheless functioned as the best available means for imagining a world literature that would, at the least, be faithful to the Bandung spirit.

The rise of Detroit's Black Arts movement coincided with a final stage of local revolutionary organization building in the Bandung era. After 1968 two new organizations appeared on the city scene: the League of Revolutionary Black Workers and the Republic of New Africa. While sharing ideological influences and in some cases personnel, each organization developed independent political and cultural fronts that synthesized and advanced key tendencies of the period. RNA was in many ways an extension and revival of the work of RAM, many of whose members had gone underground, been arrested, or were under surveillance by 1968. Like RAM, RNA was nationalist with both Marxist and internationalist leanings. Like RAM, it followed closely the writings of Robert Williams and named him president-in-exile upon its founding. Williams had thrown his support behind the organization when contacted in China by Detroit founders Milton and Richard Henry. RNA distinguished itself from RAM by arguing for black secession. It buttressed its position with the argument that blacks had never freely chosen U.S. citizenship in the United States. It compared the condition of U.S. blacks to Filipinos during "their period of subjugation" before World War II when they were U.S. residents but Philippine citizens.[84] In general, RNA attempted to translate fundamental tenets of Detroit's Bandung era activism to constitutional and governmental process. Its March 30, 1968, founding agenda proposed RNA as an embodiment of a new nonaligned black nation. It imagined a new black government with executive, legislative, and judicial branches. As a result of preliminary elections, Milton Henry was named first vice president; Betty Shabazz second vice president; Charles Howard minister of state and foreign affairs; H. Rap Brown minister of defense. Queen Mother Moore, a RAM veteran, was named minister of health and Welfare, and Brother Imari (Richard Henry) minister of information. RNA sovereignty was to be established through military action or land acquisition via negotiations with the U.S. government. The founding document also insisted that black guerrillas under arrest in the United States be treated as prisoners of war, and argued that black youth should not serve a U.S. government that failed to recognize the republic as sovereign (ibid.). Finally, RNA's founding agenda called for expansion of what it called the "Cultural Revolution." "The primary industry which is within our reach," it argued, "is the entertainment industry" (ibid.). It thus called for partial application of a 2 percent tax on citizens toward the publishing of books, magazines, pictures, and movies and the making of Afro clothes. It recommended the immediate creation of a small commercial/industrial complex in the south on a hundred-acre site to establish a printing plant, recording facility, motion picture lot, food lab, and bookstores: a kind of Motown south (ibid.).

Toward this end, the founding agenda spent considerable time on the issues of reparations and land negotiations. RNA laid claim to Alabama, Georgia, Mississippi, Louisiana, and South Carolina as territories. It demanded that the federal government relinquish these and establish the RNA as a government in exile. Two rationales accompanied the land program: RNA claimed the Black Belt as black land stolen by the United States. It also argued that the failures of northern industrialization necessitated finding a new black home, and home base, in the American South. Yet rather than thinking of the Black Belt as a return to Africa, or neo-Garveyism, RNA imagined its political relationship to the United States as akin to the National Liberation Front of North Vietnam. It thus looked to Asia as well as Africa for support. It asked the Afro-Asian world to endorse a request at the UN for a plebiscite to demand reparations and called on the "Afro-Asian world and all peace-loving people who believe in the right of peoples to self-determination, to recognize our right to self-determination (ibid.). It also looked to Asia for military models. "Our Southland, especially, is rich in military possibilities. The experience of Third World peoples everywhere, of Mao, Che, Nkrumah, Kenyata, and Giap have taught us the strategic value of the countryside" (ibid.). Regarding the status of RNA members held political prisoner by the United States, RNA declared their situation parallel to the status of U.S. military personnel held in North Vietnam even though the United States had no declaration of war there. Soon after, RNA held a regional conference in Slidell, Louisiana, reported in the issues of its new newspaper the *New African*. Acting as a state to the federal government, the Region asked the "national government" to seek a clear-cut accord with the National Liberation Front of South Vietnam to clear the way for the return of black prisoners to the United States.[85]

From 1969 to 1971, RNA struggled to purchase land somewhere in the Black Belt. In April 1971 it successfully dedicated a piece of land near the rural town of Bolton, west of Jackson, Mississippi. The land was owned by a black farmer. An RNA spokesman declared after the dedication that members would soon arrive to construct a capital, complete with a school, medical clinic, and housing. In 1972, RNA devised the "Anti-depression Program of the Republic of New Africa." It described an economy based on Tanzania's model of African socialism, Ujamma, or "cooperative economics." As Robin D. G. Kelley has shown, RNA endured repression but eventually reconstituted itself as N'COBRA, developing new reparations programs that it continued to present to the federal government. It persisted in calling for "social change, self-transformation and self-reliance" for black Americans.[86]

Like RNA, the League of Revolutionary Black Workers drew together African American radicals who since 1960 had been actively responding to events in Detroit and internationally. General Baker, a founding member, was first introduced to men who would later become members of the league at meetings of the Robert Williams Defense Committee. Of his 1964 trip to Cuba, where he met with Robert Williams, Baker later recalled:

I had read Che Guevara, Fidel Castro's *History Will Absolve Me* and Frantz Fanon's *The Wretched of the Earth*, but I still went to Cuba with a half-baked outlook and no set theory. I really was fantasizing about revolutionary theory. Going to Cuba was a real sobering experience and a real turning point in my life. Cuba was open to revolutionary fighters from everywhere. You met freedom fighters from Angola and South Africa; some had been wounded in battle and were convalescing. You met Vietnamese, Indonesians, and South Americans in struggle. It was a labor of revolutionary fervor.[87]

Upon his return from Cuba, Baker took work at the Dodge main plant in Detroit. He became a member of the Negro Action Committee, a grassroots organization that first targeted discriminatory hiring practices in Detroit banks.[88] Baker also became a member of a Marxist study group with former autoworker and Johnson-Forest Tendency member Marty Glaberman. He cofounded UHURU, a group loosely affiliated with both RAM and the Socialist Workers Party. Members of UHURU formed the league after a strike at the Eldon Dodge plant. It comprised nine black production workers from Dodge main and members of the *Inner City Voice*, including Baker and Mike Hamlin. Another precursor to the league was DRUM, the Dodge Revolutionary Union Movement, formed in 1968 after a series of segregated wildcat strikes in May 1968 led by white workers. DRUM immediately gave rise to two new revolutionary union movements, FRUM (Ford Revolutionary Union Movement) and ELDRUM (Eldon Avenue Revolutionary Union Movement). James Geschwender has aptly argued that "the league saw the black worker as the most significant element" in making a working-class revolution.[89] Because of their "superexploited" status under capitalism, black workers were, as RAM, Williams, and the Boggses had all argued before them, the most responsive to the challenge of social reorganization and revolution. "The prime focus of the League's organizing activities," writes Geschwender, "was always the black worker at the point of production."[90]

Geschwender's analysis is borne out by examination of DRUM

issues published beginning in 1968. The newsletter's inaugural issues featured demands for the hiring of black foremen and plant managers and equal pay for black workers. It also attacked and exposed black and white workers and managers it perceived as racist. The league's attempt to balance what Geschwender calls a "capitalist-colonial exploitation model" of analysis was also manifest in constant appeals to make class-conscious workers internationalists. Its equal-wages appeal for African American workers extended to black workers in South Africa Chrysler plants. Its slogans for struggle were borrowed from Mao: "Dare to Fight! Dare to Win!" As a logical extension of their proclaimed Maoism, league members Luke Tripp and John Williams organized the first branch of the Black Panther Party in Detroit[91] while at same time being critical of what it called "porkchop" or bourgeois nationalism.[92]

The league's most innovative political work, however, equally characteristic of Bandung era Detroit, was in the domain of public relations. Members were voracious media entrepreneurs. League member John Watson, for example, was elected editor of the *South End*, the Wayne State University newspaper, in 1968. In the fall of 1968, the masthead of the paper was changed to read "The Year of the Heroic Guerilla." Mike Hamlin and Luke Tripp edited a special issue of the paper on the league. In the spring of 1969, the masthead was changed again to read "One Class-Conscious Worker Is Worth 100 Students."[93] Articles in the paper ranged from reports on a wildcat strike at the Sterling automotive plant to publication of Bertolt Brecht's poem "A Worker Reads History." Borrowing the name of Marcus Garvey's repatriation ship, the league also formed its own print shop (the Black Star Press), publishing concern (Black Star Publishing), film production unit (Black Star Productions), and bookstore (Black Star Book Store). Most famously, it produced its own league documentary, *Finally Got the News*.[94] The culmination of the league's media strategies was a 1969 conference cosponsored by the *South End*, the *Inner City Voice*, and the *Fifth Estate*, Detroit's underground newspaper. The conference sought to organize a centralized news service for the Midwest and to establish a Liberation News Service as a radical alternative to mainstream news-gathering sources.[95]

These disparate political activities reflected not only the formative experiences in Cuba of league members like Baker but the catholic radicalism of members like Mike Hamlin, who counted the Communist Party, Socialist Workers Party, NAACP, RAM, and CORE as organizational influences.[96] It also reflected a loose political structure in which, according to Hamlin, personal loyalty rather than ideology gave coherence to the group.[97] In 1969, however, the league's politics took a decisive turn. Hamlin, along with league members Ken Cockrel and John Watson, collaborated with SNCC radical James Forman in shaping the agenda for the Black Economic Development Conference held in Detroit on April 25–27, 1969. The BEDC was a liberal community development conference organized by the Interreligious Foundation for Community Organization. Six league members positioned themselves on the BEDC steering committee, which also included Fannie Lou Hamer. Members of the league worked with Forman to draft the "Black Manifesto," a nationalist program for black economic development. The manifesto argued for reparations and "total control" of economic resources as the solution to black economic troubles. Specifically, the manifesto asked for $500 million in reparations from white Christian churches. It sought $200 million to be set aside for a Southern Land Bank intended to help blacks establish cooperative farms.[98] It planned to set aside $40 million to begin publishing houses in American cities, including Detroit, and another $40 million to establish four television networks.[99] Education, media images of blacks, and the role of popular culture in shaping racial perceptions were all targets of the manifesto.

The Black Manifesto represented both a continuation and a divergence for the League of Revolutionary Black Workers. It sustained its interest in advocating black economic progress but departed from its concentration on the "point of production" for black workers. This new contradiction was at least partly responsible for the league's fracture. In 1971, Mike Hamlin, John Watson, and Ken Cockrel, along with other members of the BEDC, split off with Forman to form the Black Workers Congress. The Congress published its own manifesto that year, which challenged and modified what appeared to be the more narrow nationalism of the BEDC plan. The BWC manifesto began with a call for "workers' controls of their places of work . . . so that the exploitation of labor will cease and no person or corporation will get rich off the labor of another person."[100] It advocated the right of self-determination for African people, Chicanos, Puerto Ricans, Asians, and Indians living in the United States and called for the creation in the labor movement of revolutionary black caucuses, Chicano and Puerto Rican revolutionary caucuses, and Third World labor alliances. The caucus strategy reflected recognition of contemporary liberation struggles beyond black nationalism as part of a horizontal strategy for "replacement of all class collaborators in the trade union movement with leadership that will fight for the international solidarity of all oppressed people." The BWC manifesto reiterated the BEDC call for reparations from the U.S. government and "all white racist institutions in the United States" but created a new demand that "the United States government pay reparations to the people of Africa, Latin America and Asia whom it has exploited for centuries." The document then spelled out these explicitly internationalist goals: withdrawal of all U.S. investment in South Africa; the immediate end of the U.S. war in Indo-China; the right of Palestinian people to a Middle East homeland (an issue the league had earlier addressed in the *Inner City Voice*); the ending of exploitation of workers in Africa, Asia, and Latin America by "western powers such as the U.S., France, England, Portugal, Belgium, Israel"; the end of the trade blockade of Cuba; the admission of the People's Republic of China to the UN; and the control of Formosa (Taiwan) by the Chinese mainland government.[101] The manifesto listed under "Program Objectives" the following strategies to expand the base of the organization, each an echo or iteration of an earlier Detroit strategy: building a "Black United Front and Third World Alliances" to conjoin black workers with other oppressed peoples; establishing a community newspaper that will serve the plant, the factory, and the world situation (something akin to *Correspondence*, or DRUM); organizing "according to the natural division of the city" with decentralization of activities and the creation of deep community roots; establishing bookstores and printing concerns; establishing consumer cooperatives, clinics, and schools; engaging in mass fund-raising; and organizing personal and community self-defense units. In building its united front, an obvious echo of Maoism, the manifesto cited Le Duan's *Vietnamese Revolution: Fundamental Problems, Essential Tasks*, arguing for the "unity of opposites which includes various classes." Its final recommendations were for a two-day black workers' congress for August 21–22 of that year in Detroit, dates commemorating Nat Turner's 1832 rebellion and Toussaint-Louverture's Haitian slave resolt against French planters. Finally it called for preparation of a Third World labor strike on August 8, 1972, to bring pressure to bear on the end of the Vietnam War, the restoration of a Palestinian homeland, and U.S. divestment from South Africa.[102]

The BWC manifesto was a strikingly coherent compendium of Bandung era issues as viewed from the belly of the black internationalist working class. The manifesto also reflected an evolving Marxist-Leninist perspective that would eventually cause the BWC to purge James Forman. Its influence would be felt in broader radical circles of the early 1970s that likewise must be considered continuants of U.S. Bandung struggles. On June 3–4, 1972, for example, Hamlin and James Forman represented the BWC at the Third World Summit Conference in Gary, Indiana. The conference featured more than three hundred delegates and representatives from more than fifty organizations describing themselves as "united front coalitions that represent a broad, mass base of Chicanos, Red people, Asians, Blacks and Puerto Ricans." The summit produced a series of resolutions attempting to link local struggles to attempts to end the war in Vietnam. It created a "United Treaty of Oppressed Minorities" initiated by Mad Bear, national director of the Indian Nationalist Movement of North America. It voted to establish a People's Solidarity Committee of Asian, black, Chicano, Puerto Rican, brown, and red people.[103] Conference organizers also agreed to support a Black, Asian, Brown, and Red People's Solidarity Day on August 19, 1972, an event replacing the original BWC event planned for that year. Overall, the conference strategy was to parallel struggles for national liberation among colored peoples within the United States with international struggles abroad. It was, in many ways, an end point and extension of the fundamental desire for Afro-Asian solidarity that had begun the Bandung era.

Transnational correspondence became an effective if contingent means for expanding the geographic and temporal moment of 1955 into an ongoing set of textual and political practices. It established new international linkages for the distribution of ideas, new cultural forms and ventures, particularly in publishing, and gave black literary culture an international stage of expression. It was also responsible for a powerful reconfiguration of what comprised "local" struggle, even as it made onerous, complex, and direct the charge made famous by the situationists to "act locally, think globally." That said, the ideological pressures brought to bear by corresponding transnationally produced weak links in the chain of Bandung era internationalism, particularly as it faced the logistics of political response. Maoist ethics, a bedrock of Bandung humanism, took on a pedantic and at times fundamentalist cast when translated into discourses of black struggle. What RAM called the "psychocultural" dimension of Bandung humanism was more cogently argued and applied in Fanon's *Black Skin, White Masks* than in any theoretical statement of U.S. black liberation during the Bandung era. Afro-Asianism also rebuffed racist essentialism at the same time as it often relied on contradictory and inconsistent ideas about race. The same might be said of geographic place: ideological remappings of the anticolonial world oftentimes partook of facile correspondence between politically and geographically distant points and radically different objective conditions for revolutionary struggle. Working with limited information, and handicapped by surveillance, arrest, and repression, efforts to find simultaneity and similarity often obliterated crucial questions of uneven economic conditions and varying forms of statehood, means of production, and ideology. Moreover, the presumption that military strategies and scenarios could be retrofitted merely by analogizing place was at odds with fundamental tenets of warfare, not least of which being the willingness to fight, for whom, and for how long.

The particular link between Robert Williams and Detroit, however, was indicative of the deeper centrality of dialectical thought to Afro-Asian liberation struggles of the 1960s. It symbolized a strategic antiessentialism attentive to the limits of singular narratives of liberation and demonstrated the necessarily improvisatory nature of internationalist politics. Williams was himself perhaps the single most important political text in this process of what I have been calling transnational correspondence. His words, images, and ideas became mobilized extensions of, and surrogates for, an absent persona. He humanized Bandung humanism, literally became its political face. His impact was to carry over and take astonishingly revised form in the work of two of contemporary radicalism's most seminal thinkers, James and Grace Lee Boggs.

CHAPTER 4

"Philosophy Must Be Proletarian": The Dialectical Humanism of Grace Lee and James Boggs

The Negro revolt exposes the whole American system as it has operated in regard to every sphere of the relations between human beings. Coming in the United States at a time when there is no longer any problem of material scarcity, the Negro revolt is therefore not just a narrow struggle over material necessities. It does not belong to the period of struggle over goods and for the development of the productive forces which we call the era of "Dialectical Materialism." Rather it ushers in the era of "Dialectical Humanism," when the burning question is how to create the kind of human responsibility in the distribution of material abundance that will allow everyone to enjoy and create the values of humanity.

—James Boggs, "The Meaning of the Black Revolt in the U.S.A.,"
    1963

We blacks (and I include myself as an "Afro-Chinese" in that "we") must struggle against our own individualism, our own materialism, our own tendencies to Cartesian rationalism. We must be able to think and to act dialectically, by a curved rather than an Aristotelian logic.

—Grace Boggs, "Where Do We Go from Here?"
    July 18, 1979

In June 1940, the month that France fell to the Nazis, twenty-five-year-old Grace Lee, the daughter of first-generation Chinese immigrants in New York City, graduated with her PhD in philosophy from Bryn Mawr College. Lee's graduate work had concentrated in Continental philosophy; her MA exam was on Hegel, and her dissertation a study of the work of George Mead. Upon graduating, Lee faced what she called later "a personal and intellectual crisis."[1] In 1940, no American university would consider hiring a Chinese American woman philosopher. Equally grave to Lee, "All my studies up to that time had been in European culture which was crumbling before the eyes of the whole world under the onslaught of Nazism" (22). Lee contemplated these problems at home in New York and made an abrupt decision: she would leave her family and friends and go to Chicago, where she knew no one, in order to "start afresh" (22). Once there she took a job at the University of Chicago library for ten dollars a week, living in a damp basement room, rent free. Walking one day through one of the university buildings, she happened upon a meeting of the Workers Party, a Trotskyite splinter group. By her own account, Boggs "had never given a thought to mass struggle, even though radical changes were taking place" in the United States (22). When she was fifteen, Charlotte Perkins Gilman's *Women and Economics* had made Boggs a feminist, and she had encountered acts of anti-Asian racism growing up in Jackson Heights, New York, which had taught her that "people of color are not equal in our society." The Workers Party meeting, however, concentrated on the horrible economic and living conditions of blacks in south side neighborhoods, brutalization under Jim Crow, and discrimination in the armed services. Inspired by discussion at the meeting, Boggs signed on with the South Side Tenants Organization, a community action group established by the Workers Party, and began hanging around Chicago's Washington park. The park was a regular meeting place and open-air political market for the Workers Party and other organizations seeking influence in black Chicago. There Lee took her first public political turn on a soapbox on behalf of the Workers Party. It was also there that she learned that A. Philip Randolph was organizing a march on Washington to demand jobs for blacks in the defense industry, "and suddenly everybody was talking and laughing as if the saints were marching in" (23). Lee took special heart in the example of a young black prostitute named Mary Harris, suddenly energized by the idea of the march. Spontaneously, as she recalls it, Lee came to two permanent decisions: she would become a Marxist "and . . . commit my life to bringing about revolutionary social change in the United States"

(24). She also planted her revolutionary hopes in black America, "the community of those most disinherited and dispossessed by capitalism and therefore who have the most reason to struggle to get rid of it." "From the March on Washington movement," she later wrote, "I learned that a movement begins when large numbers of people, having reached the point where they can't take the way things are any longer, find hope for improving the daily lives in an action that they can take together. I also discovered the power that the black community has within itself to change this country when it begins to move. As a result I decided that what I wanted to do with the rest of my life was to become a movement activist in the black community."[2]

Lee's transformation, at once personal and political, is best described as a moment in which a strategic antiessentialism emerges from a dialectical analysis of race and class. Her self is lost or absorbed into a collectivity that displaces existing modes of racial and class identity. At the same time, Grace Lee perceives herself as entering a new phase of historical subjectivity through these joint revelations. "For me," as she would later write, "embracing Marxism at that point meant that I could never again be content with merely interpreting American society. I must engage in the practice of struggling to change it and my ideas must come out of practice and the new contradictions which practice constantly uncovers."[3]

Though for a variety of reasons she would resist its centrality, Grace Lee Boggs's 1940 epiphany marked the beginnings of the individual political life most emblematic of the historical and political struggles informing the development of what I have been calling Afro-Orientalism. It encompasses a practical and philosophical relationship to many of its major touchstones, from the Bolshevik revolution of 1917 to the Black Power movement of the 1960s to the Asian Pacific American movement of the post-1970 period. Boggs's life is the most self-consciously lived example of the process by which radicals of color in the United States have centered, while revising and advancing, a Marxian analysis of Western capitalism and the mutual concerns of Afro-Asians within it. For Grace Boggs, this process has been a collaborative one in which interracial and transracial political work has manifested what to her is a central tenet of Marxian theory and practice: what she and her husband and collaborator James Boggs came to call after 1963 "dialectical humanism." The phrase echoes and informs Black Power's "Bandung humanism" discussed in the previous chapter, yet carries a far more local, and personal, significance. Dialectical humanism is the work of individuals across race, class, and gender lines to realize what Marx called in *The German Ideology* the fullest "productive activity" of human beings. The Boggses' collaborative work and writings, from their legal and political marriage to James's death in 1993, were in the service of discovering means toward realizing Communism's symbiotic improvement of human life. "The individual is the essence," Marx wrote in "Private Property and Communism." "His expression of life, although it may not appear in the direct form of a communal-type life carried out simultaneously with others, is therefore an expression and assertion of social living. The individual and the species of man are not distinct."[4]

Dialectical humanism is the Boggsian program for this emancipatory personal and political work. It is a Marxian interpretation of a theme that Grace Boggs has argued is central to Hegelian dialectics. Hegel, in her words, "saw the history of humanity as a continuing struggle for freedom or self-determination. Freedom itself constantly becoming more concrete and more universal."[5] In *Facing Reality*, a collaborative statement of the Detroit Facing Reality group published in 1958, this tenet was formulated in a manner that would bear permanently on Grace and James Boggs's work. Citing *The Communist Manifesto*'s famously lyrical description of "fixed, fast-frozen relations" swept away by constant changes in means of production, the book argued that "it is the working class in every country more than any other class which faces very soberly the conditions of life as they are today and knows that the future of human experience lies in the reorganization of these conditions."[6] It is the working classes and their experience of shifting social relations, in other words, that reconcretize "reality" while "all that is solid melts into air."[7] *Facing Reality*'s recurring slogan for this process, "Philosophy must become proletarian,"[8] thus urged upon the laboring classes the recognition of their own destiny as history's liberating agent. To paraphrase Césaire, dialectics are to be used in the service of the human, not the human in the service of dialectics.

The Boggses began their collaborative efforts toward these ends in 1953, when Grace moved from New York to Detroit to participate in mass struggle, particularly in the auto industry. "Proletarianizing" was leftist nomenclature for this effort to link theory and practice. One of her first acts there—to marry James—became for Grace symbolic of the necessary union of mind and body each felt manifested Marx's advocacy for "social man," a figure of disalienation whose productive manual and intellectual work is central to his or her being. Grace theorized this process in her autobiography *Living for Change:* "I decided that the main reason I married Jimmy was that I need to become whole," she wrote.

> I was still essentially a product of Ivy League women's colleges, a New York intellectual whose understanding of revolutionary struggle came mainly from books. . . . I was a Chinese American, an ethnic minority so small as to be almost invisible. He was an African American who was very conscious that the blood and sweat of his ancestors had made possible the rapid economic development of this country and who had already embarked on the struggle to ensure that his people would be among those deciding its economic and political future.[9]

The work of James and Grace Lee Boggs, however, enters more globally as an original theoretical contribution to Afro-Orientalism in its syncretic understanding of revolutionary theory. In addition to Marx and Trotsky, the two most seminal influences on their work stand at twin poles of Afro-Asian world revolution: the Trinidadian Marxist C. L. R. James, and the Chinese dialectician Mao Tse-tung. Both James and Grace Lee Boggs came to Marxism and black struggle (not to mention each other) via their enthusiasm for C. L. R. James's pioneering work in the 1930s and 1940s on the "Negro question." James's support for the autonomous struggle of African Americans within larger proletarian struggle resonated with both Grace's support for African American civil rights during World War II and James Boggs's experiences as a young black autoworker in Detroit in the late 1940s. By 1953, they had begun a collaboration with C. L. R. James through the Detroit-based Johnson-Forest Tendency, a political collective whose theoretical contributions on race, nationalism, and class struggle, I hope to show in this chapter, were far more lasting than critics have thus far noted. They were germinal to the development of a U.S.-based anticolonial theory during the Bandung era, as well as the formation of the U.S. Black Power movement. After their 1962 split with James, Maoism became the primary influence on the Boggses' work. Their break with the Johnson-Forest collective, often described by scholars as the Boggses' break with Marxism, can be better understood as a shift from a Jamesian to a Bandung or Third World analysis of global capitalism. Attendant to this shift was a vigorous interest in, and application of, Chinese Cultural Revolution theory to domestic and international struggles. The Boggses continuously distinguished, more so than James or their radical contemporaries like the Black Panthers, between "objective conditions" of First World and Third World liberation, while bringing salient points of Maoist critique to bear on dialectics, feminism, guerrilla violence, contradiction, and nationalism. Mao's insistence on placing politics before economics, on the personal as a means to political transformation, and on the central contradictions between manual and mental labor, town and country, and agriculture and industry, influenced virtually all of the Boggses' major political positions after their break with Johnson-Forest and was central to their development of dialectical humanism. At the same time, the Boggses' work articulated links or correspondences between James and Mao. It synthesized their shared proclivity for the autonomy and self-generation of mass revolutionary action, their sympathies for nonaligned colored revolutions, and their insistence on organic intellectual development of theory from practice. It was likewise sympathetic to each of their efforts to rethink Marxism in the wake of real-world limitations imposed by the failures and tribulations of the Soviet Union. Indeed, the Boggses joined the efforts of postcolonial thinkers across the globe, from Fanon to Cabral—to devise a colored revolutionary theory that would emerge directly out of indigenous (in their case U.S.) revolutionary struggles.

Since the end of Black Power, and later the death of James Boggs in 1993, Boggsism has become an even more pliable species of philosophical and political thought while remaining fundamentally true to its roots. Grace Boggs's speeches and writings demonstrate two progressive and related features of her work as an Afro-Asian theorist that might, superficially read, be seen as regressive and discrete. They involve the relationship between place and identity as the basis of what Grace and others have called a "grassroots postmodernism." Both an acknowledgment and a rebuff to contemporary identity-based political organizing, grassroots postmodernism demonstrates Boggsism as a cumulative and self-reflexive dialectic, one that, like the movements to which they have been leaders and partners, often divides into two, only to double back on its most familiar features. This chapter will thus seek to situate the work of James and Grace Lee Boggs both in the local discourse of Afro-Orientalism and in prevailing contemporary discussions of race and identity, particularly among Asian American scholars and activists for whom Grace has become an important if contested touchstone. I will attempt to show that strong misreadings of the Boggses' work that divorce or remove it from its earliest influences—including Trotsky and C. L. R. James—invariably fail to understand the protocontribution it makes to efforts to think beyond and through identity politics. It is arguable that the Boggses' work represents one of the most sustained critiques of liberal multiculturalism, and identity-based politics, produced inside or outside the academy. That they provided this critique virtually without reference to, or in playful disdain for, the wonderfully surprising fact of their own interracial marriage is merely a theoretical exclamation point for what remains to be understood as the most significant personal Afro-Asian collaboration in U.S. history.

Grace Lee Boggs first met C. L. R. James in Chicago in 1941. Though it is unclear to what extent she was familiar with his previous reputation, James's work and example would provide the most productive influence on her intellectual development for the next twenty years. Two of James's positions of the 1930s stand out in this regard: a Trotskyist critique of

the degeneration of the Soviet revolution into imperialist state bureaucracy, and the importance of African American and international black
rebellions as a dialectical complement to, and decentering of, the European (and American) working classes. James's attention to the 1937 stay-
in strike in Trinidad, which inspired similar uprisings in Jamaica and
Barbados, is a good example. James argued that Soviet sale of oil to Italy
during its 1935 campaign against Ethiopia abrogated its revolutionary
responsibility to the colonies. James offered in its place an interpretation
of the 1937 and 1938 Caribbean uprisings as signs of increasing black
self-determination and a dialectical global revolutionary movement. At
the Socialist Workers Party meeting in July 1939, James drafted two resolutions affirming the right of African Americans to self-determination.
The party also established a National Negro Department with James
directing its work.[10] Meanwhile James prepared the essay "Preliminary
Notes on the Negro Question," in which he argued that "the 14 or 15
million Negroes in the U.S.A. represent potentially the most militant
section of the population."[11] The essay was published in the ninth issue
of the SWP's internal bulletin, in June 1939. James argued that evidence
of increasing black militancy in the labor movement in the United States,
coupled with anti-imperialism in Africa, was predictive of the successful
chances of world revolution. "Many factors are in favor of a victory ultimately for those who support revolutionary socialism, when the Negro
masses are ready for it," he wrote.[12] James also defended what he called
"Negro chauvinism" as a "progressive force . . . the expression of a desire
for equality of an oppressed and deeply humiliated people."[13] The SWP
resolution at its 1939 convention articulated this position in a way profoundly figurative of 1960s black nationalism. "Black chauvinism in America today is merely the natural excess of the desire for equality while
white American chauvinism, the expression of racial domination, is essentially reactionary."[14] During 1960s Black Power, "nationalism" easily
substituted for "chauvinism" for members of the Revolutionary Action
Movement and Republic of New Africa.

In the spring of 1940, just months before Grace Lee was introduced
to it, James split with the Socialist Workers Party to form the Workers

Party. In September 1941 he attended the Workers Party national convention, where he became head of the "state capitalist" minority, which argued that the Soviet Union was a society fundamentally identical to capitalism.[15] After the convention, James traveled South to Missouri to join other Trotskyites there working with sharecroppers who were preparing to strike. James was on a return trip from Missouri when he met Grace Boggs in Chicago. According to Boggs, the C. L. R. James she met was "bursting with enthusiasm about the potential for an American revolution inherent in the emergence of the labor movement and escalating militancy of blacks."[16] In "With the Sharecroppers," a report on that experience published that same year in *Labor Action*, James enthusiastically wrote, "No working class or section of the working class hates the ruling class as these sharecroppers hate their rulers."[17] James characteristically criticized the role of the CPUSA in attempts to organize sharecroppers into the Southern Tenant Farmers Union and white landlords who sustained Jim Crow conditions. These elements had deepened his conviction that black workers themselves might lead a new interracial class struggle: "Propaganda, education, patient work, will have to be done to knit those elements that draw closer together. . . . So deeprooted a social phenomenon will only receive a serious shock by the usual way in which all serious problems of the workers' movement are solved or partially solved—by mass action."[18] Boggs was also smitten by James's insistence that it was the bottom dogs—the sansculottes in the French Revolution, the Diggers in the English Revolution, and American slaves of the nineteenth century—who were the forerunners of contemporary revolutionaries. James, for his part, was taken by Boggs's knowledge of German and dialectics, and her commitment to mass organizing in Chicago. They immediately set out on a reading course of Marx's *Capital* and Hegel's *Science of Logic*. Their study group expanded quickly to include the Russian-born Marxist Raya Dunayevskaya. These three formed the intellectual core of a new faction within the Workers Party known as the Johnsonites, after one of James's more frequent publishing pseudonyms, J. H. Johnson. Raya, known as Freddie Forest, gave the group its full moniker, the Johnson-Forest Tendency. During the war,

Johnsonite circles appeared in Workers Party branches in New York, Philadelphia, Detroit, and Los Angeles.[19] In addition to its insistence on worker self-activity, the distinguishing feature of the Johnsonite line was its support for autonomous black political struggle. The group also took a keen interest in two works by Marx: *German Ideology*, and the 1844 *Economic-Philosophical Manuscripts*. Boggs and Dunayevskaya collaborated on translating the latter, published by the group in 1947. This document was central to introducing Boggs to what she called the "noneconomist side" of Marx. In that same year, the Johnsonites left the Workers Party to rejoin the Socialist Workers Party, which they found more support-ive of black struggles generally.

The Johnson-Forest Tendency's break with Trotskyism initiated an energetic effort, as they later wrote, "to rediscover for this epoch what Marx had meant by capitalism and socialism and the philosophy of his-tory which had guided his economic writings."[20] Rereading Marx and Hegel had led them to the "essence" of Marx, namely, "his realization that side by side with the fragmentation and mutilation of the workers in the capitalist labor process, there is emerging inside the factory a new form of social organization, the cooperative form of labor."[21] In 1947 and 1948 they published several works dedicated to this theme: *Dialectical Materialism and the Fate of Humanity* (1947) and *The Invading Socialist Society* (1947); in 1948 James published his own *Notes on the Dialectic*. In 1947 the Johnsonites also published *The American Worker*, a seventy-page pamphlet, cowritten by Grace Boggs under the pseudonym Ria Stone with factory worker Paul Romano. The pamphlet distills many of the ideas developed in Johnson-Forest and foreshadows a number of others sustained by the Boggses even after their break with James.

The pamphlet is divided into two parts, roughly analogous to prac-tice and theory: "Life in the Factory," a report by Romano on working conditions, union practices, race relations, and worker stratification within the factory, and "The Reconstruction of Society," Boggs's macroanaly-sis of Romano's report. "Life in the Factory" identified production speed-ups and unemployment as the central issues for the shop floor worker. It rendered experiential alienation in unfettered terms: "The worker is compelled on the job to perform a task which can only make him rebel: the monotony; the getting up every morning, the day by day drudgery which takes its toll."[22] Unions offer little help or respite in Romano's account; they are indifferent bureaucracies looked upon with cynicism by the rank and file. Significantly, it was on the question of race that Romano reported some potential disruption to this stasis. Black workers, increasing in number, are "quiet, reserved, but deeply moved by their position in the plant" (26). Despite Jim Crow attitudes in the factory, Romano notes, "There is tremendous ferment among the Negro workers. . . . The Negro worker feels the impending depression. He burns fiercely within. He knows he will be the first to be put on the chopping block. He feels that now is the only opportunity he has to strike back somehow, some way, in the organized labor movement" (29). Static union bureaucracy and alienation are implicitly challenged by the untapped potential of black labor: "The day the Negro has the opportunity to unfold all his talents," Romano writes, "will be the day when the community as a whole will benefit" (27).

Part 2 of *The American Worker* relied heavily on Trotsky and Marx but was consistent with the Johnson-Forest imperative to create a new "humanist" history. "Today, in all strata of society," wrote Boggs on her opening page, "a search is going on for the way to create a world, a world in which men can live as social and creative individuals, where they can live as all-round men and not just as average men. Out of this search a new philosophy of life is being created. Neither the Christian Revolution nor the Protestant Reformation, the only comparable milestones in the history of Western civilization, can parallel in depth and scope the process of evaluation and re-evaluation now going on in the activity and in the thoughts of men" (42). The site of this revolution in consciousness was the factory floor. Chapter 1, "The Permanent Revolution in the Process of Production," described the "semi-skilled workers of mass production" as the vanguard of U.S. workers' struggles (43). Citing one of Marx's most famous passages from *The Communist Manifesto*, Boggs argued that the American worker "is facing 'his real conditions of life and his relations with his kind'" (44). This discovery comes about through discovery of his alienation, as described by Romano and measured by Marx in his 1844 *Economic-Philosophical Manuscripts*. The alienation of the individual, Marx contended, determined the alienation of the class: "Without the universality of the workers, the dehumanization of the whole of society was inevitable" (47). Then, in a significant departure from Marx, Boggs injected an aside: "The Negroes, the most oppressed layer and therefore the layer of society most confined to average existence in contemporary society, are the ones who reveal most clearly this contradiction between the human need for individual expression and the class need for uniformity. They hate being regarded as Negroes and yet are determined that society should recognize their growing revolutionary mobilization as Negroes" (55). Boggs's strategically antiessentialized view of race echoed James's "Historical Development of the Negroes in American Society," an essay originally circulated within the Workers Party as a memorandum in 1943 and published as "Negroes and the Revolution: Resolution of the Minority" in the *New International* in January 1945. In it James attempted to parse the "uniqueness" and "universality" of black identity via the analytic categories of race and nation:

> The Negroes do not constitute a nation, but, owing to their special situation, their segregation; economic, social, and political oppression; the difference in color which singles them out so easily from the rest of the community; their problems become the problem of a national minority. The Negro question is a part of the national and not of the "national" question. This national minority is most easily distinguished from the rest of the community by its racial characteristics. Thus the Negro question is a question of race and not of "race."[23]

James's hairsplitting was meant to define blacks as "representative" of some universalizing—read revolutionizing—potential within, but not separate from, the American working class. This is the key to Boggs's insistence in *The American Worker* that "the antagonism between the races will also find its final resolution only through the development of all-sided universal man in the process of production." African Americans, forced to fight as a racial minority, invariably undertake a "national revolt" that is "one of the most important contributing factors to the success of the proletarian revolution."[24] "It is however, in the social community, created in the heat of the class struggle, e.g., in the sitdown strikes which built the CIO, that the relations between white and Negro workers are the relations between revolutionary men, i.e. men who feel themselves bound in a social cause and therefore instinctively recognize themselves and each other as universal men, social individuals. . . . A completely new mode of production will be created which will develop the men of both races as universal all-sided men who can have human relations rather than race relations with one another."[25] This step is a precursor to a socialist emancipation directed by the will and actions of the entire working class: "When the workers take their fate into their own hands, when they seize the power and begin their reconstruction of society, all of mankind will leap from the realm of necessity into the realm of freedom."[26]

The American Worker foreshadowed a philosophical direction of Johnson-Forest that reached its culmination in *State Capitalism and World Revolution*, first published in 1950. Paul Buhle has described the book as the "definitive statement of the Johnson-Forest Tendency."[27] Coauthored by James, Boggs, and Dunayevskaya, the book is Johnson-Forest's clearest articulation of the relationship between philosophy and politics. The book declares rationalism to be the Enlightenment bourgeois worldview responsible for both state bureaucracy and the bankrupt nature of political democracy. It blames labor bureaucracy for maintaining this status quo by allowing the centralization of capital and the prevailing class structure.[28] What is needed in response is a new understanding of dialectics. It is wrong, they argued, to claim that Marx "stood Hegel on his head" by emphasizing materialism, rather than idealism, as the motive force of history. Rather, dialectics is "in Marx's hands a revolutionary theoretical weapon against bureaucracy in all its forms but primarily and particularly in the process of world revolution":[29]

> Hegel saw objective history as the successive manifestation of world-spirit. Marx placed the object movement in the process of production. Hegel had

been driven to see the perpetual quest for universality as necessarily confined to the process of knowledge. Marx reversed this and rooted the quest
for universality in the need for the free and full development of all the
inherent and acquired characteristics in productive and intellectual labour.
Hegel had made the motive force of history the work of a few gifted individuals in whom was concentrated the social movement. Marx propounded
the view that it was only when ideas seized hold of the masses that the
process of history moved. Hegel dreaded the revolt of the modern mass.
Marx made the modern proletarian revolution the motive force of modern history. Hegel placed the guardianship of society in the hands of
bureaucracy. Marx saw future society as headed for ruin except under the
rulership of the proletariat and the vanishing distinction between intellectual and manual labour.[30]

State Capitalism "proletarianizes philosophy" by making dialectics
a tool not of the master but of the slave. Breaking emphatically with state-
sponsored revolution, it rejects all sources of revolutionary impetus but
the collective. "Now the whole development of the objective situation
demands the fully liberated historical creativeness of the masses, their
sense and reason, a new and higher organization of labour, new social
ties, associated humanity. That is the solution to the problems of production and to the problems of philosophy."[31] Though the document
paid less attention to the particulars of race and gender than did *The
American Worker,* Paul Buhle's apt summary of Johnson-Forest strategies
in the 1950s was predicted by *State Capitalism:* "Against the clumsiness
and stupidity of official, bureaucratic society, the group would pose the
alternative solutions immanent in the socialization of production and the
evident capacities of the workers themselves. And it would intervene to lay
open to the workers the kernel of the internal antagonism that kept the
class divided: most prominently the aggressiveness of Blacks and women
to carve out their own, equal role in society."[32] In the same year as *State
Capitalism,* James gave a speech in Detroit titled "The Revolutionary
Answer to the Negro Problem in the United States." The speech was a
culmination of his writing and thinking on race since 1939. According to

Grace Boggs, it was intended to attract black autoworkers who had begun to come around the Socialist Workers Party seeking an organization more radical than the union or the Communist Party, particularly on the race question. James's speech reiterated two central Johnson-Forest themes: first, that "the independent Negro struggle, has a vitality and a validity of its own"; second, that "this independent Negro movement is able to intervene with terrific force upon the general social and political life of the nation."[33] The essay underscored both the unique "organic" nature of black struggle in the United States dating to the Civil War— an important precursor to Boggsism's conception of a distinctly "American" revolution. By insisting that Negro struggle "is waged under the banner of democratic rights" rather than through organized labor, it also prefigured an issue that was to divide members of Johnson-Forest some thirteen years later. Yet James's most compelling argument was that American capitalism had given the Negro movement a "fundamental and sharp relationship" to the proletariat, one that created a special animus toward the bourgeoisie and a "readiness to destroy it" that exceeded all other sectors of the working class.[34]

James's speech did indeed attract young black workers to the SWP, including James Boggs. After 1948 he began attending SWP meetings in Detroit. Initially he did not join. According to Grace Boggs, it was at a meeting in 1950 or 1951 when James Boggs discovered that a group of "Orientals" from New York had become part of a new tendency led by James that was splitting again from the SWP to form an independent organization and publish a newsletter written and edited by rank-and-file workers, blacks, women, and youths. The "Orientals" were Grace, Grace's brothers Eddie and Harry, and Harry's wife Julie. Their newsletter was to be called *Correspondence.*[35]

James Boggs moved a step closer to permanent association with Johnson-Forest via his participation in the Organic Third Layer School in New York City in the fall of 1952. The school was based on efforts to mobilize what Lenin called "third-layer" workers and peasants necessary to assist in making permanent a workers' state. Boggs was one of a number of rank-and-file workers invited to teach trade unionists and intellectuals at the school. It was there that Grace met Jimmy for the first time. In 1953, Grace decided to leave New York and move to Detroit, in part because it was a "movement" city, where as a Johnsonite she could remain close to grassroots struggle.[36] In Detroit James and Grace worked on the editorial board of *Correspondence*, and it was while Grace was driving him home from a board meeting that James proposed. The circle around *Correspondence*, known as the Committee on Correspondence, included as well the Detroit autoworker Marty Glaberman, who had been drawn to Trotskyism, and to James, in the late 1930s; Johnny Zupan, another autoworker, who from 1951 to 1955 served as editor of *Correspondence*; and, until her 1955 break with James and the group, Raya Dunayevskaya. The Committee on Correspondence undertook a number of new directions from the SWP incarnation of Johnson-Forest. The participation of Glaberman, Zupan, and James Boggs, in the organization allowed it more concentrated shop floor insight into changes in production and work conditions in the auto plant. These increasingly became the basis of their analysis of U.S. capitalism. James Boggs's presence also sharpened their attention to questions of race at the point of production. Simultaneously, international events of the 1950s, particularly in Hungary, caused another revision of the group's analysis of workers' self-activity. Boggs and Dunayevskaya also began to introduce more deliberate analysis of gender in their published writing.

"Draft Outline—Part I, VP Document," dated January 6, 1956, published a year after Dunayevskaya's departure, demonstrates these tendencies well. The document is a collective position paper centering analysis on changing union politics, the rise of Reutherism, black workers, and the family. It cites Reuther's 1950 negotiation of the five-year contract forfeiting control over shop floor conditions in exchange for a pension as contributing to the static and bureaucratic nature of the union. The report contrasts the World War II wildcat strikes with the planned strikes of the Reuther era, which lock the rank and file out of the plant.[37] It argues that spontaneous forms of "unity and organization" are the only ones in which the worker has remaining confidence, "where he can judge the situation himself and act according to his own judgment" (10). Characteristic of

Johnson-Forest work, the essay identified black workers as most apt to develop self-conscious and spontaneous resistance. They are "more advanced than the white workers in their ability to solve problems of production" (12). The vast majority of transplanted southern workers are quick to react against reenactments of former humiliations under Jim Crow. "Their speed in taking united action independently of the union apparatus to fight any specific grievance is the envy of white workers. Each Negro is fully mobilized at all times to respond to any suspicion of discrimination" (12). As a result, "It is not the union but the Negroes themselves who have won this respect and equality on the job" (12). The other progressive force identified in the essay is women in working-class families who attempt to increase male participation in domestic chores and parenting. Like African American workers, their demands exceed the union agenda, which "does nothing to change the conditions in the shop which would enable a man to come home from work and have a human relation in his family" (18). The essay then rushes to a sweeping question and answer:

> What is the problem of modern politics? It is how society can avoid the bureaucratic domination which seems inseparable from mass organization. On every issue, whether it is that of relations of production or relations between races, classes and nations, the modern worker knows he can work out an answer and an action with a freedom and spontaneity which is in complete opposition to the bureaucratic domination which threatens to overwhelm society. (20)

The 1956 draft served as a precis for the last major collaborative work between the Boggses and C. L. R. James, the 1958 Correspondence book *Facing Reality*. The book was a self-described manifesto for a "new society." It began with an enthusiastic chapter on the Hungarian Revolution and the workers' councils it produced. The authors also wrote favorably of the shop stewards' movement in England. They contrasted these with the "social death" of labor activism and "dynamic individualism" in the United States.[38] Coupled with the bureaucratic stagnation of

FACING REALITY

The New Society . . .

Where to look for it

How to bring it closer

A statement for our time

a *Correspondence* book   50¢

Cover reproduction of 1958 edition of *Facing Reality*, published by Correspondence. The book was the last collaborative effort of the Johnson-Forest Tendency.

the Left in both France and Russia, discussed in a chapter called "The Self-Confessed Bankruptcy of Official Society," the book provided a dialectical analysis of a new form of humanist crisis in a chapter called "The End of a Philosophy." This was the organization's most explicit statement yet of the relationship of philosophy and politics. Again citing *The Communist Manifesto*'s prophecy of social transformation—"All fixed, fast-frozen relations, with their train of venerable and ancient prejudices and opinions, are swept away"—the essay proceeded to argue its fundamental charge: "Philosophy must become proletarian" (67). Enlightenment rationalism had run its course. "The pressing need of society," wrote the authors, listed as Grace C. Lee, Pierre Chaulieu, and J. R. Johnson, "is no longer to conquer nature. The great and pressing need is to control, order, and reduce to human usefulness the mass of wealth and knowledge which has accumulated over the last four centuries" (68). The old "administrative elite" produced by rationalism now takes the form of oppressive bureaucracies, including Stalinist totalitarianism, fascism, and the corporate state, one-party state, and welfare State (69). By contrast, the shop floor still exhibits "the free democracy that is the natural expression of cooperative labor" (124). Unlike union bureaucracy, "In the shop floor organizations the thousands of workers in the plant make no distinction between whites and Negroes. They are concerned solely with organizing their work and their struggles with management as effectively as possible" (124). Concurrently, it is the function of a socialist or Marxist organization to understand that "socialism is nothing other than the self-organization of the proletariat carried to its ultimate limit" (90).

The second, uniquely American condition for a Marxist organization to respond to is the Negro question. In addressing this in the final section of *Facing Reality*, Johnson-Forest gave the clearest indication of its emerging internal contradictions and impending demise. Acknowledging that "Marxism has a few triumphs and many unpardonable blunders to its account on the Negro question," the authors selected two central issues affecting relations between white and black workers: first, that many white workers "continue to show strong prejudice against association with Negroes outside the plant"; and second, that "many

Negroes make race relations a test of all other relations" (151). This means not simply voting in the direction of political parties that demonstrate good intentions but judging Marxist organizations for their own position on black issues. In order to succeed, the editors recommended providing room in an organization newspaper for discussion and debate on racial questions. The paper must support the broadcast of "Negro aggressiveness on the race question" and provide that "the Negro worker shall say what he wants to say and how he wants to say it" (152). The paper should also actively campaign for black rights in the South, including voting rights (153). In total, the paper and the organization must demonstrate a "resolute determination to bring all aspects of the question into the open, within the context of the recognition that the new society exists and that it carries within itself much of the sores and diseases of the old" (154).

Facing Reality was the last major publishing collaboration of the Detroit circle. The resolute emphasis in its closing pages on not just the autonomy but the prioritization of black self-expression and self-organizing within the working class disclosed a tendency that world events between 1957 and 1961 would force into open conflict. The southern civil rights movement, the increasing layoffs and rising unemployment among black workers in the auto industry, and the announcement of the liberations of Ghana and Guineau-Bisseau, followed by Cuba in 1959, began to draw the attention of Grace and James Boggs away from Johnson-Forest. C. L. R. James's absence from the United States during this period, and Dunayevskaya's departure from the group in 1955, also weakened the collective and incited the Boggses toward more independent examination and thought. In 1961, Robert Williams's encounter with law enforcement and flight from arrest helped bring each of these tendencies into focus and demonstrated the Boggses' evolving reevaluation of their relationship to black American struggles. James Boggs's June 5, 1961, letter to Williams's attorney Conrad Lynn provides a case in point. The letter was written at a particularly crucial juncture. Just weeks before, on May 14, Freedom Riders had been attacked by mobs of angry white men armed with clubs and bats in Anniston, Alabama.[39] Inspired against

Robert Williams's work with the Monroe NAACP, the Klan had also reemerged in Monroe County, where Williams was being besieged by death threats. In his May editorials that year for the *Crusader*, Williams had criticized Martin Luther King for failing to join the Freedom Rides and for, in Williams's view, trying to exploit them for publicity for himself.[40] On June 14, 1961, Williams met with Ossie Davis, Julian Mayfield, Calvin Hicks, Amiri Baraka, and Mae Mobley to discuss the situation in Monroe. According to Conrad Lynn's minutes of the meeting, Williams argued that "the tactics of nonviolence in sits-ins, freedom rides, etc. have proved useful but has to be backed up with forceful self-defense."[41]

Boggs's June 5 letter to Lynn is both a statement of support for Williams and a challenge to devise a full-blown strategy out of the crisis. "The Negro leaders' responsibilities are first and always the aspiration and the needs of the Negroes at all times," wrote Boggs.[42] Having met briefly with Williams, Boggs declares him "that kind of a new leader" and insists that he must "set himself aside from all the rest" by a forceful demonstration of black initiative: "One can only have equality by going out and taking it." Boggs then tips his hand clearly in the future direction not only of his own politics but of the ideological direction of Black Power:

> With this program of the actual development clearly in mind, all programs for farm reform or socialism can be seen to be somewhat obsolete and abstract. The fact is that Negroes are not asking for reforms even if they say they are. They are taking rights and in the process of taking, making a total change in the social and economic structure of this country, a change much bigger than just a few rights or reforms. In fact, they are not just asking for the same rights as whites; because the rights whites have only exist because the Negroes have so little. In addition, I know of no Negroes who want what the poor Southern or Northern white has because they have nothing either. So you see, the civil rights question goes on over into economic rights and pushes that even further.[43]

James Boggs's new line on black struggle as the successor to an exhausted socialist tradition manifested itself in articles written by Grace for *Correspondence* in its fall 1961 issues. Several points were central to these pieces: first, that the majority of the white working class had been either backward or reactionary in carrying out a revolutionary line; second, that the rights of workers were as important as, if not more important than, their economic interests as a class; third, that the inevitability of socialism is a determinist argument tending to separate the objective world from the world of human activity, which included the making of black civil rights struggle. The articles were bolstered by an internal document produced by Grace for review of the collective in which she asserted for the first time that "James Boggs, a Negro and a worker, who cannot help but participate in the [civil rights] struggle, is the leader of our organization."[44]

Grace's use of *Correspondence* to articulate these positions brought angry responses from Marty Glaberman and C. L. R. James, who felt she was abusing editorial privilege to speak for the collective. Glaberman also attacked what he called the "new turn" in Grace's articles as a replica of erroneous arguments produced by the American Trotskyist Max Schactman in 1946 that had caused the Workers Party to break with the SWP. James, for his part, wrote to Grace from Barbados on October 22, 1961, to tell her, "You have struck the organization a blow from which I doubt if it will recover."[45] Between October and December 1961, acrimonious if respectful intellectual and personal exchange attempted to forestall the inevitable dissolution of Facing Reality. The December 10, 1961, resident editorial board meeting of the organization was its last stand. Grace and James opposed Marty Glaberman in passing a resolution voting down publication in *Correspondence* of an article by James intending to answer the new Boggs position. They wanted it published only as a discussion piece. Informed of the decision, James sent a statement to the board dated January 15, 1962, declaring his sundering of "all relations, political and personal, with all who subscribe to that resolution."[46] He followed with a laudatory history of the organization, a defense of Marxism, and the inclusion of several preceding letters to James and Grace challenging their criticism of the group's position on workers' control of production and the Negro question. But the die was cast. Throughout 1962 James and Grace dedicated themselves to writing new works and forming new alliances

The public if not official declaration of the Boggses' independence from Johnson-Forest came with publication of James Boggs's *The American Revolution: Pages from a Negro Worker's Notebook* in 1963. The book was published by Monthly Review Press with a preface by editors Leo Huberman and Paul Sweezy. James Boggs's introduction to the book was written and dated May 1, 1963, just months before the Grassroots Negro Leadership Conference in Detroit. Though written under James's byline, the book recasts many of the ideas Grace and James developed collaboratively after 1953 and predicts most of the major directions and episodes of Boggsism after their break with C. L. R. James. The first chapter, "The Rise and Fall of the Union," is an elaboration of the critique of both the union movement and reactionary unionism thrown into sharp relief in *Facing Reality*. It argues that a consequence of "industrial revolution" and changes in the production in the United States since World War II has been the dispersal and transformation of the traditional (i.e., Marxian) conception of the working class. The proletariat is no longer, Boggs argues, an identifiable "homogeneous segregated bloc." Another obstacle to American worker solidarity is the problem of the "permanently unemployed" caused by automation. Since 1955, the book argues, automation in the automobile industry had had several detrimental effects on worker solidarity: an increase in unemployment, particularly among young black workers; an increase in overtime; and a subsequent rise in internal worker conflict, including racism.[47] These factors had reversed Marx's prediction of a long period of industrial growth and a parallel increase in labor force. It also reversed his prediction that these conditions would produce a new world "created with human values of organization, cooperation and discipline," or what Marx called "socialized labor" (41). Such changes and challenges to Marx and Engels's notion of dialectical materialism demand that "a new theory must be evolved" (41). Chapter 3, "The Classless Society," begins this task. It opens with the declaration that "the United States is a Warfare State. The United

States is an inseparable part of Western Civilization. The United States is the citadel of world capitalism today" (42). Radicals, using Marxism, have historically analyzed capitalism, "often forgetting that their own ideas are shaped by no less a fact than that they themselves are by-products of Western Civilization." "Today," writes Boggs, "this philosophy is at the crossroads. The emerging nations of Asia and Africa, which have all these years been dominated by a little corner of the globe known as Western Civilization, are clashing head-on with that civilization. The Marxists themselves, who have done very little since the time of Marx to understand the rest of the globe, merely pigeonholing it in their minds as colonial and semi-colonial, must now do some serious re-evaluating" (42).

The passage echoes yet revises a passage from the chapter "New Society: New People" in *Facing Reality*. Describing Western civilization as the "most barbarous, the most cruel, the most sadistic, the most callous history has ever known," that chapter hyperbolically declared, "there is no more dramatic moment in the history of philosophy than that in which the young Hegel, after describing the disorder and torment inflicted on society by capitalist production, came face to face with the fact that only the proletariat could resolve it. Leaving the page forever unfinished, he turned to idealism. Marx completed it for him."[48] Boggs will now revise this page, if not the whole, of Marx, from this "non-Western" perspective, introducing a new class of subalterns. "The Outsiders," the book's next section, identifies "the new generation . . . the workless people" displaced by technological change and automation as the new revolutionary class. These people, he writes, "now have to turn their thoughts away from trying to outwit the machines and instead toward the organization and reorganization of society and of human relations inside society."[49] This new revolution will be "directed not toward increasing production but toward the management and distribution of things and toward the control of relations among people, tasks which up to now have been left to chance or in the hands of an elite" (52). Boggs's formulation retooled Marx's conception of surplus labor and James's theory of spontaneous resistance from below into a new theory of productive rebellion. It also echoed Fanon's (and Wright's) colonial conceptions of colored labor as the earth's most alienated and wretched: the Negro is the true American outsider, the "most oppressed and submerged section of the workers" (85). Boggs thus chides American Marxists for refusing to recognize this revolutionary potential, for seeing "Negroes as Negroes, i.e. in racial terms," and uses the colonial example to press his case. "The Negroes are now posing before all the institutions of American society, and particularly those which are supposedly on their side (the labor organizations, the liberals, the old Negro organizations, and the Marxists), the same questions that have been posed by the Algerian Revolution to all of French society, with this difference that Algeria is outside France while the Negroes are right here inside America" (84).

Yet rather than a Fanonian or colonial analysis, Boggs initiates what might be called a left exceptionalist, and humanist, analysis of black revolutionary potential. In the book's final chapter, "The American Revolution," Boggs stresses human rights and responsibility as the ultimate objectives of a struggle for black political power. "What is man's greatest human need in the United States today? It is to stop shirking responsibility and start assuming responsibility. When Americans stop doing the one and start doing the other, they will begin to travel the revolutionary road" (90). In an era of abundance, it is not the forces of production but the "creative imagination" of the individual that needs cultivation and change. "The American people must find a way to insist upon their own right and responsibility to make political decisions and to determine policy in all spheres of social existence—whether it is in foreign policy, the work process, education, race relations, community life. The coming struggle is a political struggle to take political power out of the hands of the few and put it into the hands of the many" (93).

These tenets informed the Boggses' development over the next ten years of the central organizing principle of their work, dialectical humanism. In 1973, their important essay "Dialectical Materialism/Dialectical Humanism" cast a retrospective glance at the ten-year interim of its development. In that essay they defined their "political conclusions" accompanying publication of *An American Revolution* as follows: the devolution of the Russian Revolution into "vulgar materialism and economism"; the bankruptcy of the U.S. labor movement; the tendency of the U.S. Left to ape the Russian Revolution; postwar affluence as a demobilizing agent for the Left; and finally, the assertion that the "black movement was introducing a new dimension into the U.S. revolutionary movement by its struggle for more human relations between people."[50] Disclosing the Boggses' ten-year path to dialectical humanism entails a close reading of the major works published in the interim. They include *Racism and the Class Struggle: Further Pages from a Black Worker's Notebook*, a compendium of the Boggses' 1960s writings and a sequel to *The American Revolution; Manifesto for a Black Revolutionary Party*, one of a number of important self-published pamphlets distributed by Advocators, a Detroit press; and *Revolution and Evolution in the 20th Century*, a historical re-evaluation of twentieth-century revolutions and their relationship to U.S. struggles. Characteristic of Boggsian thought, these books exist in dialectical, intertextual relationship to each other. Combined, they demonstrate how Black Power was for the Boggses both a local response to the specific history of African Americans in North America and a dialectical extension of Marxian questions fundamental to all major twentieth-century revolutions. They show how Black Power became an interpretive tool by which the Boggses evaluated the question of world revolution while advancing new formulations of black conditions and black struggle at home.

As with the Detroit Black Power movement generally during the 1960s, a search for correspondence between objective conditions of black struggle in the United States and those in other sites of revolution was a central strategy in the Boggses' development of the dialectical humanist ideal. Maoism and the Chinese revolution were most often touchstones in this search. In his 1965 essay "Black Power: A Scientific Concept Whose Time Has Come," first published in the *Liberator* and later in *Racism and the Class Struggle*, James Boggs argued that "Black Power in the United States raises the same question that Stalin could not tolerate from Mao: would the revolution in China come from the urban workers or from the peasantry?"[51] This analogy was central to several continuous aspects of Boggsian thought during the Black Power era. First, it foregrounded colored people's revolutions as both distinct from, and supplemental to, social movements of the European or Caucasian proletariat. Second, it underscored the affiliation between black urban workers and rural peasants, a crucial aspect of the Boggses' "city is the black man's land" thesis discussed in the previous chapter. Third, it was linked to the Boggses' admiration for Maoism's privileging of political over economic struggles. Economic overdevelopment versus political underdevelopment in the United States was the "essential contradiction in the country,"[52] they wrote, and was emendable only by adherence to Mao's challenge to the peasantry to "put politics in command of economics."[53] The latter was a means of avoiding economic determinism, or vulgar materialism, and emphasizing self- and social transformation as part of revolutionary process. Fourth, putting politics in command meant distinguishing revolutionary black nationalism from other nationalist movements, like that of the Black Panther Party, which the Boggses criticized for not developing an independent and U.S.-specific political strategy from Maoist theory. Finally, and most importantly, Mao's insistence in the essay "On Practice" that "when the whole of Mankind consciously remolds itself and changes the world, the era of communism will dawn" manifested for the Boggses the central challenge of molding philosophy and proletarianism, self- and social transformation, the individual and the species, into a dialectical unity that would advance human civilization.

These notions informed the Boggses' work with RAM and other Detroit-based grassroots organizations, sometimes in peripatetic, if not contradictory, relation to each other. Just as Mao, they argued, broke with Marxism-Leninism to devise a new revolutionary strategy "which would both break with and take advantage of the long Chinese past" (58–59), so Black Power must continuously develop its own vanguard organizations capable of creating new ideologies. Racism and capitalism had combined to make blacks especially suited to "enlarge the concept of human identity and human dignity beyond the biological or ethical limitations which have been placed upon the people" (182). In this regard, superexploitation of blacks within the United States created opportunity for *fanshen*, the Chinese concept of "overturning": Political struggle for state power can be effective, they argued, only when the most oppressed have been "set into motion to struggle against their old habits of individualism and self-interest, their old social ties to family and clan, their old ideas of right and wrong in terms of hierarchy" (61). Thus came the Boggses' 1963 formulation in "The Meaning of the Black Revolt in the U.S.A.": dialectical humanism is the era in which "the Negro revolt is . . . not just a narrow struggle over goods and for the development of the productive forces. . . . The burning question is how to create the kind of human responsibility in the distribution of material abundance that will allow everyone to enjoy and create the values of humanity" (18).

Placing black experience at the core of their concept of dialectical humanism became the Boggses' most distinctive theoretical addenda to Black Power struggle and world revolutionary theory. From it came a plethora of specific ideas about the nature of class, identity, culture, race, and gender struggle in the period of their most intense and relevant activity, from 1963 to 1974. In *Racism and the Class Struggle*, they argued that the "systematic underdevelopment" of black America was the "foundation" for the systematic development of white America.[54] Black Americans were "this country's first working class" condemned to servitude, thus destroying the possibility of "Black and White, Unite and Fight."[55] Black Power is thus the linchpin of true revolutionary black struggles, since it "opens up the possibility of a real classless society rather than the 'classless society' which has in fact rested on the class subjugation of another race."[56] Since the United States is now the "citadel" of capitalist power in the world, it is also the most pressing test or center of the legacy of revolutionary thought: "We are not faced with the task of applying the ideas of Marx or Mao to the United States," they wrote, "but with that of developing a new concept of human identity as the basis for the revolution in America, a concept which must extend the dialectical development of humanity itself."[57]

For the Boggses, this dialectical concept of human identity wedded a traditional Confucian conception of ethical responsibility and uplift rhetoric of U.S. civil rights to a Maoist dialectic of self-overturning. It required "moral rather than legal force as the foundation of political authority and legitimacy, and conceives goodness in terms of a relation between people rather than as a moral quality which an individual can have on his/her own."[58] This revision of Marxian "social man" manifests itself politically in social struggle modeled on Chinese guerrilla strategy during the war with Japan: the "distinctive style" of the Chinese revolution, wrote the Boggses, "involves the most aggressive struggle against the antihuman or antisocial behaviour of the class enemy, while always leaving the door open for the individual member of the enemy class to re-enter the social and moral universe" (66). China's Cultural Revolution subsequently provided black America the most apt and successful model of *fanshen:* by breaking down the divide between manual and mental labor, philosophy had become proletarian. The peasants "have been freed to practice the most advanced ideas" and to develop themselves as 'all-sided human beings'" (79). Thus "the Chinese revolution has demonstrated that a society built on unselfishness, on serving the people, the country, and oppressed peoples all over the world, is the key not only to social and technical advance but to personal happiness. In every Third World nation the Chinese revolution is now providing the inspiration once provided by the Declaration of Independence and then by the October Revolution" (80). Other sites of those revolutions included the United States, particularly Detroit; Guinea, under the leadership of Amilcar Cabral; and Vietnam, under Ho Chi Minh. Cabral's African Party for the Independence of Guinea and Cape Verde (PAIGC), formed in 1956, had been inspired by the examples of China and Vietnam to unite and develop the people through struggle while avoiding "economic determinism or mechanistic materialism" (84). As should good black revolutionary nationalists, the Boggses argued, Ho successfully warded off both narrow nationalism and racialism by enriching Lenin's concept of a vanguard party to incorporate Vietnamese philosophy. "The Vietnamese have never separated ethics from politics. . . . Ho conceived the party as a source not only of theoretical and political clarity but also of spiritual and moral strength" (103). Black Power should thus look to Ho—and General Giap, as well as sources like Sun Tzu's *The Art of War:* "The most urgent task for the American Revolution today is the creation of a long-range strategy by the black revolutionary movement. . . . Now the task is to do what Sun Tzu advised over two thousand years ago in the Art of War: 'Shape' the enemy, size up his strengths and weaknesses and develop strategy and tactics to win."[59]

A similar imperative informed the Boggsian argument on revolutionary culture. In the essay "Culture and Black Power," published in the *Liberator* in January 1967 in the wake of the first Black Arts Conference in Detroit, Maoism was used to leverage and distinguish between revolutionary and cultural black nationalism. James Boggs had indirectly attacked the latter at the Black Arts Conference, where he had spoken against Afrocentrism and racial romanticism: "Of what profit, then, is our history and our culture," he asked, "unless it is used in a vision of our future?"[60] He cited China's cultural riches but military defenselessness against the "gunpowder" Marco Polo introduced to the West. Mao's "power comes out of the barrel of a gun" was its corrective: "The Chinese have a great deal of culture, as all the world knows. But Mao Tsetung, cultured as he was, did not sit around and talk about the virtues of being yellow and boast about his yellow ancestors. No. He said, 'Because we have been, so we shall be.' And today the Chinese are spending their time trying to build the most powerful country in the world and developing their lands and minerals and training their people in mind and body so that they can step forward into the twentieth and twenty-first centuries with power."[61] These exemplars translated into calls for a militant Detroit and national Black Arts movement, described in the previous chapter. Boggsism reanimated the Marxian concept of productive labor as inclusive of the cultural. It countered the "vulgar materialist" line dispensed with as humanism's opposition. In short, it was a crucial piece in the formation of "all-sided man," a variation of which the Boggses had been arguing since their earlier work with Johnson-Forest.

The programmatic culmination of these advances in Boggism after 1963 was the publication of *Manifesto for a Black Revolutionary Party*. The forty-page pamphlet was published in February 1969 to coincide with the fourth anniversary of the assassination of Malcolm X. The pamphlet

MANIFESTO FOR A BLACK REVOLUTIONARY PARTY

75¢

by JAMES BOGGS

Fifth Printing With New Introduction

Manifesto for a Black Revolutionary Party. The pamphlet, written by James Boggs, was published in 1969 to coincide with the fourth anniversary of the death of Malcolm X.

reasserted "revolutionary humanist values" at a moment of competing discursive and political trends in Black Power. The manifesto was critical of the limitations of both King's nonviolence movement (it did not draw "dialectical conclusions" from its own work) and the violent response provoked by the riots in the aftermath of his 1968 assassination. It cited U.S. student protests against the Vietnam War and racism as hastening the "disintegration" of U.S. institutions.[62] Its most specific target of criticism, however, was the Black Panther Party. For a brief period, wrote James Boggs, the BPP seemed like "the kind of party which could keep the street forces from degenerating into lumpen" (iv). That did not happen because the party "did not take the time to develop the revolutionary ideology necessary to lead an American revolution" (iv). The manifesto urged a blueprint for vanguard leadership and revolutionary discipline aimed primarily at black youth. It called for a long-range strategy to mobilize the masses, not the illusion of "instant revolution," an echo of Boggisms's critique of Jamesian spontaneity. In addition, new leadership must "combat the individualism which is rampant in the United States and expose the tendency to confuse individual acts of rebellion or promotion with revolutionary struggle by masses of people" (31).

Thus the Boggses proposed a Black Revolutionary Party with three objectives: to take power for the purposes of bringing about change in the social, economic, and political institutions of society; to "establish and keep before the movement and society as a whole the revolutionary humanist objectives of the Black Revolution"; and to develop a revolutionary strategy to achieve these goals dialectically by "building on the struggles, sacrifices and achievements of the past, and learning from previous mistakes and shortcomings" (2). The BRP would reflect the combined "dynamic of a national struggle for self-determination and a social struggle to resolve the contradictions of an advanced capitalist society" (9). This synthesis of national and social struggle was the fundamental dialectic of black revolutionary nationalism. The movement, coming at a moment when the productive forces were "already sufficiently developed to establish a material basis for communism," would pursue the redistribution of resources from ability, according to need: education, transportation, work, technology, child development, medical care, and welfare would all be reconceived to meet especially the needs of the vast majority in poor urban areas (18–21). In general, the BRP would attack racism, alienation, and inequality through ridding society of "tendencies towards elitism and individualism" and by fostering local community control of resources and planning (24). These steps were linked, using the Bandung era logic of correspondence, to the BRP's larger goal of challenging U.S. imperialism: the U.S. government had "become the chief obstacle to four-fifths of mankind struggling to rid themselves of colonial and neo-colonial exploitation" (24). In response, Black Power would "recognize the right and duty of all nations to establish the kind of society which they deem suitable to their needs" (25). It would especially recognize the rights of people in Latin America, Asia, Africa, and the Middle East who likewise "are discovering and perfecting the secret of how to develop the new type of human beings" capable of world revolution (39). It would give "a sense of their growing power to improve their conditions of life through struggle and which enable them to create dual or parallel power structures out of struggle. Struggle therefore must be on issues and terrains which enable the Black community to create a form of liberated area out of what are at present occupied areas" (33). The city would thus indeed become again the black man's land, and the black revolution would be a revolution of "the majority of the world's people of which the Black Revolution in the United States is an integral part" (39).

Manifesto for a Black Revolutionary Party was both a culmination of Boggsian theorizing of U.S. Black Power and another point of dialectical transition in their work. It was an attempt to identify coherent leadership for the internal schisms and contradictions within Black Power in response to events particularly of 1965 (Malcolm X), 1967 (Detroit and Newark), and 1968 (Martin Luther King). At the same time, it anticipated a need to respond to new eruptions and disruptions in the social moment that the Boggses described: the rise of parallel ethnic nationalisms among Chicano and Asian youth; feminist dissent from both Black Power and the larger Anglo student Left; the concurrence of new Third World movements and consciousness as represented by the 1969 Third

World Conference at San Francisco State University. After 1969, the Boggses' work would resonate with each of these new developments. It would gather itself again to attempt to reconcile the manifold local and global manifestations of change. It would also coincide with a new turn in Boggsian dialectical humanism, which would encompass more firmly an inclusion of gender and particularly Asian ethnicity in their theory and practice. This third stage of Boggsism would point to a reincarnation and revision of many of their earlier themes and ideas.

Maoism's ideological influence, the emergence of the U.S. women's movement, and the beginnings of the Asian Pacific American movement in the late 1960s significantly altered the next stage of Boggsian work. Unlike the Detroit Black Power movement, the Boggses were never self-declared leaders of either of these movements. Yet from 1970 to 1984, they sought a theory and practice to encompass each. At the same time, they sought continuity of thought between these new developments and their concept of dialectical humanism. The Cultural Revolution again served as a heuristic device in this effort: "Particularly moving and instructive," the Boggses later wrote about their study of the Chinese revolution during this period, "are the cases of fanshen by Chinese women, the majority of whom had been for centuries in much the same position within Chinese societies as the blacks inside U.S. society."[63] Chinese women's response to conditions of forced marriage, enslavement, and rape demonstrated what they called the "unity-criticism-unity" model of Chinese dialectics, where women win the right to divorce, then struggle to make a new marriage work.[64] By 1970, the Boggses had added to their ongoing efforts in Black Power the formal study of Asian revolution. In that year, a group of six Detroiters, three Japanese, three Chinese, including Grace, formed the Asian Political Alliance. The group initially met weekly, screening films like *The East Is Red*, and holding demonstrations to protest the war in Vietnam.[65] With virtually no Asian American movement in Detroit to support it, the group soon ceased its weekly meetings to concentrate on the work of producing two pamphlets on Asian Americans, and to test the commitment of its small membership to serve the people in practice rather than theory. Four members of the group formed the Chrysler Workers Group passing out pamphlets and conducting revolutionary study groups in Mao's lectures on revolution.

In December 1970, Grace Boggs was invited to speak at the Asian American Reality Conference held at Pace College (now Pace University) in New York City. Boggs's speech, "Asian-Americans and the U.S. Movement," was published by the Asian Political Alliance that year. The speech is an important moment not only in the careers of James and Grace Boggs but also in the discursive trajectory of Afro-Orientalism. Boggs applied the same questions of revolutionary responsibility, dialectical humanism, race, and revolution to her Asian American audience that Boggsism had developed through years of organizational building in black America:

> What are the goals of a revolution in the United States? What are your goals? Where have you talked and written about them? What would a revolutionary government do in the United States? A revolutionist doesn't seek power just for the sake of power. A revolutionist doesn't seek power just to do what the liberals have failed to do. Most of you say that you want to "change the system." What do you mean by "the system"? Do you mean just changing property relationships or do you mean something more than that? Is your aim to create more appropriate, more human relationships between people? How would you develop those correctly? Revolution is not just rebellion, not just revolt, not just insurrection, not just a coup d' etat. . . . A revolution is for the purpose of bringing about an accelerated development in the evolution of Man, a more rapid development in the evolution of all Mankind, an evolution that has been going on now for at least 50,000 years and which is far from over. A revolution is for the purpose of creating a "New Man," new people, new men, women and children. . . . A revolution is not just a spontaneous event. It is a struggle by great masses of people seeking to make real, i.e. to translate into reality, new, more advanced concepts of themselves as human beings.[66]

Boggs's reluctance to privilege ethnicity or identity over dialectical social transformation echoes an earlier conception of dialectical humanism as a synthesis of social and national struggle. Her challenges to political spontaneity and ahistoricism reflect an attempt to distinguish the Asian American movement from its black precursors. The Asian American generation to which she speaks is the first, she notes further in the speech, to resist assimilation into what she calls "the American Way of Life" (4). Repelled by the war in Vietnam, and inspired by the black revolt, the situation of Asian Americans is thus "pre-revolutionary," but ripe. External Asian rebellions again provide the best internal model. In contemporary Vietnam and China, "a new way of life is emerging which is as inspiring to the people of the whole world as, two hundred years ago, the 'New Land' and the 'New Man' of the 'New Continent' of America were inspiring to the people of Europe" (6). As with Black Power, Boggs attempts to "center" both Asian and Asian American revolution as an organic impetus for a larger American revolution. Boggs then cites California Asian American activist Alex Hing. In 1969, with the help and under the influence of the Black Panther Party, Hing had helped to form the Red Guard in California, a Marxist-Leninist-Maoist organization. Boggs is unspecific about her support for Hing (though the Detroit collective's decisions to screen films like *The East Is Red* may have been modeled on Red Guard activity), but the speech acknowledges the Red Guard as a fraternal emergent APA movement.

Yet Boggs also argues that the American revolution will be realized only by the study of dialectics—particularly Mao's "On Practice"—and by careful articulation of how the ethnic particularity of the APA movement will distinguish its contributions to other revolutionary social movements. In a section of the essay titled "Asian Heritage, Identity, Community, and the American Movement," Boggs writes, "It is in the sphere of dialectical, or historical thinking that I believe Asian-Americans can make their greatest contribution to the American movement" (14). "In Asia," she writes, "they have been trying for at least 2,000 years to discover what are the appropriate relations between human beings" (14). Taoism and Confucianism are two examples. Mao was able to "break loose" from Confucianism and Taoism by applying dialectical thought, embodied by the Cultural Revolution's abolition of the division between intellectual and manual labor (14). Asian thought, then, is especially suited to the development of dialectical humanism, "viewed as a continuation of the struggle which the human species has been carrying on over many thousands of years to achieve appropriate human relations between people, a struggle which must be waged against both the enemy within and the enemy without, and for the revolutionary transformation not only of social institutions but of oneself" (22).

In keeping with this theme, Boggs's analysis is uncharacteristically autobiographical. She recalls her father's immigration to the United States to work on the railroads, his transformation into a shopkeeper and his support for Sun Yat-sen, and his late-in-life appreciation for Maoism before his death in Detroit at age ninety-five. She also recalls her father's advice: "Good or bad, ask eight men," an assertion that she "consult others but in the end it is up to you to decide, to choose the right course" (16). The full meaning of this moral imperative, as well as her own identity, is ultimately disclosed only through mass struggle: "This is the sort of thing that has begun to come into focus for me as I have been discovering my identity as an Asian in America. Apparently, also, I could not really internalize or make creative use of the many important truths that I have learned from non-Asians, black and white, until I was clear about my own identity as an Asian-American" (16). Boggs here writes *herself* as a subject of dialectical humanism while iterating identity as a dialectical movement between oneself and social institutions. She thus links this personal transformation for the first time to her public political persona. Marrying a black man, she confesses, defied her parents's wishes but embodied "learning from the community" (19).

Grace Boggs's fledgling commitment to the emerging Asian Pacific American movement and the question of women's choice would become recurring themes of her increasingly independent writing of the 1970s, and a more essential element in the Boggses' evolving conception of dialectical humanism. In general, her work of this period is also characterized by a more liberal conception of class and class struggle. On January 19, 1974, for example, Boggs gave a speech at Yale College titled "The Search for Human Identity in America." The speech argued that "the question before us is not whether blacks are equal with whites or women with men—although, of course, they should be treated equally. The main question is what blacks and whites, women and men, all being human, can contribute to their own search and to the search of all of us for a new more human identity and for new human social and political relations."[67] In April 1975, Boggs spoke at "A Symposium on Human Development: The Chinese View and the American View" in Denver. The conference included the report "A Background to China's Humanism," predicated on Hu Shih's "road of adaptation," or pragmatism, and Mao's "road of revolution: the creation of new men and women." In a speech titled "The Changing-Self Concept of the American People," Boggs noted that recognition of "contradiction in everything" was a Chinese strength immediately applicable to a dialectical humanist concept of human development. "We can recognize that every individual is in fact a social self, living in society in positive or negative relations with others, and that society itself does not exist except insofar as it is made up of selves."[68] This theme was elaborated on in "The Personal Is Political: The Challenge of Being a Woman in Today's America," a speech at the West Virginia College of Graduate Studies. The "personal is political" slogan, writes Boggs, "contains the potential for breaking with the whole Western philosophical and political tradition from Aristotle to Machiavelli, Descartes and Hobbes, and up to and including Marx and Lenin." Women must "enter into the creation of philosophy and the making of history."[69] Boggs's most elaborate statement on this theme from her women-centered work of the 1970s is her March 10, 1977, speech "Women and the Movement to Build a New America," delivered for International Women's Week at the University of Massachusetts–Amherst. The essay notes the objective conditions that have enabled the ongoing feminist revolution in the United States: sexual reproductive rights; work opportunities for women; the interrogation of nuclear family models. At the same time, U.S. capitalism and imperialism have simultaneously made women, blacks, and Native Americans victims of "materialism, individualism and hedonism."[70] Women must now avoid the earlier mistake of both the labor movement of the 1930s and Black Power of the 1960s, namely, bureaucratized self-interest and self-victimization—predominating themes in the Boggses' post–Black Power writing and the foes of their dialectical humanist concept. Instead, women's newly realized subjectivity makes them the logical vanguard of a new humanism:

> We/women do not have to wait upon men to begin creating this new enlarged concept of our human identity. We can begin now to use our minds to create a new philosophy and programs that will help all Americans to begin struggling for a new society that will incorporate the values and attitudes of social responsibility which we have internalized as a result of our role in the reproductive process, the raising of children and the serving of men. The ability which we as women have to subordinate self-interest to concern for the development of others, to see beyond the pleasures of the moment or the satisfaction of our egos, our sensitivity to the feelings of others, our ability to see in other individuals the potential for growth and to give them the space necessary to develop their autonomy, to deal with each problem as it arises, flexibly and without stereotyping—all these qualities which we have been developing in the private realm are today the ones most urgently needed in the public realm.[71]

The encroaching liberalism of the Boggses' dialectical humanism, evident in numerous other points of their work, is again thrown into relief by Boggs's formulations of gendered identity. Yet as should be apparent from this chapter, this tendency has always been an essential feature of their work: it is implicit in their reading of Marxian humanism, reinforced by the interpretation of Hegel as a moral idealist, and fundamental to their interpretation of the African American experience in the United States as providing a unique epistemological standpoint on race in the country. These tendencies also underpin what the Boggses and organizations like RAM called in the 1960s "progressive" nationalism. Beginning in their collaboration with C. L. R. James, the Boggses sought a distinctly *American* revolutionary politics, one that resists conventional notions of "exceptionalism" while drawing, in dialectical fashion, on U.S. national moments of revolutionary tradition. All these tendencies reconcretized and resynthesized themselves in 1978, when the Boggses led the formation of a new collective, the National Organization for an American Revolution. NOAR, as it became known, held its founding "Constitutional Convention" in Philadelphia in 1978. It drew a disparate group of adherents, as well: they included black, white, working-class, and educated activists, particularly from Detroit and Philadelphia. Those drawn to the founding convention were either previous collaborators from other Detroit circles or readers of their published works. Rick Feldman, for example, came to NOAR after reading *What about the Workers?* a pamphlet cowritten by James Boggs and James Hocker, an autoworker, in 1973. James Embry was the son of an NAACP activist mother who worked with SNCC while a student at the University of Kentucky. Sharon Howell joined NOAR and helped to author some of its early key pamphlets. No common ideological or organizational ground unified these contributors. Rather, they represented the horizontal reach of issues and ideas with which Boggsism was identifiable by the mid-1970s. Yet their congress in Philadelphia would lead to a sustained period of political work that encompassed the death of James Boggs in 1993 and has not yet diminished. This current phase of Boggsism is best understood by a reading of the first significant NOAR publication, *Manifesto for an American Revolutionary Party*, published in 1982.

Like most of their major works after 1970, the manifesto rested on yet another stated break with an earlier revolutionary incarnation—this one Black Power and black nationalism. In a chapter titled "Revolution or Counter-revolution: Our Choices Narrow," NOAR declared that Black Power had failed in the "awesome responsibilities" of leading a total revolution. "Instead of grappling with the profound human questions involved in making a second American revolution," they wrote, Black Power had become a cynical self-interest movement promoting assimilation, black capitalism, careerism, and reformism.[72] As such it had played into the hands of U.S. counterrevolution, whose goal was "to restore white male supremacy" (39).

The new American revolutionary party must provide leadership toward a "holistic" vision based on what it called a "new self-governing

Manifesto for an American Revolutionary Party. The first major pamphlet published by
the National Organization for an American Revolution appeared in 1982.

America" emphasizing new principles of responsibility, and "new forms of decentralized power" (41). The move toward local control and collective organizing was in some ways an extension of "revolution from below" tendencies vestigial to Jamesian Trotskyism, as well as to the experience of Detroit grassroots organizing. But NOAR also declared "decentralization" as a strategic response to a new phase of capitalism characterized by globalization. Chapter 1, "Naming the Enemy," begins with an echo of Marx—"A spectre is haunting the American people"— but renames capitalism's nemesis as "a new stage, the stage of multinational capitalism" (4). The relocation of U.S. multinationals to South Korea and Mexico reflects not only new exploitation of cheap labor but, more importantly and egregiously for NOAR, the abandonment of loyalty to the United States or to "any American community" (4). Classic models of industrial struggle have now been decentered; cities have been "turned into wastelands" by corporate takeovers; social and welfare programs are being dismantled; unions are being destroyed. These decenterings create a new onus for revolutionary struggle, outlined in chapter 2, "Towards a New Self-Governing America."

The chapter's epigraph is from the Boggses' 1974 book *Revolution and Evolution in the 20th Century*. It defines revolution as "a projection of Man/Woman into the future. . . . projecting the notion of a more human human being" (6). NOAR was Boggsism's most liberal and polymathic attempt to redefine this familiar conceit. NOAR cited the labor movement, black movement, ecology movement and even "human potential movement" as sources of "the need for inner transformation" (9). NOAR's innovation was to link capitalism's multinational decentering to local grassroots and community organizing. The "New Self-Governing America" was to be built on three foundations: local self-government, families, and communities (14). Education, housing, energy conservation, health reform, and public transportation were all issues to be taken up by regional self-reliance councils and neighborhood responsibility councils. What the Boggses called in a previous pamphlet the "awesome responsibility of intellectuals" was to be converted into forms of organic self-activity and theoretical innovation from below. The regional and neighborhood councils were to be community incarnations of the 1956 Hungarian workers' councils, or the 1963 grassroots leadership conference in Detroit. They would achieve the "from the masses, to the masses" imperatives of Maoism, refashioned to a populist conception of self-activity. The emphasis on issues pertinent to families—education and health care, for example—bore the distinctive fingerprints of 1970s feminism. The absence of attention to industrial sites and unions was a concession to multinational capitalism's new diffuseness.

NOAR buttressed its analysis with theoretical statements on what it attempted to define as neoimperialism. In 1983, Grace Boggs spoke on "transnational" capitalism in a speech entitled "Beyond Imperialism." It refuted Lenin's thesis on imperialism by arguing that "internationalization of production and of finance capital," rather than the expansion of capitalist forms, was the specific and different essence of multinational capitalism. This was the result of several features of post–World War II capitalism: development of communications and transportation technology, the U.S. creation of a free trade economy, and the Marshall Plan. This "gigantic socialization of production across national frontiers" did not necessarily create the objective conditions for socialism; rather, it demanded a "second" revolution dedicated to community and regional self-governance recommended by NOAR. NOAR did not assess in depth in their studies of multinationalism what have become essential tenets of globalization analysis: uneven development, the exportation of U.S. cultural imperialism, and the effects of transmigration on wages and working conditions. It concentrated its organizational efforts instead on American cities, establishing local branches in Boston, Detroit, Lexington, New York, Philadelphia, San Francisco, and Syracuse, among others. It continued to publish works written by the Boggses or members of NOAR's collective, for example, "Liberation or Revolution?" published in 1980, a speech given by James Boggs at Stanford University in 1978; and "What about the Workers?" and *"Uprooting Racism and Racists in the U.S.A.,"* published in 1982. The latter pamphlet reiterated numerous Boggsian themes, most especially the uniqueness of black experience as a means of leading a struggle to put politics in command of economics.[73] In Detroit,

NOAR also formed community alliances to resist proposals for casino gambling and worked with Save Our Sisters and Daughters (SOSAD), an organization to combat youth violence. In 1984, NOAR organized support for Jesse Jackson's presidential campaign, refitting its rhetoric to its original mission statement. This support coincided with speeches and articles on black leadership published in the *Awakening*, NOAR's bi-monthly newsletter. As with other radical and left groups that coalesced around Jackson, like I Wor Kuen and the Revolutionary Communist Party, NOAR ended up disillusioned and damaged by engagement with mainstream electoral politics. Not long after the 1984 election, the group disassembled.

In 1984, Grace Boggs traveled to China for the first time. As she recounts in her autobiography *Living for Change*, the trip was unremarkable except for her own disillusionment with the lack of political sophistication and knowledge among younger Chinese. Her notes for a speech entitled "The Chinese and Marxism" from early 1985, however, indicate a sympathetic relationship between NOAR's attempts to reconsider socialism and China's era of Deng Xiaoping reform. Her strongest criticism, one dating back to the late 1970s, appears in correspondence with her friend Louise Tsen: Boggs argues that China still needs the equivalent of an intellectual Reformation or Renaissance to release individual creative thought to identify existing contradictions under socialism and between socialist and capitalist nations.[74] Thus what is necessary but missing from Deng Xiaopingism is a democratic centralist party that is constantly learning and "seeking truth from facts" as a means of developing theory on the basis of practice.[75] Boggs's configuration of Maoism as the Renaissance impulse necessary to advance Chinese (and American) revolutionary theory was most ably theorized later in a speech entitled "Beyond Eurocentrism" delivered at the Socialist Scholars Conference in New York City in 1989. The occasion for the address was a panel discussion organized by the *Monthly Review* featuring Harry Magdoff, Sami Amin, and Val Moghadam. The speech is a circular and dialectic reconsideration of the stages of her own intellectual development framed by its relationship to Eurocentrism. The first stage is her conversion to

NATIONAL ORGANIZATION FOR AN AMERICAN REVOLUTION

LIBERATION
or
REVOLUTION
?

$1

**We can change
the way it is!**

Liberation or Revolution? Published by the National Organization for an American
Revolution.

Marxism as a first-generation Chinese American woman born during World War I "after many years of study in Western and particularly Hegelian philosophy"; the last is her thirty-six years in Detroit, once hailed as the "Arsenal of Democracy," a city now "as devastated as any city at capitalism's periphery."[76] These personal coordinates of political development find their correspondence in the century's endeavor to move beyond what Boggs calls the "culture of capitalism" (40) "Objectively," she writes, "the world has been moving beyond Eurocentrism ever since World War I" (41). World War II and the extermination of the Jews followed by five decades of Third World peoples' struggles, the defeat of the United States in Vietnam, the mass migration of Third World peoples into First World cities, the resurgence of Islam, and now the emergence of Japan as a world economic power "have made it clear that we are living in a multipolar world" (41). Boggs tips her hand toward a postmodernist conception of globalization here, as well as in her characterization of Marxism's relationship to the Enlightenment: "Marxism criticized the Enlightenment for its linear concept of progress, but his concept of Scientific Socialism as a potential world system shows how much he shared its faith in Reason and Science" (41). Third World liberation struggles, she continues, have "helped us to see how the belief in the universal validity of the ideas of the Enlightenment has provided legitimacy to the imperialist destruction of indigenous cultures." Boggs in turn calls for "philosophies which go beyond the anthropomorphism and reductionism of Scientific Rationalism. . . . which emphasize our interconnectedness with one another and with other livings things . . . which will empower us to transform ourselves and our relationship with one another and with Nature":

> Today and for the foreseeable future the historic project of humanity is not to conquer Nature but to live in harmony with it; not to free the individual from feudal controls but to create community and social justice in a world in which people have been transformed into individualists and materialists by the expansion of capitalism. Under these circumstances how do we go beyond the concepts of Individual Freedom and Equality

which we have inherited from the French Revolution? This is very difficult to do precisely because these concepts have been so empowering in our historical struggle and are therefore bound up with our sense of self or our identity. (42–43)

Boggs's tentative conclusions for addressing this dilemma make up some of her most independent writing and work. She notes that the "post–World War II revolutionary struggles in the Third World"—those of the Bandung era—were led mainly by Western-educated leaders who "could not help but see the world through Western categories of Race, Class and Nation, categories which reinforced the fragmentation of human beings and their estrangement from their primary and community relationships" (44). The next generation, she argues, born after the Vietnam era, like leaders of the West Bank Intifada, or antiapartheid activists in South Africa, "are coming to maturity in a world which has objectively gone beyond Eurocentrism of both the Western and Eastern variety" (44). Boggs's notion of a bipolar or global Eurocentrism to be resisted and remapped is a useful restatement of ideological struggles through which both Xiao Mei Chen's Occidentalists and the Afro-Orientalists I have been discussing have passed. It also undergirds her call in the essay for a "multipolar" world capable of balancing the needs of hemispheres and communities (43). This vision and the attempt to sustain and realize it have motivated the final stage of Grace Boggs's political career. Her conception of self and social transformation since the death of James Boggs on July 22, 1993, has been located in the dialectical relationship between roots and place. Boggs's name for this strategy is "grassroots postmodernism." It is a synthesis of several key influences: Gustavo Esteva and Madhu Prakash's 1998 book *Grassroots Post-Modernism*, her own reflective view of her life's work, and the critical body of thought of Immanuel Wallerstein, particularly his book *After Liberalism*.[77] Each of these influences, as described by Boggs, is a synthetic continuation of her collaborative, lifelong work with James, particularly as extensions of their evolving conception of dialectical humanism. Esteva and Prakash's book calls for a globalized, placed-based resistance to the politics and philosophical practices of Western capitalist modernity: the authors' postmodernism challenges Western-defined notions of human rights and epistemology while criticizing self-sufficient individualism as a Eurocentric remnant of capitalism's five-hundred-year history in the West. They call, instead, for independent, local, and indigenous political responses specific to local objective conditions. Their program is a challenge to both national and ethnic-based politics, reimagining the political as the interrelation between micro- and macrocosmic struggles. For Grace Boggs, Wallerstein's work provides a historical frame for thinking about the fate of Marxism and capitalism after liberalism. Wallerstein argues that fundamental capital-labor relations are no longer the central dilemma posed for revolutionaries by capitalism, and centralized vanguard political leadership is thus no longer a necessary or favorable political response. Instead, Wallerstein argues for a politics concerned with capitalist production's effects on ecology, quality of life, and rampant (i.e., global) commodification. In her own synthesis of these positions, Boggs has argued that indigenous movements in underdeveloped nations formerly known as the Third World should become reciprocal models of grassroots organizing in overdeveloped countries like the United States. In yet another return of faith to "people at the bottom," Boggs has likewise argued that decentralized grassroots movements like the Zapatistas in Chiapas, or the Tree Huggers in India, offer the best hope and model for activists in developed nations as well.

Grace Boggs's orientation to grassroots postmodernism is also a direct response to events in Detroit. It was Detroit's deindustrialization of the 1980s, destructive megaprojects like the GM Poletown plant, which bulldozed 1,500 houses, and the effort by Coleman Young to introduce casinos that caused the city's present urban crisis. In the early 1990s, before the death of James Boggs, neighborhood alliances, veterans of NOAR, newcomers to Boggsism, and others began a series of programs to try to rebuild the city piece by piece. These included the Detroit Agricultural Network, a program to build community, youth, church, and school gardens on Detroit's vacant lots; Detroit Summer, a program to engage young people in community leadership and participation; and the Mural Message Movement (AC3T), bringing artists and schoolchildren together. In the wake of James Boggs's death, these same organizers formed the Grace and James Boggs Center for Community Leadership. The center is housed on the second floor of Grace and James's roomy and solid brick home on Detroit's east side, not far from the area of the city that was among the most animated by the Detroit riots of 1943 and 1967. Grace Boggs lives alone in the home now but is rarely without local, national, or international visitors to the Boggs Center.

Meanwhile, Boggs has become something of a reluctant icon for the newest generation of Asian Pacific American activists and students. In some ways, the reluctance is reciprocal. APAers have been critical of Boggs for not adhering permanently to the first wave of APA rebellion in the early 1970s, a charge to which she pleads guilty. They have also criticized her for not more forcefully joining local and national protests that erupted in 1980 after the killing of Detroit autoworker Vincent Chin. Boggs cites taking part in at least one Chin march as her second encounter with the APA movement up to that time. Yet Boggs's long-term usefulness to the APA movement more likely lies elsewhere. As Arif Dirlik, one of Boggs's ardent admirers, has written, she is "a link to an Asian American radicalism that once was capable of transcending ethnic and racial boundaries to engage in political activity that envisioned as its end not just the reaffirmation of ethnic presence but a broader goal of human liberation."[78] Dirlik places Boggs with Yuri Kochiyama, the Japanese American companion and colleague to Malcolm X, and Philip Vera Cruz as members of a premovement era in APA history. Boggs's example of interracial Asian American collaboration with African American struggle also predates and anticipates the work of figures like Richard Aoki and Alex Hing, who in the mid- to late 1960s had a similarly dialectical response to Black Power, and especially to the Black Panther Party in California, in part the subject of the next chapter. Boggs's lifelong dedication to the study of Maoism, particularly as an addendum and antidote to both Asian and African American political theories of liberation, also bears a compelling—if, for some, musty—path of study for today's generation of APA activists. Just as it is difficult to imagine contemporary

African American studies without the fertile theoretical grounding of Fanon, Padmore, Nkrumah, the Pan-Africanist Du Bois, the negritude writers, and others, so it should be equally difficult to conceive of an Asian Pacific American studies or APA movement that isn't grappling with the legacy of Maoism, arguably, after Gandhism, the most influential body of Asian thought outside of Asia produced in this century. Put another way, Grace Boggs's radicalism embodies an intellectual diaspora to which few contemporary ethnic studies movements have yet caught up. That said, the numerous contradictions in Boggsism—from its at times inchoate liberalism, to its redundant faith in humanism, to its at times contradictory means of assessing American capitalism—also merit enormous areas of study and review for young radicals, Asian American and others, as a means of assessing the impact of Asian America's most influential left thinker of the twentieth century.

These tasks, and the work of James and Grace Lee Boggs, await a still more complete explication. What can be said in the context of this study of Afro-Orientalism about Grace Boggs is this: her work, both inclusive and exclusive of her relationship to James Boggs, defines many of the major coordinates of our evolving if provisional map of the Afro-Asian century. Up to and including her present newspaper columns for the *Michigan Citizen*, which touch on everything from sweatshop labor to casino gambling, and inclusive of her remarkably consistent fidelity to the liberation of peoples of color, Grace Boggs has steadfastly made good on Afro-Orientalism's potential for redrawing the shape of the color line, and the shape of Marxism as it has steadfastly negotiated that line. The final chapter of her life, not yet completed, points the way toward the final chapter of this book, where her groundbreaking work on Afro-Asian liberation finds a worthy heir and successor.

CHAPTER 5

Making Monkey Signify:
Fred Ho's Revolutionary Vision Quest

The culture and Arts of the oppressed owes nothing, needs not be
thankful to, the culture and art of the oppressor. What oppressor
cultural aspects there are have been refashioned and transformed, and
dare we say, violated and miscegenated. This has been the way of the
oppressed masses: the field slave, the coolie, the savage, the bandit, the
heathen, the guerilla.

—Fred Ho

Music is our bomb!

—Ron Sakolsky and Fred Ho

Afro-Orientalism's familial relationship to other discourses of liberation
is revealed by its fondness for the revolutionary imagination. W. E. B.
Du Bois's midsummer night's dream of a colored world's revolution nods
affectionately to Communism's wedding to happy endings. Grace and
James Boggs's dialectical humanism enacts the human potential movement integral to Marxism's vision of a workers' paradise. Richard Wright's
ambiguous utopias described in *The Color Curtain* and *Black Power* bear
the scars of Western modernity's brute force and the healing hopes of
its demise. Robert Williams's rhetorical transformation of China into a
world without police and without race signifies how far he physically and
mentally traveled from dystopic America. For the Revolutionary Action
Movement or the Nation of Islam the American city was the black man's
land, the mountaintop come to (Elijah) Muhammad.

Afro-Orientalism's utopian and speculative thrust is central to the
work of Chinese American baritone saxophonist, composer, and cultural
worker Fred Ho. A longtime participant in Asian Pacific American and
African American political movements, Ho's performances and recordings

for disc and theater provide a staging ground, literally and figuratively, for key moments in the history of Afro-Asian liberation struggle. Ho is founder and director of Big Red Media, Inc. He has released more than a dozen albums and is the founder and leader of both the Monkey Orchestra and the Afro-Asian Music Ensemble. He has coedited two books, *Sounding Off! Music as Subversion/Resistance/Revolution* and *Legacy to Liberation: Politics and Culture of Revolutionary Asian Pacific America*. His operas and staged theatrical productions have debuted at significant American venues such as the Brooklyn Academy of Music and the Walker Art Center in Minneapolis. They include the recordings *Monkey: Part One and Part Two*, an adaptation of the epic Chinese fable *Journey to the West*; *The Black Panther Ballet Suite*, a multimedia narrative history of the Black Panther Party; and *Warrior Sisters: The New Adventures of African and Asian Womyn Warriors (A New American Opera)*, a prolonged dramatic musical essay on African and Asian sheroes. In these works and others, Ho synthesizes African and Asian archetypes, myths, fantasies, and real-world

Promotional photograph of Fred Ho and the Afro-Asian Music Ensemble, with Esther Iverem and Alma Villegas. Photograph by Juan Sanchez; courtesy of Fred Ho.

acts of heroism with a revolutionary optimism born from a longtime engagement with Marxism-Leninism-Maoism, Third World liberation theory, and radical feminism. Ho's name for this strategy, his own creative archetype, is "revolutionary vision quest." It is a dramatic metaphor for what he perceives as the urgent necessity of discovering and reclaiming "indigenous" Afro-Asian cultural expressive forms suitable as vehicles for revolutionary politics. "Afro-Asian New American Multicultural Music" is Ho's provisional title for this cultural work. The "Afro-Asian" designation echoes the self-description of anticolonial organizers at the Bandung Conference of 1955, a major touchstone for Ho's theory and practice of cultural critique. Ho's music correspondingly incorporates both folk and traditional African American and Asian American formic structures, instrumentation, and themes to produce "a musical analogy for the Chinese American identity or, even further, something Afro Asian in sensibility."[1]

The "something" Ho's work seeks to articulate in dramatic and musical terms is solidarities of politics and culture between people of color in the face of white supremacy, capitalist domination, patriarchy, and old and new forms of colonial imperialism. At the same time, his strategy of finding "analogy" in music for the historical experiences of blacks and Asians bespeaks a strategic antiessentialism and dialectical approach to culture and identity. Ho founded the Afro-Asian Music Ensemble, for example, "to musically express a vision of unity between the cultural-socio-political struggles of African Americans (the originator and innovators of 'jazz') and Asian Americans."[2] For Ho, this aesthetic link emerged with the influence of black nationalism and the Black Arts movement on late-1960s and early-1970s Asian Pacific American political and cultural self-determination movements. Ho's own interpretation of African American music, for example, derives much from Amiri Baraka's *Blues People*, a seminal statement on the national character of ethnic cultural forms. Baraka's conception of the "changing same" to describe an aesthetic of revision and reinterpretation in black music reflects a dialectical materialist perspective commemorating black American expressive culture's grounding in slavery. Likewise, Ho approaches black music as a vernacular form with working-class roots always evolving in the direction of liberation. He has argued, for example, that the "entire history" of black music "has been the freeing of time, pitch and harmony from fixed, regulated, predictable standards. Every major innovation in the history of the music has been from the struggle of musicians to attain greater and greater levels of expressive freedom through liberating the two basic fundamentals of music: time (meter) and sound/pitch/temperament/harmony)."[3] Ho takes a parallel approach to Asian American cultural forms, including literature, work songs, poetry, and music. His analysis of Chinese and Asian immigration patterns, exclusion laws, labor struggles, and independent radical political movements has disclosed to him "a working class, even revolutionary tradition" in APA cultures.[4] Chinese Shaolin fighters, Japanese women cane workers, and Filipino *manong* (pioneers) form a pantheon of indigenous heroes and sheroes each productive of both transformative transnational labor and international cultural work. Ho's revolutionary vision quest synthesizes these interpretive threads, embedding Asian immigrant cultural forms—Cantonese opera, woodfishhead chants, talk-story traditions—within jazz and blues motifs and structures. By grounding his own creolization in working-class indigenous forms produced by Afro-Asian diasporic labor, Ho attempts to combat and resist what he calls the "Christopher Columbus syndrome," the casual and commercial appropriation by the dominant mainstream (and marketplace) of ethnic cultures. For Ho, "True kreolization, the free and voluntary intermingling, cultural synthesis and crossfertilization, occurs at the bottom of society, among the varying oppressed peoples."[5]

Ho's political aesthetics are particularly guided by anticolonial, anti-imperialist, and Third World theorizings of the Bandung era. Amilcar Cabral and Frantz Fanon's view of culture as a first terrain of national liberation struggles informs Ho's syncretic appropriation of African American and Asian Pacific American literature and music as sources for his work. Ho is yet critical of political art that avoids the "national" question of self-determination or adheres to antiquated models of agitprop. Likewise, his cultural work as producer, composer, musician, and artistic director is guided by a rigorous autonomy, self-control, and self-representation and a desire to work outside the mainstreams of avant-garde culture, a box into which his work is often placed. Inspired in large part by the strategies of both the black liberation movement and Black Arts movement, Ho challenges and refutes avant-gardism itself as a "Eurocentric" conception. Ho even rejects the term "jazz" to describe his music.[6] Ho contends that the term is a colonialist one synonymous with "Negro, Oriental, or Hispanic."[7] In Ho's Afro-Asian New American Multicultural Music, rather, "every feature of the music is an expression of revolutionary dialectics."

> Demarcations are dissolved between soloist and ensemble; Among the elements of melody, time, and harmony; between composition and improvisation; between "traditional" and "avant-garde"; between "artist" and "audience;" between "art" and "politics"; between "Western" and "Eastern," etc. If there is any "tradition," it is the continual exploding of time and pitch in quest of a deeper spiritualizing of the music that is fundamentally rooted in the struggle to end all forms of exploitation and oppression and to seek a basic "oneness" with life and nature.[8]

Ho's revolutionary vision quest ultimately understands Afro-Asian collaboration as a deconstructive tool for destroying racial, cultural, and geographic binaries undergirding Orientalism and the Western metaphysic that is its foundation and platform. At the level of practice, Ho's Afro-Asian Multicultural Music provides an aesthetic third way beyond the limits of both Euro-centered commercial ideas of world music and liberal multiculturalism's strategies of cultural containment—Ho refers to this as a journey "beyond" both East and West. New Afro-Asian Multicultural Music is thus best understood as Ho's sui generis genre for a new Third World proletarian internationalism. At the same time, Ho's savvy manipulations of contemporary commercial forms, from kung fu films to comic books, offers a decisively post-Bandung (but not postmodern) revision of prior models of revolutionary culture, from Soviet socialist realism to Yenan. Ho's dramatic operas and martial arts productions gleefully exploit the slapstick and anarchist spirit of fairy tales and children's cartoons in order to stake out the broadest possible terrain for his art. Mass work and mass culture are the reconcilable antinomies of his guerrilla musical theater. Close study of Ho's life and work thus helps to disclose not only an important contemporary legacy of the black world revolution theorized by earlier generations of Afro-Asian activists and theorists, like those in Detroit and at Bandung, but to consider what the cultural revolutions of a twenty-first-century Afro-Orientalism might be.

Coming to Black and Yellow Consciousness

Like the life of W. E. B. Du Bois, Fred Ho's biography is a key text to understanding his evolutionary views on race, art, and politics. Ho frequently tells his own life story in distinctive dialectical "stages" indicating transitions from patriarchal petit bourgeois to feminist revolutionary consciousness. Ho was born to Chinese American parents in 1957 in Palo Alto, California. His father was a professor of Chinese political science. His mother appears in his life recountings as a victim of domestic violence. Ho links his father's violence to a Chinese form of double consciousness. He was "culturally schizophrenic," Ho has written, a man who "self-identified as a Confucian scholar" and "had to lower himself to function" in the university while "frustrated by the professional/career politics required to advance."[9] His father's assimilationist angst, Ho believes, caused the man to beat his mother for failing to speak English and for seeking the independence "that she perceived white middle-class wives possessed" (196). At age seventeen, in one of his "first revolutionary insurrections," Ho fist fought his father for beating his mother. Ho links this act to his later feminist works: *Warrior Sisters, Bound Feet, Night Visions*, and a number of his individual compositions addressing patriarchal forms of oppression against women, including rape and domestic violence. *Yes Means Yes, No Means No, Whatever She Wears, Wherever She Goes!* an album released in 1998, is dedicated entirely to issues of women's resistance to male domination. Ho perceives these compositions and recordings not only as tribute to his mother's victimization but as correctives to feudalist treatments of women in China before (and after) the

1949 revolution, as well as to blatant examples of sexism in the 1960s Left, including the black liberation movement. Ho also finds sympathy against victims of masculine violence via his experiences in the U.S. military. While serving in the army, Ho suffered repeated racist insults, often being used as the "enemy" for training exercises. When a lieutenant used the word "gook" in his presence, Ho responded by knocking him out. His military training in hand-to-hand combat allowed him to "turn pain into power," a phrase that would become the title of a 1997 recording by the Afro-Asian Music Ensemble.

Ho's own brand of Afro-Asian double consciousness was formed out of a struggle against acts of anti-Chinese racism in Boston in the 1960s. He describes segregated sandboxes at public schools and mockery from white-majority peers at his taste for Chinese snacks like *baos* (fried and steamed buns). Ho attempted to win majority acceptance by parting his hair and trying to become a fan of white popular music. During this same period, Ho identified with *Star Trek*'s Mr. Spock, the half-human, half-Vulcan character who suppressed his emotions. *Star Trek*'s Asian character, Sulu, was an impossible source of identification: "he was so token, his Asian-ness completely peripheral or nonexistent" (196). Likewise, 1960s TV shows like *Hawaii Five-O* or *Kung Fu* presented demonic or "yellow-face" caricatures of Asian culture. The one exception for Ho, significantly, was Bruce Lee's Kato on *The Green Hornet*. "Raised in the boys-will-be-boys heterosexual socialization of male aggressiveness and heroism," he later recalls, "I craved an action-adventure hero like Kato, who could really kick ass" (197). Ho's later martial arts dramas, to be discussed later, would take up these themes.

Ho's awakening to racialized consciousness was a Black Experience class in high school, where he read for the first time *The Autobiography of Malcolm X*. The course was taught by Marilyn Lewis, according to Ho the first African American teacher hired by the Amherst public school system. The book's searing analysis of U.S. racism became a means of analogizing his own plight to that of African Americans in the United States: "that I/ we are victims of a system of white supremacy and racism" (198). "For the first time," Ho later wrote, "I began to theorize my personal experience to the level of social analysis and radical political concepts; it never could remain at the level of feel-good politics or 'identity politics'" (198). Following the class, Ho joined the Nation of Islam for a brief time and was known as "Fred X." Later he would title his first opera *A Chinaman's Chance* to commemorate Malcolm's reversal of that racist stereotype to describe the probabilities of a revolution of Asian peoples.

At the age of fourteen, in 1971, Ho acquired a secondhand baritone saxophone from his public school band. He characterizes the horn as a tool to "give voice to my exploding radicalism, my hatred of oppression and my burning commitment to revolutionary struggle."[10] Black music, specifically free jazz, provided an entrée into expression of these themes. He cites Calvin Massey's extended suites, such as *The Black Liberation Movement Suite* (written for a fundraiser for the Black Panther Party), as an early influence,[11] as well as Massey works with "Fanonic titles" like "The Damned Don't Cry." Ho's own *Black Panther Ballet Suite* is comprised of fifteen separate movements on distinctly political themes—"The March of the Oppressed . . . Loving the People," a distinctive echo of Massey's eight-part suite structure chronicling the black liberation movement. Ho recalls retrospectively hearing "Afrocentric" rhythms in Massey's compositions: "One could hear the Black Panthers marching inside the music itself."[12] In the 1980s, Ho organized two tribute concerts to Massey where Ho's own arrangements of Massey compositions were performed. Ho also credits other Black Arts movement figures as early sources of musical inspiration: Sun Ra, Gil Scott-Heron, the Last Poets, and Archie Shepp. Of these, Shepp has had the most lasting impact on Ho's work. Ho studied with Shepp at the University of Massachusetts–Amherst. Shepp's 1972 album *Attica Blues* combined free jazz and spoken-word arrangements on political themes, including "Malcom, Semper Malcolm," an extended suite sampling Malcolm X's speeches. Ho's own *Turn Pain into Power* includes "Essay to X," a free jazz composition featuring spoken-word tribute to Malcolm by African American poet Esther Iverem.

In combination with early free jazz influence, it was the Black Panthers' example that was a crucial moment in the formation of his

Afro-Asian cultural politics. The Panthers were the primary source of inspiration for the Asian Pacific American organizations I Wor Kuen and Red Guard Party, formed respectively in New York City and the Bay Area in the early 1970s. Ho was a student at Harvard University majoring in sociology when he joined the Boston chapter of IWK. At Harvard he took the first courses offered at the university in Asian American studies, helped to create Asian American Awareness Month, and in 1978 helped to form ECASU (East Coast Asian Students Union). Yet he describes his decision to join IWK as a respite from the elitist and racist white liberalism at Harvard. Retrospectively, Ho identifies this first stage of his political development as "Yellow Revolutionary Nationalism," though the organization's politics were informed by Marxism-Leninism and other sources. IWK took its name from Cantonese Boxers during the Boxer Rebellion. Like the Panthers, it was primarily a working-class grassroots organization. It started "Serve the People" programs inspired by the Panthers' Survival Program and created a "Twelve Point Platform Program" modeled closely on the Panthers' own ten-point program.[13] The latter's opening statement insisted that "Asian people in Amerika have been continually oppressed by the greedy, traitorous gangsters of our own communities and by the wider racist exploitation of Amerikan society."[14] Despite efforts to improve living conditions and to use "peaceful means" of reform, the statement added, "our situation remained the same. We are not free."[15] Like the Revolutionary Action Movement, IWK invoked a plan to abolish the U.S. government and begin a new one "which is without class distinctions and is based upon the love and unity of all peoples."[16] Self-determination, liberation of all Third World peoples, an end to male chauvinism, community control of institutions and land, an education system "which exposes the true history of western imperialism in Asia and around the world," decent housing and health care, freedom for political prisoners, an end to the American military, an end to racism and national boundaries, and a call for a socialist society were among IWK's demands.[17]

Ho worked as a cultural organizer for IWK in Boston's Chinatown, assigned to organize the Asian American Resource Workshop (AARW), a community-based educational and cultural group.[18] Much like the Black Arts movement had done in Detroit, Newark, and New York City, AARW organized Asian American cultural events, poetry readings, and agitprop theater. The group's outreach was to working-class Chinese in Chinatown, and its directive was to unite immigrant and American-born Asians. Ho attributes his understanding of Asian Pacific American culture as primarily working-class forms from these encounters and organizing experiences. IWK also promoted the formation of a Pan-Asian identity among diverse APA nationalities: Japanese, Chinese, Korean, and Filipino most especially. Because some of its founding members had participated in the Third World Liberation Front strike at Berkeley in 1969, IWK also helped lead the demand for Asian studies at American universities like San Francisco State and Berkeley and was instrumental in the development of Asian studies at City College. Ho often cites the merging of black, Asian, and Chicano Third World struggles during the 1969 strike as an incipient model of his Afro-Asian activism and an integral foundation of his internationalist "multiculturalism."[19] For example, IWK's and the Red Guard's support for Asian Pacific American community centers and autonomous cultural organizations still informs Ho's insistence on self-determining cultural activism: to this day, he describes himself and his Big Red Media, Inc., production company as demonstrative of what it means to be a "guerrilla cultural entrepreneur."

In 1978 IWK merged with the Chicano August 29 Movement to become the League of Revolutionary Struggles. It subsequently merged again with the Revolutionary Communist League, formerly the Congress of Afrikan Peoples. The league formed its own newspaper, *Unity*, to which Ho was a contributor, and published an Asian Pacific American magazine called *East Wind*. Yet sometime in the early 1980s, Ho became disillusioned with what he perceived as the LRS's accommodationist and assimilationist politics. In "The Personal Is Political: Lessons," Ho writes that he was "thrown out" of IWK/LRS after criticizing its central committee for announcing that it was "reevaluating" Marxism and socialist revolution. In the same essay, he acknowledges criticisms leveled against him of "severe weaknesses of arrogance and individualism."[20]

The falling out may have coincided with, or inspired, Ho's decision in the fall of 1981 to go to New York City to attempt a career as a musician. Yet IWK's struggles in the 1970s to promote and sustain new Asian Pacific American cultural forms influenced what Ho describes as the next phase of his career, from 1982 to 1989, the exploration of "Asian American jazz." Several key figures in the movement, including pianist Jon Jang and bassist Mark Izu, had roots in IWK and helped to establish the West Coast Kearney Street Workshop and AsianImprov Records, along with Francis Wong and Glenn Horiuchi. Both institutions provided early performing and recording support to Asian American jazz musicians on the West Coast. Ho meanwhile remained mostly on the East Coast, working as a sideman with Jang and writing numerous articles and reviews promoting Asian American jazz. Ho's sense of Afro-Asian jazz as a vanguard force also emerged in his music: he became the first Asian American to record as a leader for the important experimental jazz Soul Note/Black Saint label of Italy. His first albums released on Soul Note are *Tomorrow Is Now!* (1986) (whose title is drawn from Ho's poem "A dialogue: Tomorrow is Now!" a manifesto on music "THEY can't clone"),[21] and *We Refuse to Be Used* (1989). Ho describes Asian American jazz as the combination of "actual Asian traditional instrumentation and Asian-inspired or influenced stylistic elements with predominantly 'free' or modal improvisation in the African American avant garde context."[22] Ho also formed the Afro-Asian Music Ensemble during this period and dedicated himself to exploring Asian American cultural forms based in immigrant and working-class traditions. He became a self-described polemicist as well, arguing in articles for journals, newspapers, and magazines for an Asian American art and music that would distinguish itself from Eurocentric, white, or petit bourgeois culture. His separation from European avant-garde conceptions likewise coincided with his critique of LRS for its "mainstream" accommodationist politics in support of Jesse Jackson. Both of these "breaks" by Ho, one political, one cultural, are recorded in allegorical form in *Once Upon a Time in Chinese America*, Ho's marial arts opera. The story's protagonist, Gar Man Jang, conspires with Manchu imperial forces to sack the Shaolin Temple and to steal the

Shaolin Secret Scrolls, the accumulated knowledge of all martial arts. In response, five Shaolin monks go on a twenty-year adventure to create new martial art forms and schools. Gar Man Jang is a comprador opportunist in the tale, and the Shaolin monks something like the "authentic" renegades of a true revolutionary history. Ho calls *Once Upon a Time* "a radical allegory about the betrayal of late-20th century activism in the Asian American movement by the role of sell-outs internal to that movement. . . . The story also educates about the necessity to discard old forms and techniques that have been co-opted and appropriated, and to innovate new forms and methods in order to achieve transformation and liberation."[23]

Ho describes the year 1986 as a significant turning point in his career and thought. He was, he acknowledges, frustrated with the Asian American jazz designation to describe his work. "I was continuously struggling with the question," he writes, "what makes Chinese American music Chinese American? What would make for an Asian American musical content and form that would be transformative of American music as well, and not simply be subsumed in one or another American musical genre such as 'jazz.'"[24] Following the lead of composer Mark Izu, Ho began to explore the use of Asian instrumentation in a composed and orchestrated rather than jazz setting. A year earlier, Ho had composed music for the multimedia work *Bound Feet* for Jodi Long, a member of his Asian American Art Ensemble. The piece incorporated Chinese double-reed *sona* and the Chinese two-stringed fiddle, the *erhu*, orchestrated with Western woodwinds, contrabass, and multiple percussion.[25] Ho found the integration of Chinese nontempered and Western tempered instruments liberating. The echoes of his own jazz training in the piece also suggested to him a synthesis of Chinese and African American components symbolic of an Afro-Asian sensibility. Inspired by this hybrid, Ho composed *A Chinaman's Chance*, the first modern Chinese American opera. The choice of genre pays tribute to the flourishing of traditional Chinese opera in Chinatown communities before World War II. Musically, the piece fuses Cantonese and Beijing opera melodic styles and African American rhythms and harmonies. The story entails the immigration experiences of a Chinese immigrant god, Kwan Gung; Ho calls the story the "transformation of the Chinese to becoming Chinese American"[26] and describes it as an "unconventional, experimental multicultural docu-opera."[27] The story describes an enslaved utopia, Fusang, where "the rule of iron and gold is supreme."[28] It is among other things an allegory of ideology; the script proposes: "In this transformed land demon ghosts live in the flesh and enslave through Dreams. And when the unreal is taken for the real, then the real becomes unreal. And where are gods then to be found?"[29] The piece also includes verse by Ho collaborator Genny Lim and foreshadows feminist themes of later plays in pieces like "White Men Are a Pain in the Ass (A Whore's Song)."[30]

A Chinaman's Chance enjoyed a single performance at the Brooklyn Academy of Music in 1989, another watershed year for Ho. Poised for a radical new direction in his work, Ho was commissioned by the late Jack Chen, then president of the Bay Area–based Pear Garden in the West, to compose the music for an episode from the Chinese serial classic *Journey to the West*. Ho formed the Journey beyond the West Orchestra, a chamber ensemble again combining traditional Chinese and Western jazz instrumentation. Ho's adaptation of *Journey to the West* premiered as "Monkey Meets the Spider-Spirit Vampires," the first Chinese American opera-ballet with a libretto sung exclusively in Mandarin Chinese. Ho later developed additional episodes from *Journey* into *Journey beyond the West: The New Adventures of Monkey*. By that time, the Journey beyond the West Orchestra's name had become the Monkey Orchestra. It consisted of three Chinese instrumentalists playing *pipa*, *sona*, and *erhu*, multiple percussion combining Chinese opera and jazz-trap set (featuring Ho's regular drummer and percussionist Royal Hartigan), and a special tenor saxophone part by Hafez Modirzadeh. Ho notes that the Monkey Orchestra included no piano so as "not to be bound by western temperament and harmony."[31]

Nineteen eighty-nine also produced a public crisis in world socialism that for Ho came to symbolize the lost direction of the U.S. Marxist-Leninist Left that had emerged in the 1970s. The institutionalization of corporate and academic multiculturalism compounded his challenge of making a radical interethnic art that might escape easy co-optation. Ho recalls, "Without an organized movement, I was trying to understand how my music would support the revolutionary struggle beyond the aesthetical and ideological."[32] He began to associate with younger radicals particularly attuned to a critique of the New Left and black liberation movement's failure to address sexism, patriarchy, and homophobia. Ho had already produced works on feminist themes (*Bound Feet*) and collaborated with women artists (*Rockin' in Revolution/Drowning in the Yellow River,* based on Janice Mirikitani's poetry). Around 1992, Ho says, he began "a very extensive Marxist and radical feminist study of patriarchy as rooted in the very beginning of class society, the overthrow of womyn's matriarchy, the rise of the state as an instrument of patriarchal class rule, and the cultural and social domination, oppression and exploitation of gender."[33] These influences led to the current phase of Ho's political self-identification: matriarchal socialism. Ho joined ORSSASM (Organization of Revolutionary Socialist Sisters and Some Men), a collective of anarchists, socialists, radical feminists, and Marxists. The collective comprised primarily women of color and majority women. Ho turned these new political experiences into a collaboration with Ann T. Greene on *Warrior Sisters: The New Adventures of African and Asian Womyn Warriors,* based partly on the escape from a New Jersey prison of Black Liberation Army leader Assata Shakur. Ho describes the opera as "politically matriarchal socialist, musically new Afro Asian, and theatrically an action-adventure epic."[34]

This three-stage sketch captures and synthesizes the evolutionary stages of Ho's political autobiography to date. Indeed, an analysis of Ho's wide body of cultural work discloses a continuously self-reflective artist aware of the need to both question and act out the terms of his evolving political commitments. Like Grace Boggs, each step of Ho's development as an Afro-Asian activist and theorist exists in dialectical relationship to the others. Ho's matriarchal politics are both intensely personal yet at the same time bound to premises of dialectical materialism. His anti-essentialism likewise offers myriad ways of rethinking subjectivity, racial identity formation, and the necessity of cross-racial alliances. His astute attention to the relationship between mass culture, consumerism, and cultural hegemony provides a constant state of alert to the limits of either a postmodern or commercial rendering of Afro-Asian experience. In short, Ho's corpus of writings, compositions, performances, and public activisms offers a characteristically genre- and gender-bending analogue to Afro-Orientalism's own vision quest for third ways, third spaces, and new journeys beyond the West.

Practicing Theory/Theorizing Practice

Joseph S. C. Lam has argued that Asian American panethnicity has complicated and obscured the definition of what might be called "Asian American music." Because the term "Asian American" homogenizes the heterogeneity of Asian American experience, it has tended to blur the categories, genres, and ethnic features of music written, produced, and played by Asian American musicians. Lam insists, in response, that Asian American music be recognized as a "heuristic device" toward more carefully delineating the historical and political content of Asian American experience. "Indeed, only by confronting heterogeneity," writes Lam, "can Asian Americans expose class, gender, and cultural inequities in their communities, articulate distinct challenges and demands developed from their experiences, and join other American ethnic groups in their efforts to counteract 'various specific forms of domination.'"[35] Ho's work may be understood as a constantly shifting engagement with this concern. His earliest recordings for Soul Note and AsianImprov records adopted jazz timbres and conventions to the expression of distinctively Asian American themes and ideas. At the same time, the attempt to locate a panethnic Asian jazz sound corresponded with his participation in both I Wor Kuen and the League of Revolutionary Struggle. Ho's 1987 album *Bamboo That Snaps Back* is a good example of the results. The album emerged out of Ho's work with the Asian American Art Ensemble, a collective of Asian American jazz musicians whose namesake invoked the pioneering Art Ensemble of Chicago. The album's title is Ho's recurring metaphor for defining a resistant Asian American expressive culture that flies in the face of the Orientalist stereotype of passive accommodationism and "model minority" discourses (Ho has argued that the model minority myth is an assimilation strategy of U.S. imperialism). As such the album is a compilation of panethnic Asian music. It features among others the Asian American composer and arranger Jon Jang. Though their work has evolved in different directions, both Jang and Ho veered in the direction of African American culture as a means of expanding their conceptions of expressive ethnic cultures. Indeed, Lam's analysis of this aspect of Jang's work can also be applied to Jang's 1980s collaborations with Ho. Their Asian American jazz innovations challenge taxonomic attempts "to discuss the music of Asian Americans with established labels and analytical concepts. For example, by essentializing Asian American works into autonomous objects of sound with formalistic concepts of styles and compositional structures, the works are taken out of their cultural and ethnic contexts and are forced to 'speak for themselves.' By referencing the works with established labels, such as Chinese music or African American jazz, the works are interpreted in specific sites of cultures and peoples. In contrast, when a musical work of an Asian American composer is categorized as jazz or rap, it will be understood within the meta-narrative of that genre, rendering its Asian American issues secondary or irrelevant."[36]

Ho's Afro-Asian jazz of the 1980s worries both generic and ethnic categorization by at once foregrounding the racial and ethnic content of the music as consistent with its formalistic hybridity. Yet Ho's 1980s work also troubles definitions of hybridity that remain at the level of celebrationist multiculturalism. In the preface to *Sounding Off*, for example, published by Autonomedia in 1995, Ho calls for "radical hybrids" or "guerrilla musicians" seeking "subversive beauty and marvelous diversity."[37] Ho's manifesto owes a debt to the surrealist experiments of the negritude writers—Aimé Césaire, for example—whose subversive recombination of Eurocentric cultural forms created an aesthetic of anticolonialism. He rejects what he calls "chop sueyism," touristic eclecticism and pirating characteristic of world music (Paul Simon and David Byrne are frequent examples he provides). Hybridity, for Ho, implies rather an aesthetic reproduction of "multinational unity" between oppressed peoples.

One of Ho's frequent sidemen and an original member of the Afro-Asian Music Ensemble is Hafez Modirzadeh, a saxophonist, ethnomusicologist, and associate professor of music at San Jose State University. Modirzadeh is Iranian. His own hybrid musicality fuses Persian, Chinese, and other Eastern timbres and tonalities in his playing with experimental jazz and blues rhythms. Modirzadeh has written about Chinese cyclic theory and modal jazz practice as sources for John Coltrane's later compositions. Coltrane is seminal in two ways to Ho's Afro-Asian music conception: it was Coltrane's turn to Asian tonalities, and Asian religiosity, that Ho identifies as a Bandung era aesthetic turn. Coltrane's Eastern experiments and Malcolm X's hajj to Mecca are for Ho parallel pilgrimages symbolic of the anticolonial era's quest for resonance between politics and culture. "Mao and Cabral/Mingus and Coltrane/Variations on the same tune," he has written in his part-time capacity as poet. Modirzadeh likewise pays homage to Malcolm and Bandung era politics in his music: his album *By Any Mode Necessary* playfully suggests a Third World bridge across the sounds of two of the black liberation movement's most distinctive voices.[38] "Chromodal discourse" is Modirzadeh's coinage for this bridge, "where one culture moves towards another but doesn't forfeit what they are about and vice versa."[39]

Ho's original Afro-Asian Music Ensemble also includes the ethnomusicologist Dr. Royal Hartigan. Hartigan is a master of West African drumming. An Irish American, he has played and studied with Max Roach, Archie Shepp, Abraham Adzenyah, and Freeman Donkor. Hartigan shares Ho's critique of "chop suey" or Christopher Columbus appropriations in particular of African- and Asian-influenced musical forms. "I believe in never doing music of any culture until I've studied it for many years, and, if possible, have lived with the people for a long time . . . to live with the people as much as possible, to try to understand their cultures as much as possible, and to feel it. You need to do more than understand it, because you can understand it and still rip it off. You must feel it, commit to it and feel connected with it, and feel like you'd give yourself up for it if you had to."[40] Other early members and long-time collaborators of the Afro-Asian Music Ensemble include the alto and soprano saxophonist Sam Furnace; Allen Wong and David Bindman, tenor saxophonists; Peter Madsen on piano; and Kityoto Fujiwara on bass. Bindman, Furnace, Ho, and Chris Jonas also make up the Brooklyn Sax Quartet, another ensemble.

Tomorrow Is Now! the ensemble's first recording for Soul Note in 1986, included liner notes by Amiri Baraka. It is generically elusive, drawing from blues, swing, and avant-garde traditions. Ho's second album with the ensemble, *We Refuse to Be Used and Abused,* also with Soul Note, included spoken-word poetry by Sonia Sanchez. The Asian American jazz musicians of the 1980s movement, demonstrating the lingering influence of Black Arts aesthetics, made collaboration with Asian American writers a regular feature of their music: Jon Jang's *The Dance of the Gold World* on the Spoken Engine label was a collaboration with Maxine Hong Kingston. Ho's *Bamboo That Snaps Back* included poetry by Janice Mirikitani, and he also played with spoken-word accompaniment by Genny Lim. Ho's next album with the ensemble, *A Song for Manong,* was released by AsianImprov Records. The label has been host to records by pianist Vijay Iyer, Jon Jang, and Anthony Brown, the latter a member with Mark Izu of the Afro-Asian group United Front. Ho's 1988 album featured the influence of Filipino folk music, a recurring component of Ho's panethnic Asianism. The album was produced with the support of Kularts, a San Francisco–based arts support organization dedicated to supporting Asian and Filipino cultural work.

Ho's work in building Asian arts organizations and collaborations with Asian American writers, his use of jazz as a vehicle for panethnic Asian struggles, and his close collaborations with other members of the West Coast Asian American jazz music circle created an impressive platform for his ascent to prominence as a vanguard Asian American composer, saxophonist, and cultural worker. But it was a platform he claims to have kicked out through a dialectical process of self-questioning. The unsatisfactory designation of "Asian American jazz," with its suggestion of cultural or ethnic subordination to genre, subsequently motivated Ho's quest for "Afro-Asian New American Multicultural Music." Ho's first album after this turn, *The Underground Railroad to My Heart,* released in

1994 on Soul Note, indicates the consequences of this shift. The album comprises eleven tracks. The first nine are played by the Afro-Asian Music Ensemble. The last two, "The Monkey Theme" and "The Pig Theme," are played by the newly formed Journey beyond the West Orchestra. The album opens with "Joys and Solos," an impromptu studio jam session for the Chinese double-reed *sona* and string bass and drum kit. Ho's liner notes describes the "free" jazz playing as a "cross-cultural first." The jam has the effect of liberating the hyphenated space between African American and Asian aesthetics. The stark contrasting registers of the high-end *sona* and low-end bass suggest a meeting of musical "tops" and "bottoms" in the coming together of Asian and black musicians. (Ho has joked that his own radical aesthetics and choice of baritone sax often place him at the "bass" or "bottom" of both the mainstream and avant-garde musical worlds.) Song 2, "The Underground Railroad to My Heart," is a swinging tribute to that seminal freedom institution and its legacy. Madsen's freewheeling barrelhouse piano lends sonic credence to Ho's description of the tune as "an anti-bourgeoisie boogie woogie."[41] Running bass lines and staccato blasts from the horn section provide a kind of musical metaphor for flight to a jazz Canada. The song is long—13:35 minutes—and driven by propulsion and locomotion. Described as a "suite," it is divided into chapters or sections, with themes suggesting the shape of Ho's revolutionary vision quest: Trail of Tears, Sanctuary, Making Love in the Moonlight before Socialism Comes, Insurrection, Here's Better Yet to Come, Making Love Making Reprise. In his liner notes, Ho writes that "today's underground railroads include the Pro-Choice movement, the Sanctuary Movement of the 1980s which assists Central American refugees facing political persecution, and the current struggle (1994) of Haitian refugees fleeing Haiti after the coup that exiled Jean Aristide." The choice of the suite for Afro-Asian themes also points to the influence of Duke Ellington, who composed frequently in the form. Ellington's influence as composer hovers between the lines and liner notes of many of Ho's extended compositions.[42]

Song 3, "An Bayan Ko" (For My Country), is the anthem of the Katipunan, the nineteenth-century nationalist labor movement that fought for Philippine independence from Spanish colonial rule. Royal Hartigan plays the southern Philippine kulintang in the introduction, a chimelike percussion whose call is answered by the roaring response of Ho's baritone. Again contrasting pitch, high and low registers, fuse in a kind of sound dialectic. The song is sweetly lyrical and Old World, with waltz tempos starkly interrupted by urgent but tender calls to love and nationhood. Song 4, "Kang Ding Love Song," is a traditional Chinese love song that, according to Ho, connects "wishes for personal joy and happiness with the struggles for a better society." Vocalist Cindy Zuoxin Wang sings of a "New Moon" endowed with seasonal rebirth. Withered blossoms give way to new growth, suggesting the coming of a brighter day. Ho calls the choice of songs on the album a "continuing distancing from 'Jazz standards' and the conventionality of a 32 bar, ABA head-solo-head formula."[43] Having laid down that rule, Ho bends or breaks it with the following tune, "Strange Fruit Revisited," a six-minute adaptation of the canonical antilynching song. The tune opens with slow, draggy bass riffs, ominous drum patter, and low-end piano rolls, along with flute quotations from Coltrane's "Naima." Over these Veatrice Williams reads Brian Auerbach's "Making a Long Sound Short (for Billie Holiday)," a poem, which is followed by a cacophony of percussion that introduces the lyrics proper to "Strange Fruit." Williams's vocal stylization is blues opera, a conjunction frequent in Ho's work. An expressive horn interlude fills the break between verses. In the last verse, Williams's voice literally falls the register to convey the falling fruit of black bodies. The song renders lynching horror and violence commensurate with its 1939 moment of protest intended by Communist lyricist Lewis Allen, so cited in Ho's liner notes.[44]

"Lan Hua Hua" (Blue Flower) is a Chinese folk song in which peasant women sing in protest against arranged feudal marriage. It is an Asian strange fruit in its way, its pastoral scenes interrupted and scarred by oppressive social convention:

Bright blue flower as blue as day
Loved both near and far

None so bright and none so gay
As our pretty Lan Hua Hua

Tall and graceful grows the grain
Many stems there are
Of the maids who live on the plain
None so fair as Lan Hua Hua

Brief the time and harsh the law
Hard the bargain driven
One fine day is Lan Hua Hua
To the highest bidder given.[45]

Cindy Zuoxin Wang's singing of the lyrics in Mandarin offers poignant call and response to Sam Furnace's alto lament. Ho's liner notes insist on the album's bilingualism or use of "indigenous" languages as a countervailing force against English-only American popular music (his rendition of "Auld Lang Syne," originally a Scottish melody, is sung in English, Spanish, Chinese, and Japanese). The next song, "Bambaya," is a duet for alto saxophone and percussion, with Royal Hartigan playing African doono drum and bass drum. "Bambaya" is the name for the indigenous rhythms of Ghana used to "express cultural resistance to neo-colonialism":[46] in Ho's New American Multicultural Music, the subaltern speaks in many rhythmic tongues. The album's culminating piece is Ho's 9:18 rendering of "Caravan," the 1937 Duke Ellington, Juan Tizol, and Irving Mills collaboration, jointly arranged by Hartigan and Ho. The song is up-tempo, played in 15/8 meter. The momentum, writes Ho, suggests history's forward march, or caravan, "heading into the 21st century filled with the spirit and struggle for justice and revolutionary socialism."[47] The album ends with samples of the work-in-progress that would constitute Ho's next major recording project: "The Monkey Theme" and "The Pig Theme" from his four-episode epic score *Journey beyond the West: The New Adventures of Monkey*. The Chinese libretto and combination of Chinese and Western instrumentation, the hallmarks of his work ever since, leave the reader and listener to *Underground Railroad* grappling with the shape of his own jazz to come: "One may ask," Ho writes in his liner notes, "Is this a new form of Chinese music or a new form of western 'jazz'? Depending on one's stand, I am either leaving 'jazz' or expanding it. In any case, my current musical direction defies easy categorization, formula and convention and the neo-conservative retrograding of 'jazz' tradition."[48]

Ho's challenge to jazz neoclassicism, a movement led by the Marsalis school of the 1980s and 1990s, underscores the speculative thrust of his revolutionary vision quest in relation to jazz tradition. Ho's subversive interest in the Chinese classic epic *Journey to the West*, particularly the central figure of Monkey, may also be seen as an allegory for his own place in relationship to the master narratives, or cultural texts, that he seeks to disrupt. *Journey to the West* is Wu Cheng'en's (1500–1582) three-volume novel based on traditional folktales written during the Ming dynasty. The story relates the picaresque adventures of a Buddhist priest, Sanzang, and his three disciples: Monkey, Pig, and Friar Sand. Their mythic quest leads them west in search of the text of Buddhist Sutra. The story begins with the birth of the Monkey King and his rebellion against Heaven. In traditional Chinese interpretation, Monkey is a heroic if conventional embodiment of the apex of Ming culture and the desire for spiritual perfection. He is also a symbol of the perpetual underdog. On his journey with Pig and Friar, according to classic convention, they meet and must vanquish demons and monsters, cross extravagant unknown territories, and conquer death and destruction before reaching their destination—the Thunder Monastery in the Western Heaven, where they find the Sutra. Monkey is also something of a Chinese Huckleberry Finn, and *Journey to the West* something of China's *Wizard of Oz*, especially in the nation's burgeoning contemporary mass culture: numerous storybooks, cartoons, games, toys, icons, and imagery marketed to children especially purvey the country's post–Deng Xiaoping, post–Cultural Revolution commercial landscape.

Monkey's renegade pursuit of sacred text is a natural symbol for Ho's own recontextualizing approach to jazz tradition. All too familiar with the myth of the "signifying monkey" in both West African and African American folklore and music, Ho has adopted Monkey as the seminal touchstone and figuration of his artistic and political project. Legba, the high priest of Vodun, is the prophetic spirit at the crossroads between heaven and earth; equivalent to Mercury, or the Messenger, as Henry Gates Jr. notes in his study *The Signifying Monkey*, he is the archetype for subversive meaning making in the service of a subaltern vision and revision of orthodoxy, hegemony, and dominance.[49] Monkey/Legba signifies with irony, wordplay, and sarcasm, directed against overlords of standard exclusionary meaning practices: the pantheon of gods against whom the Satan/Legba/Monkey figure must rebel. Signifying is quite literally Monkey's turning inside out the discourses on which his desire for reversal of social power depends. For Ho, Monkey signifies both his own place at the crossroads of Afro-Asian culture and his penchant for signifying practices upon racist, Eurocentric, and capitalist practices. In their preface to *Sounding Off*, Ho and Ron Sakolsky render this multiplicity of cultural and political tasks via allusion to a variety of visionary cultural practices. "Come all you guerilla musicians: Native Warriors and Tricksters; Kreoles and Majority-World revolutionaries; womynist monkeywrenchers, punks, hiphoppers, and ravers; surrealists, noisicians and plunderphiles; socialists, anarchists, utopians and all the vibrant and complex racial hybids therein."[50] Ho and Sakolsky end their signifying shout out by inviting readers of *Sounding Off* to "construct your own musiopolitical identity." Monkey, a trickster figure, signifies this capacity for identity improvisation. Ho's melding of Asian and African musical forms into a "truly Chinese American music" is thus a form of what might be called trickster jazz.

Monkey: Part One, Ho's first adaptation of *Journey to the West*, was released in 1996. The album is the score for a live-stage martial arts performance of Ho's version of the tale. It is the first recording of the Monkey Orchestra, formerly the Journey beyond the West Orchestra. Like JBTW, the Monkey Orchestra melds African, American, and Chinese instrumentation: Pei Sheng Shen's sona, You Qun Fu's erhu, Ting Yi Lin's erhu, Pauline Hong's San Shuen. Hafez Modirzadeh plays chromodal sax; Jim Norton plays alto sax and flute; Francis Wong and David Muro-take share duties on tenor sax and flute; Martin Wehner plays trombone; John Shifflett contrabass. The all-Mandarin lyrics are sung by Cindy Zuoxin Wang. Royal Hartigan plays both drum set and Chinese percussion, and Ho plays baritone sax and flute. The album features a cover illustration of Monkey by Jack Chen, who died in 1995 and to whom the album is dedicated. Ho admits to having "freely reinterpreted" the story of the seventeen-year quest by Monkey and his companions for the Buddhist scriptures. He has conceived the "four-part serial fantasy action-adventure multimedia work" as a "living comic book" akin to old silent movies with continuous live music, visuals, and movements onstage. The shift to speculative genres is consistent with Ho's utopian rewrite of Wu-Cheng'en's predominant themes. Act 1, "Uproar in Heaven," retells Sun Wu Kong's birth from a rock and his adoption as leader of the monkeys on the Flower and Fruit Mountain, a utopian paradise. Ho notes that he drops the "King" from Monkey's appellation to designate the feudal, pre-class conditions on the Mountain. Monkey soon goes to the undersea world of the Dragon King after hearing of his new weapon—a great staff. Monkey steals the staff as an act of defiance against "private ownership of property."[51] Dragon King sends an undersea army to battle and retrieve it. Monkey defeats them, but Dragon King goes to the Jade Emperor to complain about the theft. Jade Emperor, "the top god in heaven," is the ersatz ruling class: he sends the "Great White Planet" to tempt Monkey to return the staff by offering him the title "Protector of Horses," a bogus appellation for a "lowly janitorial job."[52] When Monkey learns the title is a trick, he rebels and sings a song against private ownership. The climactic scene of act 1, "Monkey Wreaks Havoc in Heaven," is a cacophonous eighteen-minute battle sequence in which Monkey overturns a celestial banquet to which he is not invited. Jade Emperor again sends an army to conquer Monkey and his new consortium of monkey soldiers. Monkey wins again. This pitched allegorical class struggle rewards Monkey's hedonism and loyalty to socialist ideals. In scene 5, Buddha exploits Monkey's trickster arrogance and conceit to imprison him under a mountain for five hundred years. The serial format includes a "break" or missing scene; Ho jumps directly to act 3, "Monkey Meets the Spider Spirit-Vampires." This partial section describes Pig's seduction by the spider spirit-vampires, sirens who seduce with their song and live off of human blood and flesh. The vampiric figure recurs often in Ho's dramaturgy as a figure of rampant greed. Pig and Monkey barely escape and are able to move on to the second part of their quest.

Monkey Part Two begins with a Beijing opera chant as the journey resumes. The story is picaresque: Monkey and Tang Seng are tied by devil demons, chased by bandits, freed, and meet up with Pig in a village marketplace. Monkey aids a maiden pursued by the lecherous Pig. The benevolent goddess of mercy, healing, and medicine, Kwan Yin, intercedes to persuade Pig to join Monkey and Tang Seng on their quest for the Buddhist scripture. In the next scene, they pick up Friar Sand after a battle with an ogre. The four comrades continue their journey west. In act 4, "The Journey Home—the Struggle for Heaven on Earth," the pilgrims arrive in India and receive the Buddhist scriptures. They also learn that Monkey's home, Flower and Fruit Mountain, has been colonized and corrupted by Heaven. According to Ho's liner notes, "For the first time, Monkey's great individual powers are insufficient to wage this battle, and so Monkey must undertake the process of building a revolutionary movement" (ibid.). His defiance is responsible for Heaven's vengeance on his home, which includes "class stratification, carpet baggers, poverty, prostitution, drug addiction, crime and other social evils" (ibid.). Monkey's former allies are now "aping" Heaven's elitist ways, and Kwan Yin has been imprisoned and shackled in a cage. Monkey must choose between immortality and social justice for the homeland. Monkey decides abruptly to return home "to Right the Great Wrongs" and to rebuild paradise. When he arrives there, home has become a "smoggy, garbage-strewn, dark, gaudy colony with beggars, prostitutes, drugs—a neon-like Mahogony/Third World city, a place where the gods from Heaven come for their perverse recreation" (ibid.). Monkey attempts to win back the hearts and minds of the common folk by going into exile and forming a guerrilla cave base. They read scriptures "as well as other texts," including equations and concepts about surplus value and capital. The guerrilla band is sitting around the campfire one day when an army of allies arrives; it is led by Monkey's former comrades, each joined with a new force: Pig with Coyote, the Native American trickster, and Eshu, from Vodun, as well as guerrilla gorillas and other tricksters. Tang Seng is joined by Buddhist Shaolin monks and nuns, and the ogre with a group of wretched humans "including the white-haired woman warrior and a troop of witches"—an obvious allusion to Maxine Hong Kingston. They carry banners that read "Unite the World's Exploited and Oppressed!" and "End the Tyranny of Heaven and the Rule of Profit!" The revolution erupts in battle: Monkey and his comrades seize the Jade Emperor's palace; Kwan Yin is freed and dispenses medicine and healing for all creatures on earth. Ho's epilogue pronounces, "The adventures of Monkey and the pilgrims have earned them immortality in songs, stories and legends. Though there have been many interpretations of the world, the point, however, is to change it" (ibid.).

Ho's agitprop comic book reads the Tang dynasty epic backwards through China's anticolonial history. It also recognizes in Tang myth a source for building a dialectical interpretation of mass culture. The story's exaggeration is utopian, and its self-referentiality a means for Ho to tell the "story" of his own guerrilla theater: the score for Monkey is the "book" that Monkey seeks. Ho's white-haired womyn warrior pays homage to Maxine Hong Kingston's appropriation of *Journey to the West* in her novel *Tripmaster Monkey: His Fake Book*, which like Ho's performance rewrites the original into a tale of Asian American resistance to both essentialist and assimilationist Asianism.[53] Ho's multicultural revolutionary army of heroes and sheroes stands in not just for his assembled cast of musicians in the Journey to the West Orchestra but for the audience he hopes to create for his work. Musically, *Monkey: Part Two* performs its disruptive themes through controlled cacophony, the naturally eruptive sound of Afro-Asian instrumentation: "The Revolution Begins/ The Liberation of Flower and Fruit Mountain" features strong bass lines provided by Ho's baritone, and ominous registers reminiscent of suspense or horror films. The arrival of the allies is announced with fanfarelike brass, counterposed with Chinese opera percussion and Yu Shan

Min's soprano vocals. The dramatic action sequences are driven by a musical pulse reminiscent of the martial arts sequences of Beijing opera. Free or improvisational dissonance always stays within the more formal narrative. "Victory! Kwan Yin Is Free!" the penultimate song of *Monkey: Part Two*, is a subdued and almost mournful freedom song that gives way to the album's primary motif, a four-blast refrain from the brass section that lifts off with the introduction of Modirzadeh's and Shen Pei Sheng's Chinese sonas. The "Epilogue," a reprise of "Happiness Is Being a Monkey," is a rollicking restatement of uptempo themes, a kind of Dixieland Beijing opera punctuated by Hartigan's cymbals and Yu Shan Min's clarion soprano. The album leaves no doubt that a brighter musical and political day is just around the corner.

Released in the same year as *Monkey: Part Two*, Ho's 1997 album *Turn Pain into Power!* looks forward and backward in Ho's oeuvre. The album prominently features the words and voices of women of color and predicts Ho's dedication to that theme in *Warrior Sisters*. It also broadens the spectrum of Ho's Afro-Asian political themes by foregrounding Latino and Latina politics. Poet Alma Villegas's "Puerto Rican Woman" is a spoken-word poem, in Spanish, with brooding accompaniment from the Afro-Asian Music Ensemble. The poem reverses masculinist nationalist tropes calling for two-stage revolution:

There is a captive people
Not only of body but rather of soul,
That we love profoundly.
A people for which the Puerto Rican woman
Has been prepared to fight.
That people is simply happy
And it could almost be said innocent . . .

. . . Puerto Rican woman
who has embroidered our first flag,
who has written our revolutionary anthem
who has resisted heroically in the struggle,

who has challenged the enemy . . .
Puerto Rican woman . . .

. . . Puerto Rican woman . . . we'll overcome.[54]

Villegas is also featured on "A Song to My Liberation," a spoken-word poem in Spanish. Ho's dedication to Puerto Rican national liberation struggles reflects a longtime dedication to the support of autonomous indigenous movements as a first step toward international solidarity. Thus other songs and tunes on the album systematically point toward this next step: "Essay to X" and "Essay to Us," two spoken-word poems by the African American poet Esther Iverem, deliberate on two-stage struggle: the former is an homage to Malcolm and an assault on Bush I. The poem is situated historically on "this precipice at the close of the century, / we either fall or fly." The poem attacks Willie Horton ads, Clarence Thomas, the antiabortion right: "Locking women's wombs. Funding bombs, not / babies." Malcolm's spirit is invoked as a prayer for a new beginning: "now more than ever, it is necessary by any means." "Essay to Us" invokes a history of capitalist assaults on racial unity fostered at the level of the state and the marketplace:

We stand here witnessing the turning of the tide,
Feeling split in two. Which America is America?
Which way will we march? How life is sucked from us
As we breathe to a bass and video beat.[55]

The poem invokes key moments in radical racial protests—Little Rock, Watts, Newark, Harlem—as touchstones for a new social movement to "turn pain into power." The spoken-word venue for the album's key themes pays direct tribute to the Black Arts movement's word experiments, particularly the experiments of Archie Shepp. Shepp gave Ho one of his first breaks as a musician, calling his home in 1974 to ask him to perform in the musical *Lady Day*. Shepp was also a student of theater and playwriting, having had his plays produced in New York during the

1960s. Shepp's dramatic poetry on politically charged themes foreshadows primary and indirect influences on Ho's penchant for agitprop lyrics in his operas and stage production. Shepp's poem "A Poem for Mama Rose" became part of the libretto to Ho's opera *A Chinaman's Chance*, which includes a tribute poem to Vincent Chin. Ho also cites as influence on his spoken-word experiments Sonia Sanchez's poetry (he sat in on her poetry workshop at Amherst College and later recorded her poems) and the work of Kalamu ya Salaam. Salaam, a veteran of the Congress of Afrikan Peoples, an internationalist Pan-African group of the 1970s with whom Ho is in some political sympathy, was a key member of the New Orleans Black Arts movement and later founder of Runagate Press. After meeting in 1989, Ho and Salaam began the "Afro-Asian Arts Dialogue." In their music and spoken-word collaborations, Ho credits Salaam as the writer best attuned to the demands of live improvised jazz performance.[56]

In a larger sense, Ho's commitment to spoken-word artists bespeaks his larger goal of forging and sustaining a bridge between the Black Arts movement and a viable and continuous radical Asian Pacific American culture. *Turn Pain into Power!* pays specific tribute to Janice Mirikitani's role in this endeavor. Ho originally recorded with Mirikitani in the 1980s, using her poem "Awake in the Yellow River." The last two tracks on *Turn Pain into Power!* feature music by Ho and text by Mirikitani: "What's a Girl to Do?" and "The Earth Is Rockin' in Revolution/Drowning in the Yellow River." Mirikitani is widely known in American poetry circles and Asian American literature for her three books of poems: *Awake in the River* (1978), *Shedding Silence* (1987), and *We the Dangerous* (1995). She is also an anthology editor, San Francisco's poet laureate, and founder of Third World Communications. Her experience as a university student (she has degrees from UCLA and Berkeley) provides parodic material for "What's a Girl to Do?" a poem that, like Alice Walker's *Meridian*, lampoons the socializing pressures for women of color in higher education in the pre–women's rights, pre–civil rights era. The speaker of the poem is "cloistered" in academic towers where she learns "art for art's sake" theories that preach that life is but an objective correlative for transcendent art objects. The native speaker of Asian words is rendered mute in the academy, taught to "act white on demand." This socializing/intellectual narrative is interrupted in the poem by Vietnam, Selma, East Oakland, and the 1960s, marked by sudden dissonance in the Afro-Asian Music Ensemble's backing of Jodi Long's vocal rendering of Mirikitani's verse. The speaker, too, suddenly speaks: I "tore out my tongue of cement in a fit," cried, attempted suicide. All this is prelude to the speaker's real education: at poem's end, she "began to remember" that which, the poem implies, will remain relevant, like the personal and political disruptions that make possible the retroactive critique of her university experience. Jon Jang accompanies on piano on this and the following track, "The Earth Is Rockin' Revolution," which opens with mock-doo-wop blasts from Ho's saxophone and faux-boogie-woogie piano. The time of the composition is a satirical now and then: the speaker recalls "necking in backseats of convertibles with white boys" while Elvis "screams out your pain" on the radio: "You ain't nothing but a hound dog." The playful ventriloquizing use of Elvis's "white boy" antics to articulate Asian American female angst is a formidable keynote in the poet/speaker's search for a liberating consciousness within the poem. Unable to tell her white lovers to stop sucking on her neck so she can use the restroom, and haunted by the image of Chinese American men acting as wallflowers at high school dances, the speaker finally screams out her own pain at poem's end: "You ain't nothing but a white boy." The reversal of racial and pop cultural fortunes in Mirikitani's poem dovetails with Ho's revisionist cultural politics and makes Mirikitani a forerunning warrior sister of APA self-determinist aesthetics, a natural touchstone for retracing and retelling the history of race and culture through Asian eyes.[57]

The latter is the objective of Ho's only lyric contribution to *Turn Pain into Power,* the savagely satirical "The Climbers." Originally written as a poem, the piece launches an attack on the academic and corporate assimilation of the Black Arts movement under the refrain "New Black Aesthetic for Sale!" The title "NBA" refers to academic celebration of the Black Renaissance of the 1980s (from the preeminence of Henry Louis Gates's pioneering efforts in African American studies, to the ascent of

Wynton Marsalis to national prominence as jazz spokesman). Ho is unequivocally critical: the divorce from grassroots, radical, indigenous, Third World orientations in the NBA represents the ascent of a new black cultural elite that forbodes ill for American multiculturalism:

> I say
> Don't be afraid, you haven't got it made.
>
> Calling all tragic mulattos!
> Calling all tragic mulattos!
> Calling all model minorities!
> Calling all model minorities!
> Calling anyone who's a credit to their race!
> Calling anyone who's a credit to their race!
> Calling all role models!
> Calling all role models!
> Calling the talented tenth!
> Calling the talented tenth![58]

Ho's ironic reference to the NBA as a "model minority" movement is the tragic reversal of his argument elsewhere that a radical or revolutionary APA culture rests on capturing the national, racial, and political militancy of the original Black Arts movement. The need to reproduce worker-student alliances, the attachment between grassroots activism and cultural work, are lost in the "'80s megabuck generation," which relies on corporate and institutional support and university sanction. Ho's targets are so obvious as to remain unnamed—"Some just skipped out / and quickly became / superstar signifying monkeys justifyin' / 2 Live Crew's doo doo"—but underlying his ad hominem critique is the structural question of where a New American Multicultural Music rooted in liberation ideology might find space in even the so-called avant-garde world. Ho's answer is to call for a redistribution of cultural ideas to follow the redistribution of material wealth: "We heard it before: / climb to the top to help the trickle down / trick us down / trick us down." Only an art that can truly turn pain into power is worthy of bearing the mantle of vanguardism, something akin to his own New American Multicultural Music.

The Subaltern Sings: Sheroes among Us

Trickster identity often includes sexual shape-shifting, gender crossing, or the celebration of sexual desire as a politically subversive force. In Ho's *Journey to the West*, a female hero, or sheroe, Kwan Yin, provides medicinal and spiritual aid that helps turn the battle against Heaven. The "woman warrior" is not an underling but central to revolutionary battle. Ho's adoption in the 1980s of the designation "womyn," spelled with a *y* to take out the "men," reveals the significant influence of 1970s and 1980s feminism on the development of his revolutionary vision quest. Just as New American Multicultural Music challenges the racial and generic essentialism of jazz and world musics, so Ho's body of creative and critical work on the relationship of culture to politics asserts the primacy of a sexually decentered, antipatriarchal program for liberation. Feminism is a heuristic device for Ho's rereading in particular of popular Afro-Asian narratives of both cultural affirmation and political struggle. In general, Ho perceives patriarchal feudalism as casting an even longer shadow over Afro-Asian liberation than more-vaunted exploitations celebrated by Marxist, nationalist, and anticolonialist champions. In "Matriarchy: The First and Final Communism," written in 2002, Ho lays out a template of ideas explored in allegorical form in *Warrior Sisters*. The essay draws on Marxist feminism and feminist critiques of Marxism to argue for a radically womynist historiography: it contends that precapitalist society was matriarchal, female centered, and nonexploitative, and that the struggle to overthrow matriarchy was the first "class struggle." Marxism and historical materialism are thus fundamentally feminist tools to rewrite history's long nightmare of patriarchal capitalism. At the end of this historical vision quest is the dialectical reversal not only of materialism but of Western myth: the recovery of Mother Earth and a "plethora of goddesses across cultural groups who were associated with nature, creation, and life."[59] This vision also has a distinctive anticolonial edge in Ho's account: following Ward Churchill and other indigenists, Ho claims that "for indigenous peoples, a 'feminine' nature is to be loved and venerated. For the predator cultures, a 'feminine nature' is to be dominated, controlled and conquered. Thus, the interconnected triple struggle to save the planet indigenous peoples and womyn is the struggle to stop ecocide, genocide and matricide."[60] The objectives of these struggles find their pragmatic analogue in endeavors to promote womyn's self-defense, to erode the primacy of the nuclear family, and to ban private ownership and the commodification of life-forms, and in the offering of reparations to indigenous peoples, and the redrawing of imperialist U.S. borders.

Ho thus works to recover not just important theoretical reflections on "the woman question" in the canon of male-dominated writings on national liberation but real-world acts of sheroic struggle by women who practice and invent corresponding theories of liberation. Albums like *Turn Pain into Power!* and *No Means No Wherever She Goes* represent aspects of these themes. However, it was not until the 1998 production of *Warrior Sisters: The New Adventures of African and Asian Womyn Warriors* that Ho recast the political and aesthetic strategies of his entire career in a womynist light. The result is one of his most complex collaborative works, one that displaces and replaces many of the masculinist myths of liberation struggles that Third World feminisms have themselves struggled to overturn.

African American librettist Ann T. Greene collaborated with Ho on *Warrior Sisters*, described as a "new American opera in three acts." She is credited with the book and libretto for the opera. Fundamentally, *Warrior Sisters* is a womynist recasting of masculine archetypes naturalized by narratives of anticolonial Third World struggle and national liberation movements. The story is a gynocentric creation myth of the making of revolutionary history. The opera telescopes and leaps sites of feminist struggle from nineteenth-century China and Africa to the 1970s United States. Accordingly, the story celebrates "herstory" as a playful disrespecting of historical representation. Lines between the real and imaginary are, like Trickster sexuality, easily crossed. Indeed, *Warrior*

Sisters is itself a feminist retelling or signifying on Ho's earlier seminal text *Journey to the West:* the pantheon of four female figures at its center—the Chinese heroine Fa Mu Lan, the Ashante princess Nana Yaa Asantewa, the Chinese Boxer leader Sieh King King, and the Black Panther leader Assata Shakur—replaces Monkey, the Friar, Pig, and the Buddhist Priest. Their own journey is not primarily one beyond Western, Eurocentric conceptions of race but one that enters a new territory or Third Way beyond patriarchal conceptions of color, power, sexuality, and empire. Like female science fiction writers Ursula K. Le Guin and Joanna Russ,[61] Ho and Greene deploy speculative fiction as a genre for previously unthinkable conceptions of gender. Likewise, the newness of their American opera is its use as an expression of vanguard political ideals that unravel and rewrite Eurocentric history. Going well beyond the territory of even D. H. Hwang's *M. Butterfly,* with its exposition of Orientalist gender myth,[62] Ho and Greene smash the vestiges of virtually all the generic and political placeholders that secure high culture's (or modernism's) fears of racial or other forms of contamination. Thus consistent with Ho's larger political vision, *Warrior Sisters* is less "postmodern" than a Third World reconfiguration of the capitalist, colonialist, and patriarchal premises of modernity. At the same time, it recasts the history of Afro-Asian liberation and Afro-Orientalism as walking on bound feet that only a twenty-first-century womynism can truly teach to dance.

Liner notes to *Warrior Sisters* describe the plot as "the imaginary meeting of four legendary revolutionaries." They are Fa Mu Lan, the Chinese Boxer leader; Nana Yaa Asantewa, queen mother of the Ashante nation, what is now Ghana; Sieh King King, the early twentieth-century Chinese American feminist; and Assata Shakur, also known as Joanna Chesmir, the former Black Panther member arrested and charged with killing a New Jersey police officer in 1973. The choice of legendary characters befits the play's utopian dramaturgy. Comprised of three acts, the opera begins in late nineteenth-century China as Fa Mu Lan drills the Boxers for an attack against American and European armies, merchants, and missionaries. "Let the Red Rain Fall" is Fa Mu Lan's song of lament for the dead and dying already killed in battle. She vows to fill the sky with the "red rain" of foreign devils. Act 1's prelude is an extended anthem as the Boxers prepare for battle armed only with their martial arts weapons and skills:

Chorus: Foreign devils steal our land
This would never happen
In the dynasty of the Ming!

Drink canals until bled dry
This would never happen
In the dynasty of the Ming!

Foreign devils preach of Christ.
This would never happen
In the dynasty of the Ming!

We must
We must
We must restore the Ming!
This thievery will be halted
By the dynasty of the Ming![63]

The Ming dynasty is a touchstone both for precolonial China and for the opera's revision of *Journey to the West*. Monkey's heroic exploits are invoked as subtext and pretext for Fa Mu Lan's second-wave anticolonial rebellion. This leap of historical faith suggests the serial nature of historical struggle represented formally by the rapid "jump cut" narrative itself. Scene 2 of *Warrior Sisters* takes place in Kumase, the Ashante nation of the 1890s. The synchronized global melodrama invokes sentimental conventions of nineteenth-century feminist and abolitionist fiction, here given a decidedly Third World spin. In Kumase, Ashante chieftains sing of the golden stool, sacred object of Ashante sovereignty. The British governor, named Hodgson, demands that the stool be forfeited. The compliant male chiefs are goaded into preparation for battle to preserve the stool by the appearance of Nana Yaa Asantewa. Like Fa Mu Lan, she is figured as the leader of national liberation struggle:

> So this is the state of affairs,
> My brothers!
> I come to the Council
> All the way from Ejisu
> To hear that my son is gone!
> To hear that my King is in chains!
> To see my brothers wring their hands
> As if stung!
>
> If this is the state of affairs,
> My brothers,
> Ashante will perish as surely as
> Gold now dances in our rivers
> And millet spills from our granaries
> And babies sleep from our milk.[64]

Nana's invocation of "natural" resources threatened, including children's food, recasts the conventional nationalist rhetoric of blood and soil into images of sustenance, not self-determination. Her nickname, "Queen Mother" (also adopted by the famous Communist shero Audley Moore), proposes national liberation as women's work for womyn warriors. Scene 3 again jump-cuts the action, this time to San Francisco's Chinatown, 1902, a synchronous site of Afro-Asian Third World struggle within the First World. The scene is a dimly lit warehouse. Inside, Chinese stowaways to America are being liberated from packing crates. From one emerges Sieh King King. New World patriarchy replays Old World feudalism as she finds herself struggling to speak in an all-male (tong) society:

> Gold Mountain!
> I am Sieh King King!

I come seeking freedom!
On my unbound feet
I walk electric streets
Of the . . .

Male Chorus:
Gum San! (Gold Mountain)
Hungry men ride hungry seas
To fall in your embrace.
The land of plenty
Where poor men get rich
With gold for many wives
We'll buy back home[65]

Ho and Greene configure Chinese immigration within a larger matrix of capitalist patriarchy: the men have "come to you / to become rich"; Sieh King King, the product of a Jesuit foreign school in China, a speaker of English, "the tongue of Christian men," has arrived in the United States "to learn the new ways / to be Chinese." "I ride the street-car, / to meet those who / can teach me the ways / of the modern / who are not slaves to the past or oppressors!" Seeking audience, she turns to a young Chinese prostitute named Bad Luck, who intones with Old World solemnity: "It is a curse to be / born / female." Undeterred, Sieh King King insists that she "learn the new ways / to be a Chinese womyn."[66]

Act 1 thus establishes parallel yet converging plotlines bespeaking a radical reconception of twentieth-century national liberation struggle. The discrete staging of scenes also dramatizes a stagist progression from nationalism to internationalism: Ho and Greene must resolve ways of merging and "acting out" synchronically rebellions along multiple weak links of Western imperialism. In scene 5, the last of act 1, the dynamic duo again leap time and space to crash an address by Sieh King King in San Francisco to the Baohuanghui (Protect the Emperor Society). A segregated audience—pigtailed men on the floor, wives and the prostitute Bad Luck in the balcony—is being treated to a rousing oratory on the future emancipation of Chinese womyn when Fa Mu Lan and Nana Yaa Asantewa arrive together on Fa Mu Lan's trusty steed, no longer lone rangers. The liner notes comment: "The audience is confused and shocked after they realize that this is not an operatic episode common to Chinese opera."[67] The transgression of genre sets a revolutionary stage for a dramatic Wild West showdown between womyn warriors: Fa Mu Lan challenges Sieh King King for speaking "in the Devil's tongue." She retorts, "I am Sieh King King / Modern Chinese womyn. / Sister, my feet are big / like yours." Sorority, not filial piety, wins out as Sieh King King gives propers to her radical elder: "I respect you like / my father / my mother / my ancestors." Fa Mu Lan and Nanan then sing their appeal for Sieh King King to join them in order to "plunge our hands" into the rotting wounds of Earth Mother. When she agrees, they throw her on the steed and set out to complete their journey:

> The fourth of four
> Completes the square.
> The proper configuration for righteous war![68]

The proper four, of course, are Monkey, Teng Seng, Pig, and Friar Sand, themselves accompanied by a white stallion in *Journey to the West*. The end point of their quest, however, is the matriarchal socialist future: "Tearing a hole in the universe," write Ho and Greene in their prefatory plot summary, "the three womyn warriors vanish from the 19th century, and travel through time and space to 1970s Amerikka." Act 2 takes place as the mother ship sets down on the New Jersey Turnpike, where Assata Shakur, Zayd Shakur, and Sundiata Acoli are in desperate flight from New Jersey state troopers. Their Black Panther Party meeting in the basement of a Harlem brownstone has just been interrupted by police. The modern-day trio have fled in a white Pontiac. When Fa Mu Lan and her compatriots arrive, the car has broken down on the roadside and appears to the state trooper as a "demonic and flaming white horse and rider." Fa Mu Lan, in spectral white-haired form, chases the troopers. Shots are fired. Zayd Shakur is killed. Sundiata and Assata are captured.

The next scene catapults the action to the Middlesex County courthouse, where Assata is chained to a hospital bed, tortured by armed troopers for a confession, and threatened with rape. She is then led down a corridor to visit with Sundiata. They profess their "black revolutionary love" and declare their commitment to resistance. It is not enough. In the next scene, Assata is found guilty. The act ends with a Womyn's Chorus describing an underground training camp where Nana Yaa Asantewa is training womyn revolutionaries, and King is organizing and educating womyn inmates in the prison to which Assata will be sent.[69]

Act 3 is a dialectical climax and synthesis of the temporal and spatial unities invoked in the preceding stages of the drama. All four protagonists converge at the Clinton Correctional Facility for Women in Clinton, New Jersey. Assata, pregnant, is held in an isolation cell. In the prison yard, Sieh King King foments a protest, and prison guards prepare for riot. Back inside, Nana Yaa Asantewa beats two prison guards, frees Assata from her cell, and dons the male guards' clothing to lead her to freedom. The Womyn's Chorus sings behind the action its collective import: "She who runs when the sun is sleeping will stumble many times." Two soloists then emerge from the chorus to urge their sisters on: "You better go, Girl! / Get out of here, Girl!" Sieh King King, in call and response, sings her reiteration:

> You better go, Girl!
> No looking back, Girl!
> Leave us behind, Girl!
> Fuck this Amerikkka![70]

The next scene is the Florida coast, where the triumphant foursome are reunited, joined now with the militia from the underground prison camp. Fa Mu Lan vows that the time is to retreat and take the struggle underground. She sends Assata "over water to your freedom," where "the General is waiting / to be born." Fa Mu Lan then "divests herself of the last spell," and in a blinding burst of light akin to their breaking through, the warriors disappear. The final scene of *Warrior Sisters* occurs

synchronously in centers of First and Third World liberation: Cuba and
New York City. Assata nurses her newborn daughter, the new general,
in a rural Cuban village. She has named the daughter Nana. Her working body, Earth Mother's body, nurtures the child of revolution: "Mamar
la leche! / Mamar la leche" (Suckle the milk / Suckle the milk). Suddenly
report of a massive street demonstration in New York City comes across
the radio. Womyn of many nationalities carry multilingual banners proclaiming VIOLENCE AGAINST WOMYN WILL ONLY END WHEN WOMYN DEFEND
THEMSELVES! WOMYN CONTROL OUR BODIES! There is another sudden burst
of light, and through the membrane of space and time bursts the demonstration's vanguard, led by Sieh King King, the ghost of an aged Fa Mu
Lan, and Nana Yaa Asantewa, followed by a disciplined cadre of womyn
warriors. They sing, in chorus, "Oh Earth Mother / We fight to heal you
/ To kill the parasite / capitalism!"

> Our work is never ending
> We fight back!
> To protect the Divine
> Birthing the New World
> Of justice!

Their chant continues, the women march, and the opera ends with
a final call and response, the dialectical completion of a revolutionary
century:

> Womyn's Chorus:
> All power to the womyn!
> Daughters of the Earth!
> We who have been last
> We shall be first
> (repeat)

> Men's Chorus:
> All power to the womyn!

Daughters of the Earth!
We who have been last
We shall be first! (repeat)[71]

The transgendered voicing of the collective "we" puts the "men" back in womyn. The performance not only exposes the masculinism of traditional Chinese opera (where men, as in Shakespeare, often play

Promotional photograph of Fred Ho. Photograph by Jack Mitchell; courtesy of Fred Ho.

women's roles) but discloses traditional agitprop as a forbidden action-adventure genre now open to women warriors. It recasts *Journey to the West*'s search for "enlightened" text—the Buddhist scrolls—as the search for a new "book," a radical Afro-Asian womynist libretto and a new American opera. More pointedly for Ho's political development and his larger oeuvre of New American Multicultural Music, *Warrior Sisters* customizes his themes and generic inventions to a new corpus or body politic. The opera's reliance on ecological, environmental, and maternal metaphors for a "new world" challenges a masculinist essentialism in tension with its pretexts and subtexts: WOMYN CONTROL OUR BODIES! Indeed, the opera recovers the bound and raped bodies of Afro-Asian womynhood as evidence of the need for a transracial feminist dialectic; Ho and Green's cross-race, cross-gendered collaboration is also acted out in the struggle for control over the body of the text itself. These features of *Warrior Sisters* make it a crucial addition to the corpus of Afro-Asian cultural texts inaugurated by the confluence of Black Arts/APA struggles dating to the Panthers and I Wor Kuen. Ho and Greene pay homage to collaborative precursors like Ishmael Reed and Frank Chin, editors of the ground-breaking *Yardbird Reader*, leaders of the first wave of new American literary multiculturalism. Yet *Warrior Sisters* also recalls some of the gender exclusions concomitant with that first-wave project. For all these reasons, *Warrior Sisters* must be reckoned among the more important contemporary womynist interventions not only in Afro-Asian/Afro-Orientalism but in the wider pantheon of multiculturalist texts. Its womynist serial adventure leaves few icons from twentieth-century mass culture, and anticolonialism, untouched by what was once called, in a time before the time of womynist historiography, the woman question. *Warrior Sisters* answers the call of that early history with a revolutionary vision quest that is unmatched in the largely masculine time of Afro-Orientalism and portends another alternative modernity worth waiting and fighting for.

Fred Ho Discography

As Leader

All Power to the People! The Black Panther Ballet Suite. Afro-Asian Music Ensemble, recorded March 1998 (completed but unreleased).

Bamboo That Snaps Back. Asian American Art Ensemble, Finnadar/ Atlantic, 1987.

Monkey: Part One. The Monkey Orchestra, Koch Jazz, 1996.

Monkey: Part Two. The Monkey Orchestra, Koch Jazz, 1997.

Night Vision: A Third to First World Vampyre Opera. Book with double CD. Autonomedia and Big Red Media, Inc., 1999.

Voice of the Dragon: Once Upon a Time in Chinese America: A Martial Arts Ballet. Fred Ho and Ruth Margraff, Innova, 2001.

A Song for Manong. Asian American Art Ensemble, AsianImprov Records, 1988.

Stranger Than Fiction. CRI–Blue Shift, 2003.

Tomorrow Is Now! Afro-Asian Music Ensemble, Soul Note, 1986.

Turn Pain into Power! Fred Ho and the Afro-Asian Music Ensemble, O O Discs, 1997.

The Underground Railroad to My Heart. Fred Ho and the Afro-Asian Music Ensemble, Soul Note, 1994.

Warrior Sisters: The New Adventures of African and Asian Womyn Warriors. Double CD, Koch Jazz, 1999.

The Way of the Saxophone. Innova and Big Red Media, Inc., 2000.

We Refuse to Be Used and Abused. Afro-Asian Music Ensemble, Soul Note, 1989.

Yes Means Yes, No Means No, Whatever She Says, Wherever She Goes! Koch Jazz, 1998.

DVD

All Power to the People! The Black Panther Ballet Suite. Innova and Big Red Media, Inc., 2003.

Notes

Introduction

1. Richard Wright, *12 Million Black Voices* (New York: Thunder's Mouth Press, 1991), 4, 47.

2. Robin D. G. Kelley, *Freedom Dreams: The Black Radical Imagination* (Boston: Beacon Press, 2002). In the context of Afro-Asia, see especially "Roaring from the East: Third World Dreaming," 60–109.

3. Edward Said, *Orientalism* (New York: Vintage Books, 1978), 67.

4. Malcolm X , *The Autobiography of Malcolm X* (New York: Ballantine Books, 1993), 266.

5. W. E. B. Du Bois, "Indians and American Negroes," *Aryan Path*, December 1935, 1.

6. Xiaomei Chen, *Occidentalism: A Theory of Counter-discourse in Post-Mao China* (New York: Oxford University Press, 1995), 5.

7. See Homi Bhabha, *The Location of Culture* (New York: Routledge, 1994). Bhabha's hybridity theory rests in part on the in-betweenness experienced by colonizer and colonized. There are numerous outstanding critical studies of Orientalism, and of Said's seminal text. Those with which I am particularly sympathetic are Aijaz Ahmad's *In Theory: Classes, Nations, Literatures* (London: Verso, 1992); Arif Dirlik's "Chinese History and the Question of Orientalism," *History and Theory* 35, no. 4: 96–118; and Evelyn Hu-DeHart's *Across the Pacific: Asian-Americans and Globalization* (Philadelphia: Temple University Press, 1999). Feminist criticism of Said has been especially astute about describing his work's patriarchal epistemology; see, for example, Meyda Yegenoglu, *Colonial Fantasies: Towards a Feminist Reading of "Orientalism"* (London: Cambridge University Press, 1998).

Other applications of feminism in Orientalist theory include Reina Lewis, *Gendering Orientalism: Race, Femininity, and Representation* (New York, 1996); and Billie Melman, *Women's Orients: English Women and the Middle East, 1718–1918; Sexuality, Religion, and Work* (Basingstoke and London, 1992). See also Antoinette M. Burton, *Burdens of History: British Feminists, Indian Women, and Imperial Culture, 1865–1915* (Chapel Hill: University of North Carolina Press, 1994).

8. See Mary Louise Pratt, *Imperial Eyes: Travel Writing and Transculturation* (New York: Routledge, 1992).

9. Vijay Prashad, *Everybody Was Kung Fu Fighting: Afro-Asia and the Myth of Cultural Purity* (Boston: Beacon Press, 2002), 58.

10. Ibid., 61.

11. Ibid., 69.

12. Arif Dirlik, "Chinese History and the Question of Orientalism," *History and Theory* 35, no. 4:117.

13. Ibid., 117–18.

14. Evelyn Hu-DeHart, *Across the Pacific: Asian-Americans and Globalization* (Philadelphia: Temple University Press, 1999), 47.

15. Said, *Orientalsim.*

16. Karl Marx, "Genesis of the Industrial Capitalist," chap. 31 of *Capital*, vol. 1, quoted in Karl Marx and Friedrich Engels, *On Colonialism: Articles from the New York Tribune and Other Writings* (New York: International Publishers, 1972), 292.

17. Marx and Engels, *On Colonialism*, 7.

18. Said, *Orientalism*, 45.

19. Marx, "Revolution in China and in Europe," in *On Colonialism*, 19.

20. Frederick Douglass, "Our Composite Nationality: An Address Delivered in Boston, Massachusetts, on 7 December 1869," in *The Frederick Douglass Papers*, vol. 4 (New Haven: Yale University Press, 1991), 253–54.

21. Engels, "Persia and China," in *On Colonialism*, 124.

22. Ibid., 120.

23. Ibid., 20.

24. Robert Young, *White Mythologies: Writing History and the West* (London: Routledge, 1990), 3.

25. Ibid., 4.

26. Sanjay Seth, *Marxist Theory and Nationalist Politics: The Case of Colonial India* (New Delhi: Sage Publications, 1995), 220.

27. Ibid., 206.

28. Ibid., 221.

29. Robin D. G. Kelley and Tiffany Ruby Patterson, "How the West Was One: On the Uses and Limitations of Diaspora," *Black Scholar* 30, nos. 3–4:13.

30. Paul Gilroy, *The Black Atlantic: Modernity and Double Consciousness* (New York: Oxford University Press, 1993), 39–40.

31. Paul Gilroy, *Against Race: Imagining Political Culture beyond the Color Line* (Cambridge: Harvard University Press, 2000), 356.

32. Peter Linebaugh and Marcus Rediker, *The Many-Headed Hydra: The Hidden History of the Revolutionary Atlantic* (Boston: Beacon Press, 2000).

33. Kate Baldwin, *Beyond the Color Line and the Iron Curtain: Reading Encounters between Black and Red, 1922–1963* (Durham: Duke University Press, 2002), 158.

34. Gilroy, *Black Atlantic*, 2.

35. See Marcial Gonzalez, "A Marxist Critique of Borderlands Postmodernism: Adorno's Negative Dialectics and Chicano Cultural Criticism," in *Left of the Color Line: Race, Radicalism, and Modern Literatures of the United States*, ed. Bill V. Mullen and James Smethurst (Chapel Hill: University of North Carolina Press, 2003). Other critics to have taken up the critique of biological essentialism in multiculturalist theory include Scott Michaelson, *The Limits of Multiculturalism: Interrogating the Origins of American Anthropology* (Minneapolis: University of Minnesota Press, 1999).

36. Gilroy, *Against Race*, 30.

37. Ibid., 123–24.

38. Brent Edwards, "The Uses of Diaspora," *Social Text* 19, no. 1 (Spring 2001): 61.

39. Hu-DeHart, *Across the Pacific*, 43.

40. Wilson Moses, *Afrotopia: The Roots of African American Popular History* (Cambridge: Cambridge University Press, 1998), 16.

41. Sudarshan Kapur, *Raising Up a Prophet: The African-American Encounter with Gandhi* (Boston: Beacon Press, 1992), 17.

42. Ibid., 18.

43. Prashad, *Kung Fu Fighting*, 31. See also Gerald Horne, *Race War! White Supremacy and the Japanese Attack on the British Empire* (New York: New York University Press, 2003), 45–46, 57.

44. Ibid., 31.

45. David Levering Lewis, "Race in the Service of Civil Rights: Du Bois in Germany, China, and Japan, 1936–1937," *Black Renaissance/Renaissance Noire* 4, no. 1:10.

46. Ibid., 19.

47. Ibid., 20.

48. Ibid., 22–23.

49. Ali A. Mazrui, "Black Orientalism? Further Reflections on *Wonders of the African World*," *Black Scholar* 30, no. 1 (Spring 2000): 15.

50. In "How the West Was One: On the Uses and Limitations of Diaspora," Robin D. G. Kelley and Tiffany Patterson caution against diaspora theory that ameliorates the impacts of capitalism and racism on the formation of diaspora studies (*Black Scholar* 30, nos. 3–4:31–35).

1. W. E. B. Du Bois's Afro-Asian Fantasia

1. W. E. B. Du Bois, "Color Line Belts the World," *Collier's Weekly*, October 20, 1906, 20.

2. W. E. B. Du Bois, "World Problem of the Color Line," *Manchester (NH) Leader*, November 16, 1914.

3. W. E. B. Du Bois, "Forum of Fact and Opinion," *Pittsburgh Courier*, February 20, 1937.

4. Wilson Jeremiah Moses, *Afrotopia: The Roots of African Popular History* (Cambridge: Cambridge University Press, 1998), 96.

5. Ibid., 97.

6. *Pamphlets and Leaflets by W. E. B. Du Bois*, ed. Herbert Aptheker (White Plains, NY: Kraus-Thomson, 1986), 162.

7. Ibid., 207.

8. W. E. B. Du Bois, *The World and Africa* (Millwood, NY: Kraus-Thomson, 1986), 115.

9. *Newspaper Columns by W. E. B. Du Bois*, ed. Herbert Aptheker, vol. 2, 1945–1961 (White Plains, NY: Kraus-Thomson, 1986), 1085.

10. Du Bois, *The World and Africa*, 117.

11. Sudarshan Kapur, *Raising Up a Prophet: The African-American Encounter with Gandhi* (Boston: Beacon Press, 1992), 26.

12. Du Bois, *Darkwater: Voices from Within the Veil* (Millwood, NY: Kraus-Thomson, 1975), 60.

13. Alys Eve Weinbaum, "Reproducing Racial Globality: W. E. B. Du Bois

and the Sexual Politics of Black Internationalism," *Social Text* 19, no. 2 (Summer 2001): 15–39.

14. Kapur, *Raising Up a Prophet*, 26.

15. W. E. B. Du Bois, "The Massacre of East St. Louis," *Crisis* 14, no. 5 (September 1919): 223.

16. Lala Lajpat Rai, *Unhappy India* (Calcutta: Bana, 1928), 124.

17. Quoted in Herbert Aptheker, introduction to *Darkwater: Voices from Within the Veil* (New York: Kraus-Thomson, 1975), 6.

18. Ibid., 7.

19. Ibid., 19.

20. Du Bois, *Darkwater*, 49.

21. Ibid., 95.

22. Ibid., 97.

23. Excellent recent books shedding light on this subject include Winston James, *Holding Aloft the Banner of Ethiopia: Caribbean Radicalism in Early 20th Century America* (London: Verso, 1999); Bill Maxwell, *New Negro, Old Left: African-American Writing and Communism between the Wars* (New York: Columbia University Press, 1999); James Smethurst, *The New Red Negro: The Literary Left and African American Poetry, 1930–1946* (New York: Oxford, 1999); Kate Baldwin, *Beyond the Color Line and the Iron Curtain* (Durham: Duke University Press, 2002).

24. W. E. B. Du Bois, *Dark Princess: A Romance* (Jackson: University Press of Mississippi, 1995), 228.

25. Ibid., 21.

26. Ibid., 22.

27. Ibid., 3.

28. David N. Druhe, *Soviet Russia and Indian Communism, 1917–1947* (New York: Bookman Associates, 1959), 21.

29. Maxwell, *New Negro, Old Left*, 81.

30. Ibid., 90.

31. Harry Haywood, *Black Bolshevik: Autobiography of an Afro-American Communist* (Chicago: Liberator Press, 1978), 158.

32. Du Bois, *Dark Princess*, 16.

33. John Patrick Haithcox, *Communism and Nationalism in India: M. N. Roy and Comintern Policy, 1920–1939* (Princeton: Princeton University Press, 1971), 33.

34. Ibid., 18.

35. "Gandhi and India," *Crisis* 23, no. 5 (March 1922): 205.

36. Du Bois, *Dark Princess*, 285.

37. Du Bois, "The Black Man and Labor," *Crisis* 31, no. 2 (December 1925): 59–62.

38. Ibid.

39. Du Bois, *Dark Princess*, 285.

40. Du Bois, *Darkwater*, 40.

41. Du Bois, *Dark Princess*, 29.

42. Ibid., 228.

43. Ibid., 227.

44. Ibid., 220.

45. Paul Gilroy, *The Black Atlantic: Modernity and Double Consciousness* (New York: Oxford University Press, 1993), 144.

46. W. E. B. Du Bois, *The Souls of Black Folk*, ed. Henry Louis Gates Jr. and Terri Hume Oliver (New York: Norton, 1999), 11.

47. Du Bois, *Dark Princess*, 286.

48. David Kimche, *The Afro-Asian Movement: Ideology and Foreign Policy of the Third World* (New York: Halstead Press, 1973), 4.

49. Ibid., 4, 5.

50. Du Bois, *Dark Princess*, 286.

51. "The Pan-African Congresses," *Crisis* 34, no. 8 (October 1927): 263–64.

52. W. E. B. Du Bois, "As the Crow Flies," *Crisis* 34, no. 3 (February 1932): 80.

53. W. E. B. Du Bois, "Postscript," *Crisis* 40, no. 1 (January 1933): 20.

54. W. E. B. Du Bois, "Forum of Fact and Opinion," *Pittsburgh Courier*, February 20, 1937.

55. See Ernest Allen Jr., "When Japan Was 'Champion of the Darker Races': Satokata Takhashi and the Flowering of Black Messianic Nationalism," *Black Scholar* 24 (Winter 1994): 23–46.

56. W. E. B. Du Bois, "Postscript," *Crisis* 40, no. 12 (September 1933): 293.

57. Ibid., 293.

58. W. E. B. Du Bois, "Forum of Fact and Opinion," *Pittsburgh Courier*, February 27, 1937.

59. Ibid.

60. W. E. B. Du Bois, "Forum of Fact and Opinion," *Pittsburgh Courier*, September 25, 1937.

61. W. E. B. Du Bois, *Worlds of Color: The Black Flame; A Trilogy* (Millwood, NY: Kraus-Thomson, 1986), 69–70.

62. W. E. B. Du Bois, *Newspaper Columns by W. E. B. Du Bois*. ed. Herbert Aptheker, vol. 2, 1945–1961 (White Plains, NY: Kraus-Thomson, 1986), 654.

63. Ibid., 654.

64. Ibid., 331.

65. W. E. B. Du Bois, "As the Crow Flies," *Crisis* 37, no. 9 (September 1930): 315.

66. W. E. B. Du Bois, *Black Folk Then and Now* (New York: Henry Holt, 1939), 401.

67. W. E. B. Du Bois, *The Autobiography of W. E. B. Du Bois: A Soliloquy on Viewing My Life from the Last Decade of Its First Century* (New York: International, 1968), 400.

68. George Padmore, *Pan-Africanism or Communism* (London: D. Dobson, 1956), 11.

69. W. E. B. Du Bois, "China and Africa," *Peking Review*, March 3, 1959, 11.

70. Ibid., 12.

71. Ibid.

72. Ibid., 13.

73. W. E. B. Du Bois, "I Sing to China," *China Reconstructs* 8 (June 1959): 24–26.

2. The Limits of Being Outside

1. Paul Gilroy, *The Black Atlantic: Modernity and Double Consciousness* (Cambridge: Harvard University Press, 1993), 186.

2. See Arnold Rampersad, "Du Bois's Passage to India: *Dark Princess*," in *W. E. B. Du Bois on Race and Culture*, ed. Bernald W. Bell, Emily Grosholz, and James Stewart (New York: Routledge, 1966), 161–76. The Chiwengo, Shankar, and Hakutani essays on Wright are all collected in *Richard Wright's Travel Writings: New Reflections*, ed. Virginia Whatley Smith (Jackson: University Press of Mississippi, 2001). See Chiwengo, "Gazing through the Screen: Richard Wright's Africa," 20–44; Hakutani, "*The Color Curtain:* Richard Wright's Journey into Asia," 63–77; and Shankar, "Richard Wright's Black Power: Colonial Politics and the Travel Narrative," 3–19. Gilroy's more sympathetic account of Wright's travel writing appears as the chapter "'Without the Consolation of Tears': Richard Wright, France, and the Ambivalence of Community," in *The Black Atlantic:*

Modernity and Double Consciousness (Cambridge: Harvard University Press, 1993), 146–86.

3. Richard Wright, *White Man, Listen!* (New York: HarperCollins, 1995), 6.

4. Ibid., 6.

5. Amritjit Singh, introduction to *Black Power: A Record of Reactions in a Land of Pathos*, by Richard Wright (New York: HarperCollins, 1995), xiv.

6. Bryan S. Turner, *Marx and the End of Orientalism* (London: George Allen and Unwin, 1978), 81.

7. Richard Wright, "How Bigger Was Born," in *Native Son* (New York: HarperPerennial, 1995), xiv.

8. See Ernest Allen Jr., "When Japan Was 'Champion of the Darker Races': Satokata Takhashi and the Flowering of Black Messianic Nationalism," *Black Scholar* 24 (Winter 1994): 23–46.

9. "Is Japan the Champion of the Colored Races?" (International Publishers, 1937).

10. Wright, "How Bigger Was Born," xxvi.

11. Wright, *Native Son*, 364.

12. Richard Wright, *12 Million Black Voices* (New York: Thunder's Mouth Press, 1991), 146.

13. Ibid., 147.

14. Richard Wright, *Black Boy (American Hunger)* (New York: HarperPerennial, 1993), 43.

15. Ibid., 445.

16. Ibid., 435.

17. Ibid., 435–36.

18. Richard Wright, *Black Power: A Record of Reactions in a Land of Pathos* (New York: HarperCollins, 1995), xxxvi.

19. Ngwarsungu Chiwengo, "Gazing through the Screen: Richard Wright's Africa," in *Richard Wright's Travel Writings: New Reflections*, ed. Virginia Whatley Smith (Jackson: University Press of Mississippi, 2001), 21.

20. Ibid., 38.

21. Wright, dedication to *Black Power*.

22. Muhammad Hallaj, "Afro-Asian Politics in the United Nations" (PhD diss., University of Florida, 1966), 18.

23. Ibid.

24. Ibid., 48.

25. Richard Wright, *The Color Curtain* (Jackson: University Press of Mississippi, 1994), 43.

26. George McTurnan Kahin, *The Asian-African Conference: Bandung, Indonesia, April, 1955* (Port Washington, New York: Kennikat Press, 1972), 47.

27. Wright, *The Color Curtain*, 13–14.

28. Ibid., 20.

29. Ibid., 18.

30. Ibid., 15.

31. Aijaz Ahmad, *In Theory: Classes, Nations, Literatures* (London: Verso, 1992), 304–5.

32. Wright, *White Man, Listen!* 5.

33. Alaba Ogunsanwo, *China's Policy in Africa, 1958–1971* (London: Cambridge University Press, 1974), 7.

34. Ibid., 19.

35. Kahin, *The Asian-African Conference*, 41.

36. Wright, *The Color Curtain*, 54.

37. W. E. B. Du Bois, *The World and Africa* (Millwood, NY: Kraus-Thomson, 1976), 257.

38. Ibid., 258.

39. Wright, *The Color Curtain*, 219.

40. Ibid., 209.

41. Adam Clayton Powell Jr., "Afro-Asian Meet Puts U.S. on Spot," *Pittsburgh Courier*, April 30, 1955. Other reports in the black press on Bandung were more sympathetic. See, for example, Ethel L. Payne, "Afro-Asian Parley Blasts S. Africa's Racial Policies," *Chicago Defender*, April 30, 1955. In general, black U.S. response to Bandung was contradictory, mixing appreciation for colored self-determination movements with uncertainty and phobia about the consequences of, for example, China-Africa ties.

42. Willard S. Townsend, "Labor Front: Commies Punish Workers," *Pittsburgh Courier*, May 14, 1955.

43. Manning Marable, *Race, Reform, and Rebellion: The Second Reconstruction in Black America, 1945–1982* (Jackson: University Press of Mississippi, 1984), 31–33, 54–55.

44. Ibid., 31, 55.

45. Quoted in Michel Fabre, *The Unfinished Quest of Richard Wright* (Urbana: University of Illinois Press, 1993), 517.

46. Cedric Robinson, introduction to *White Man, Listen!* xx.

47. For more on Wright's relationship to Marxism, see Cedric Robinson, *Black Marxism: The Making of the Black Radical Tradition* (London: Zed Press, 1983).

48. Wright, *White Man, Listen!* 126.

49. Robinson, "Introduction," xxii.

50. Yoshinobu Hakutani, "*The Color Curtain:* Richard Wright's Journey into Asia," in *Richard Wright's Travel Writings: New Reflections,* ed. Virginia Whatley Smith (Jackson: University Press of Mississippi, 2002), 64.

51. Ibid.

3. Transnational Correspondence

1. *Shijie Wenxue* (World Literature) 9 (September 1963), box 3, Robert Franklin Williams Papers, Bentley Historical Library, University of Michigan, Ann Arbor.

2. *Monroe, North Carolina . . . Turning Point in American History* (Detroit: Facing Reality Publishing, 1962).

3. *Correspondence,* October 1963, box 3, James and Grace Lee Boggs Collection, Walter P. Reuther Library of Labor and Urban Affairs, Detroit. See also Dudley Randall, "Roses and Revolution" and "Ballad of Birmingham," in *Cities Burning* (Detroit: Broadside Press, 1968).

4. Randall, *Cities Burning,* 3.

5. *SAGA,* undated article, box 7, Robert Franklin Williams Papers, Bentley Historical Library.

6. "Urban Guerilla Warfare," *Black America,* August 1965, 6.

7. James Boggs, *Racism and the Class Struggle: Further Pages from a Black Worker's Notebook* (New York: Monthly Review Press, 1974), 41.

8. Larry Neal, "The Black Arts Movement," in *The Norton Anthology of African American Literature* (New York: W. W. Norton, 1997), 1963.

9. Revolutionary Action Movement, "The World Black Revolution," 31, box 2, Robert Franklin Williams Papers, Bentley Historical Library.

10. Ibid., 31.

11. For more on the Afro-Asian Writers Movement, see "Organizational File, Afro-Asian Writers Bureau," New York University Bobst Library, Tamiment Collection.

12. See Mary L. Dudziak, *Cold War Civil Rights: Race and the Image of American*

Democracy (Princeton: Princeton University Press, 2000); and Penny Von Eschen, *Race against Empire: Black Americans and Anticolonialism, 1937–1957* (Ithaca: Cornell University Press, 1997).

13. Timothy Tyson, *Radio Free Dixie: Robert F. Williams and the Roots of Black Power* (Chapel Hill: University of North Carolina Press, 1999), 132–33.

14. Robert F. Williams, "The Sino-Soviet Dispute and the Afro-American," box 2, Robert Franklin Williams Papers, Bentley Historical Library.

15. Suzanne Smith, *Dancing in the Street: Motown and the Cultural Politics of Detroit* (Cambridge: Harvard University Press, 1999), 172.

16. "Subscription List," box 3, Robert Franklin Williams Papers, Bentley Historical Library.

17. Quoted in Robert Mast, ed., *Detroit Lives* (Philadelphia: Temple University Press, 1994), 306.

18. Smith, *Dancing*, 114.

19. *Correspondence*, November 1963, 1, box 3, James and Grace Lee Boggs Collection, Walter P. Reuther Library of Labor and Urban Affairs.

20. Ibid.

21. *Malcolm X Speaks*, ed. George Breitman (New York: Grove Press, 1963), 14.

22. *Correspondence*, 2.

23. Quoted in *Correspondence*, 2.

24. See Robin D. G. Kelley and Betsy Esch, "Black like Mao" *Souls* (Fall 1999): 6–41; and Robin D. G. Kelley, "'Roaring from the East': Third World Dreaming," in *Freedom Dreams: The Black Radical Imagination* (Boston: Beacon Press, 2001), 60–109. See Thomas L. Blair's account of RAM and the 1960s black Left in *Retreat to the Ghetto: The End of a Dream?* (New York: Hill and Wang, 1977).

25. Maxwell C. Stanford (Muhammad Ahmed), "Revolutionary Action Movement (RAM): A Case Study of Urban Revolutionary Movement in Western Capitalist Society" (MA thesis, Atlanta University, 1986).

26. Ibid.

27. Robert F. Williams, "Revolution without Violence?" *Crusader*, box 5, Robert Franklin Williams Papers, Bentley Historical Library.

28. Stanford, "Revolutionary Action Movement."

29. Ibid.

30. Ibid.

31. Ibid.

32. *Black America*, Fall 1964, 6–12.

33. "Greetings to Our Militant Vietnamese Brothers," *Black America*, Fall 1964, 21–22.

34. *International Conference for Solidarity with the People of Vietnam against U.S. Imperialist Aggression and for the Defence of Peace*, box 3, Robert Franklin Williams Papers, Bentley Historical Library.

35. Ibid.

36. Ibid., 85.

37. Ibid., 48.

38. Robert F. Williams, "U.S.A.: The Potential of a Minority Revolution," *Black America*, August 1965, 8.

39. Ibid., 9.

40. "Notes on the Philosophy of Self-Defense Warfare," *Black America*, August 1965, 11–12.

41. Ibid., 3–4.

42. Ibid., 5.

43. Revolutionary Action Movement, "World Black Revolution," 3.

44. James Boggs, "Integration and Democracy: Two Myths That Have Failed," *Black America*, Fall 1964, 4–5.

45. *Black America*, Fall 1964, 32; italics mine.

46. Ibid., 32.

47. Inner City Organizing Committee Papers, James and Grace Boggs Collection, box 5, folder 7, Walter P. Reuther Library of Labor and Urban Affairs.

48. Ibid., 3.

49. Mao Tse-tung, "Talks at the Yenan Forum on Art and Literature (May 23, 1952)," in *Mao-Tse Tung: An Anthology of His Writings*, ed. Anne Fremantle (New York: Mentor Books, 1962), 260.

50. "The Relationship of Revolutionary Afro-American Movement to the Bandung Revolution," *Black America*, Summer–Fall 1965, 11–12.

51. Ibid., 11.

52. James Smethurst, "The Origins of the Black Arts Movement in Chicago and Detroit." Unpublished manuscript, 7. Forthcoming in *The Black Arts Movement: Literary Nationalism in the 1960s and 1970s* (University of North Carolina Press).

53. Julius E. Thompson, *Dudley Randall, Broadside Press, and the Black Arts Movement in Detroit, 1960–1995* (Jefferson: McFarland, 1999), 26.

54. Rosey E. Poole, ed., *Beyond the Blues: New Poems by American Negroes* (London: Hand and Flower Press, 1962).

55. Quoted in Thompson, *Dudley Randall*, 28.

56. Ibid.

57. Dudley Randall and Margaret G. Burroughs, eds., *For Malcolm: Poems on the Life and the Death of Malcolm X* (Detroit: Broadside Press, 1969).

58. Quoted in Mast, *Detroit Lives*, 290.

59. Mao, "Talks at Yenan," 247.

60. Ibid., 252.

61. Ibid., 259.

62. Ibid., 254.

63. Robert F. Williams, "Speech, 25th Anniversary of Mao's 'Talks at the Yenan Forum on Literature and Art,'" box 3, Robert Franklin Williams Papers, Bentley Historical Library.

64. Smith, *Dancing*, 175.

65. Ibid.

66. Inner City Organizing Committee, 1.

67. Ibid.

68. Mao, "Talks at Yenan," 258.

69. Smith, *Dancing*, 191.

70. "Black Arts Conference Statement," James and Grace Lee Boggs Collection, box 19, folder 4, Walter P. Reuther Library of Labor and Urban Affairs.

71. Ibid.

72. Ibid.

73. Mao, "Talks at Yenan," 254.

74. Quoted in Mast, *Detroit Lives*, 292.

75. James Boggs, "Birth of a Nation," *Inner City Voice* 1, no. 1 (October 20, 1967), box 1, Detroit Revolutionary Movements Collections Newsletters and Newspapers, Walter P. Reuther Library of Labor and Urban Affairs.

76. *Inner City Voice* 1, no. 1 (November 9, 1967): 2.

77. *Inner City Voice* 1, no. 2 (November 16, 1967).

78. *Inner City Voice*, February 29, 1968, 6.

79. Ibid.

80. *Inner City Voice*, December 15, 1967.

81. Robert F. Williams, "The Nationalist Anthem," *Crusader*, December 1967, box 5, Robert Franklin Williams Papers, Bentley Historical Library.

82. *Sauti* 1, no. 9 (September 9 1969).

83. Sonia Sanchez, "Buy American," *Red Flag*, March 6, 1968, box 7, Robert Franklin Williams Papers, Bentley Historical Library.

84. "Agenda—Saturday 30 March 1968," box 4, Robert Franklin Williams Papers, Bentley Historical Library.

85. *New African* 2, no. 2 (August 17, 1968), box 4, Robert Franklin Williams Papers, Bentley Historical Library.

86. Kelley, "Roaring from the East," 124–25.

87. Quoted in Mast, *Detroit Lives*, 307.

88. Ibid., 290.

89. James A. Geschwender, *Class, Race, and Worker Insurgency: The League of Revolutionary Black Workers* (London: Cambridge University Press, 1977), 128, 135.

90. Ibid., 137.

91. Ibid., 142.

92. Mast, *Detroit Lives*, 313.

93. *South End* 21, no. 104 (April 14, 1969).

94. Geschwender, *Class*, 146.

95. *South End*.

96. Geschwender, *Class*, 146.

97. "Interview with Mike Hamlin," Dan Georgakas and Marvin Surkin, Dan Georgakas Collection, Walter P. Reuther Library of Labor and Urban Affairs.

98. Kelley, "Roaring from the East," 121.

99. Ibid., 122.

100. Black Workers Congress, "Manifesto," box 14, folder 15, Martin and Jessie Glaberman Collection, Walter P. Reuther Library of Labor and Urban Affairs.

101. Ibid.

102. "Third World People: Unite," box 1, Detroit Revolutionary Movements Collection, Walter P. Reuther Library of Labor and Urban Affairs.

103. Ibid.

4. "Philosophy Must Be Proletarian"

1. Grace Boggs, "I Must Love the Questions Themselves," in *Selected Speeches by Grace Boggs* (Detroit, 1990), 22.

2. Ibid., 24; Grace Lee Boggs, *Living for Change: An Autobiography* (Minneapolis: University of Minnesota Press, 1998), 39.

3. Boggs, "Questions," 24.

4. Quoted in Paul Romano and Ria Stone (Grace Boggs), *The American Worker* (New York, 1947), 59.

5. Todd L. Duncan and Kathryne Lindberg, "The Continuity of Living for Change: An Interview with Grace Lee Boggs," *Social Text* 67, no. 2 (Summer 2001): 55.

6. *Facing Reality* (Detroit: Facing Reality, 1958), 67.

7. Ibid., 66.

8. Ibid., 67.

9. Boggs, *Living for Change*, xii.

10. Scott McLemmee, introduction to *C. L. R. James on the Negro Question*, ed. Scott McLemmee (Jackson: University Press of Mississippi, 2001), xxii.

11. *C. L. R. James on the Negro Question*, ed. Scott McLemmee (Jackson: University Press of Mississippi, 2001), 3.

12. Ibid., 10.

13. Ibid., 11.

14. Ibid. 86.

15. McLemmee, "Introduction," xxiii.

16. Boggs, *Living for Change*, 43.

17. James, *Negro Question*, 28.

18. Ibid., 32.

19. McLemmee, "Introduction," 28.

20. *Facing Reality*, 168.

21. Ibid., 169.

22. Romano, *The American Worker*, 1–2.

23. James, *Negro Question*, 71.

24. Romano, *The American Worker*, 61.

25. Ibid., 61.

26. Ibid., 70.

27. Paul Buhle. "C. L. R. James: The American Period," draft, 1973, box 21, folder 4, Martin and Jessie Glaberman Collection, Walter P. Reuther Library of Labor and Urban Affairs.

28. Ibid., 46.

29. *State Capitalism and World Revolution*, 3rd ed. (Detroit: Facing Reality, 1969), 96.

30. Ibid., xx.

31. Ibid., 104.

32. Buhle, "C. L. R. James," 59.

33. James, *Negro Question*, 139.

34. Ibid., 147.

35. Boggs, *Living for Change*, 77.

36. Ibid., 79.

37. "Draft Outline—Part I, VP Document, 1/6/56," box 4, folder 8, Martin and Jessie Glaberman Collection, Walter P. Reuther Library of Labor and Urban Affairs.

38. *Facing Reality*, 59.

39. Timothy Tyson, *Radio Free Dixie: Robert F. Williams and the Roots of Black Power* (Chapel Hill: University of North Carolina Press, 1999), 245.

40. Ibid., 246–47.

41. Ibid., 250.

42. James Boggs, "Letter to Conrad Lynn," June 5, 1961, box 6, folder 10, Martin and Jessie Glaberman Collection, Walter P. Reuther Library of Labor and Urban Affairs, 1.

43. Ibid., 2.

44. Box 6, folder 11, Martin and Jessie Glaberman Collection, Walter P. Reuther Library of Labor and Urban Affairs.

45. C. L. R. James, "Letter to Grace," October 22, 1961, box 6, folder 11, Martin and Jessie Glaberman Collection, Walter P. Reuther Library of Labor and Urban Affairs.

46. "Statement," box 6, folder 13, Martin and Jessie Glaberman Collection, Walter P. Reuther Library of Labor and Urban Affairs.

47. James Boggs, *Pages from a Negro Worker's Notebook* (New York: Monthly Review Press, 1963), 33–34.

48. *Facing Reality*, 76.

49. Boggs, *Pages*, 52.

50. James and Grace Boggs, "Dialectical Materialism/Dialectical Humanism," box 5, folder 1, Grace and James Boggs Collection, Walter P. Reuther Library of Labor and Urban Affairs, 8.

51. James Boggs, *Racism and the Class Struggle: Further Pages from a Black Worker's Notebook* (New York: Monthly Review Press, 1970), 56.

52. Ibid., 156.

53. James Boggs and Grace Lee Boggs, *Revolution and Evolution in the Twentieth Century* (New York: Monthly Review Press, 1974), 60.

54. Boggs, *Racism*, 156.

55. James and Grace Boggs, *Revolution*, 173.

56. Boggs, *Racism*, 126.

57. Ibid., 196.

58. James and Grace Boggs, *Revolution*, 60.

59. Boggs, *Racism*, 132.

60. James Boggs, "Culture and Black Power," *Liberator*, January 1967.

61. James and Grace Boggs, *Revolution*, 69.

62. *Manifesto for a Black Revolutionary Party* (Detroit, 1969), 16.

63. James and Grace Boggs, *Revolution*, 68.

64. Ibid., 69.

65. Grace Boggs, *Living for Change*, 196.

66. Grace Boggs, *Asian-Americans and the U.S. Movement* (Detroit: Asian Political Alliance, 1971), 3–4.

67. Grace Boggs, "The Search for Human Identity in America," speech delivered January 19, 1974, box 6, folder 10, James and Grace Boggs Collection, Walter P. Reuther Library of Labor and Urban Affairs.

68. Grace Boggs, "The Changing Self-Concept of the American People," speech delivered April 11, 1975, box 6, folder 11, James and Grace Boggs Collection, Walter P. Reuther Library of Labor and Urban Affairs.

69. Grace Boggs, "The Personal Is Political: The Challenge of Being a Woman in Today's America," speech delivered June 9, 1978, box 6, folder 16, James and Grace Boggs Collection, Walter P. Reuther Library of Labor and Urban Affairs.

70. Grace Boggs, "Women and the Movement to Build a New America," speech delivered March 10, 1977 (Detroit: National Organization for an American Revolution).

71. Grace Boggs, *Selected Speeches*, 17.

72. *Manifesto for an American Revolutionary Party* (Philadelphia: National Organization for an American Revolution, 1982), 31–32.

73. *Uprooting Racism and Racists in the U.S.A.* (Detroit and Philadelphia: National Organization for an American Revolution, 1982), 21.

74. Grace Boggs, "Letter to Louis Tsen," box 17, Grace and James Boggs Collection, Walter P. Reuther Library of Labor and Urban Affairs.

75. Ibid.

76. Grace Boggs, "Beyond Eurocentrism," in *Selected Speeches by Grace Boggs*, 40.

77. Gustavo Esteva and Madhu Suri Prakash, *Grassroots Post-modernism:*

Remaking the Soil of Cultures (New York: Palgrave/Macmillan, 1998); Immanuel Maurice Wallerstein, *After Liberalism* (New York: New Press, 1995).

78. Arif Dirlik, "Dare to Cross the Color Line" (manuscript provided to the author by Grace Boggs), 4.

5. Making Monkey Signify

1. See Fred Ho, "Mao, the Black Panthers, and the Third World Strike," a speech delivered at the 30th anniversary conference on the Berkeley Third World Strike, April 9, 1999, box 19, folder "Drafts 1999–1993," Fred Ho Papers, Thomas J. Dodd Research Center, University of Connecticut Libraries.

2. Fred Ho, "Nobody Knows the Trouble I've Seen: The Roots to the 'Black-Asian Conflict' through a Socio-historical Comparative Analysis between Asian Americans and African Americans," box 19, folder "Drafts 1992–1978," Fred Ho Papers, Thomas J. Dodd Research Center, University of Connecticut Libraries.

3. Fred Ho, "What Makes 'Jazz' the Revolutionary Music of the 20th Century, and Will It Be Revolutionary for the 21st Century?" *African American Review* 29, no. 2 (1995): 285.

4. Ibid.

5. Fred Ho, "Kreolization, Cross-Fertilization, or Cultural Imperialism," box 19, folder "Drafts 1999–1993," Fred Ho Papers, Thomas J. Dodd Research Center, University of Connecticut Libraries.

6. Ho, "What Makes 'Jazz,'" 283.

7. Ibid.

8. Ibid., 286.

9. Fred Wei-han Ho, "From Banana to Third World-Marxist," in *Boyhood, Growing Up Male: A Multicultural Anthology*, ed. Franklin Abbott (New York: Crossing Press, 1993), 196.

10. Fred Ho, "Beyond Asian American Jazz: My Musical and Political Changes in the Asian American Movement," *Leonardo Music Journal* 9 (1999): 45.

11. Ibid.

12. Ibid.

13. Fred Ho, "The Inspiration of Mao and the Chinese Revolution on the Black Liberation Movement and the Asian Movement on the East Coast," speech for the 30th anniversary conference on the Third World Strike, box 19, folder "Drafts 1999–1993," University of California, Berkeley, April 9, 1999, Thomas J. Dodd Research Center, University of Connecticut Libraries.

14. Ho, *Legacy to Liberation*, 405.

15. Ibid.

16. Ibid.

17. Ibid., 405–7.

18. Ho, "Beyond Asian American Jazz," 46.

19. See Ho, "The Inspiration of Mao." Ho continues to perceive the 1969 Third World Strike as an exemplary model of intellectual activism and a salient moment for contemporary academic discussions of multiculturalism.

20. Fred Ho, "The Personal Is Political: Lessons," box 19, folder "Drafts 1972–2001," Fred Ho Papers, Thomas J. Dodd Research Center, University of Connecticut Libraries.

21. Fred Ho, "A dialogue: Tomorrow is Now!" box 2, series 25, Folder K, Fred Ho Papers, Thomas J. Dodd Center, University of Connecticut Libraries.

22. Fred Ho, "No Longer Resistance, but Revolution! My Musical and Political Changes in the Asian American Movement," manuscript in possession of the author.

23. "Script: Once Upon a Time in Chinese America," box 3, Series 38, folder L, Fred Ho Papers, Thomas J. Dodd Research Center, University of Connecticut Libraries.

24. Ho, "No Longer," 12.

25. Ho, "Beyond Asian American Jazz," 13.

26. Ibid., 47.

27. "Script: A Chinaman's Chance," box 3, series 38, folder I. Fred Ho Papers, Thomas J. Dodd Research Center, University of Connecticut Libraries.

28. Ibid.

29. Ibid.

30. Ibid.

31. Ho, "No Longer," 18.

32. Ho, "Beyond Asian American Jazz," 48.

33. Ibid., 48.

34. Ibid., 49.

35. Joseph S. C. Lam, "Embracing Asian American Music as an Heuristic Device," *Journal of Asian American Studies* 2, no. 1 (1999): 3.

36. Ibid., 4.

37. Ho and Sakolsky, "Preface," 9.

38. Modirzadeh elaborates in "The Story of Maqam 'X': Musical Archetype of the People," essay in possession of the author.

39. Taylor Bynum, "Cross Cultural Musical Discourse: Fred Ho and the Development of Afro-Asian American Music," box 3, series 43, folder B, Fred Ho Papers, Thomas J. Dodd Research Center, University of Connecticut Libraries, 3.

40. Fred Wei-han Ho, "Playing Other People's Music: An Interview with Royal Hartigan," in *Sounding Off! Music as Subversion/Resistance/Revolution* (Brooklyn: Autonomedia, 1995), 332.

41. Liner notes to *The Underground Railroad to My Heart* (Soul Note, 1994).

42. Ibid.

43. Ibid.

44. Ibid.

45. "Lan Hua Hua," *Underground*.

46. Liner notes, *Underground*.

47. Ibid.

48. Ibid.

49. See Henry Louis Gates Jr., *The Signifying Monkey: A Vernacular Theory of African American Literature* (New York: Oxford University Press, 1988). There are numerous other articles and books on the topic of signifying.

50. Ho and Sakolsky, "Preface," 9.

51. Liner notes to *Monkey: Part One* (Koch Jazz, 1996).

52. Liner notes to *Monkey: Part Two* (Koch Jazz, 1997).

53. See Maxine Hong Kingston, *Tripmaster Monkey: His Fake Book* (New York: Vintage, 1990). Ho pays tribute to Kingston as a signifying feminist/artist here and later in *Warrior Sisters*. The title derives most obviously from Kingston's groundbreaking book on Asian American women, *The Woman Warrior*.

54. "Puerto Rican Woman," *Turn Pain into Power!* (OO Discs, 1997).

55. "Essay to Us," *Turn Pain into Power!*

56. Fred Ho, interview with the author, February 20, 2002.

57. "What's a Girl to Do?" *Turn Pain into Power!*

58. "The Climbers," *Turn Pain into Power!*

59. Fred Ho, "Matriarchy: The First and Final Communism," box 19, folder "Drafts: 1992–1998," Fred Ho Papers, Thomas J. Dodd Research Center, University of Connecticut Libraries, 9.

60. Ibid., 22–23.

61. For two futuristic/speculative allegories of gender, gender reversal, or genderlessness, see Ursula K. Le Guin, *The Left Hand of Darkness* (New York: Ace, 1991); and Joanna Russ, *The Female Man* (Boston: Beacon, 2000).

62. D. H. Hwang, *M. Butterfly* (New York: Penguin, 1994).

63. Act 1, "Prelude," *Warrior Sisters: The New Adventures of African and Asian Womyn Warriors* (Koch Jazz, 1999).

64. Act 1, scene 3, *Warrior Sisters*.

65. Ibid.

66. Ibid.

67. Ibid.

68. Act 1, scene 5, *Warrior Sisters*.

69. Act 2, scene 1, *Warrior Sisters*.

70. Act 3, scene 1, *Warrior Sisters*.

71. Act 3, scene 3, *Warrior Sisters*.

Index

Adzenyah, Abraham, 179

Africa, 55, 57

African American Party of National Liberation, 85–86

African Blood Brotherhood, 81

African National Congress, 28

African Party for the Independence of Guinea and Cape Verde (PAIGC), 141

African self-determination, 58

Afrikan Peoples, 191

Afro-American Student Conference on Black Nationalism, 86

Afro-American Student Movement Conference, 86, 92

Afro-Asian jazz, 173, 178

Afro-Asian Journalists Association, 78, 88

Afro-Asian liberation, 77, 162

Afro-Asian Multicultural Music, 167

Afro-Asian Music Ensemble, 164–65, 169, 173, 179–81, 192

Afro-Asian New American Multicultural Music, 180

Afro-Asian Solidarity Fund, 67, 79

Afro-Asian Writers Bureau, 78

Afro-Asian Writers' Movement, 68, 95, 102

Afro-Asian Youth Movement in Cairo, 68

Afrocentric Marxism, 3

Afrocentrism, xx, xxxiii, 142

Afro-Orientalism, xv–xviii, xix–xx, xxvi–xxxii, xxix–xxx, xxxii, 51, 58, 71, 115, 117, 119, 147, 159, 162, 163–64, 168, 177, 204

Ahmad, Aijaz, xvii, xxviii, 61

Allen, Ernest, 24, 48

Allen, Lewis, 182

American Congress for Cultural Freedom, 66

American Hunger (Wright), 52

American Negro Labor Congress, 19

Amin, Sami, 156

Amsterdam News, 81

Antiessentialism, 111, 115, 124, 176

Anti-imperialist League, 59

Aoki, Richard, 161

Art Ensemble of Chicago, 177
Aryan Path, 1
Ashanti, 57
Asian American Art Ensemble, 174, 177
Asian American Awareness Month, 171
Asian American jazz, 173, 180
Asian American music, 177
Asian American panethnicity, 177
Asian American Resource Workshop (AARW), 171–72
Asian American Reality Conference, 147
AsianImprov Records, 173, 177, 180
Asian Pacific American (APA) movement, xliv, 115, 149, 161–62, 204
Asian Political Alliance, 146–47
Association of Afro-Asian Journalists, 88
Association of Afro-Asian Writers, 88
Association of Oppressed Peoples, 21
Auerbach, Brian, 182
Autobiography of Malcolm X, xii
Awakening, 156

Baker, General, 81–82, 86, 104–5, 107
Baldwin, Kate, xxix
Bamboo That Snaps Back, 177
Bandung, 69
Bandung Conference, 54, 59–63, 78, 81, 165
Bandung era, xxv, xviii, 71, 77–78, 79, 90, 98, 102, 106, 110, 118, 159, 166, 179

Bandung humanism, 92, 110–11, 116
Bernal, Martin, 5
Bhaba, Homi, xvii
Big Red Media, Inc., 164, 172
Bindman, David, 180
Birmingham church bombings, 87, 88
Black America, 87, 88–91, 102
Black Arts Conference, 96, 97–98, 142
Black Arts movement (BAM), xxv, xliii, 77, 93–96, 98, 102, 165, 167, 170, 172, 180, 190, 191–93, 204
Black Belt, 103–4
Black Belt rhetoric, 69, 88
Black Belt thesis, 22, 50, 69
Black Boy, 51–52
Black Dragon Society, xxxvi
Black Economic Development Conference (BEDC), 107, 108
"Black Manifesto," 107
Black Metropolis, 66
Black nationalism, 142
Black Panther Party, 30, 106, 118, 139, 144, 164, 170–71, 196, 200, 204
Black Power, xliii, 54–58, 68, 71, 97–98
Black Power movement, 115–16, 118–19, 120, 133, 138–41, 144, 145, 148, 150–52, 161
Black Renaissance (1980s), 192
Black Revolutionary Party (BRP), 143–45
Black Star Book Store, 106
Black Star Press, 106
Black Star Publishing, 106

Black studies, xl

Black Workers Congress (BWC), 107–8, 109; manifesto, 108–9

Blair, Thomas, 85

Blyden, Edward Wilmont, xxxiii

Boggs, Grace (Grace Lee), xli, xviii, 30, 113–16, 117, 119–25, 127, 128, 133–35, 147–50, 156–62, 176. *See also under* Boggs, James

Boggs, James (Jimmy), xxv, xliii, 30, 113,116, 117, 121, 127–28, 129, 132–37, 143–44, 159; and Grace Lee, 68, 75, 76, 82, 84, 86, 91, 92, 94, 96, 98–99, 105, 111, 113, 117, 127–28, 129, 132–35, 136–40, 145–46, 151–52, 154–55, 162

Boggsism, 116, 119, 135, 138, 142, 145, 146, 147, 152, 162

Bolshevik revolution of 1917, 115

Bontemps, Arna, 93

Boone House, 93, 94

Bound Feet, 174

Boxer Rebellion, 7, 8, 171

Boxers, 196

Brecht, Bertolt, 106

Broadside Press, 93–94, 101–2

Brooklyn Sax Quartet, 180

Brooks, Gwendolyn, 93, 94

Brown, Anthony, 180

Brown, H. Rap, 103

Brown, Sterling, 93

Buhle, Paul, 125–26

Burroughs, Margaret, 94

Bush I, 190

By Any Mode Necessary, 179

Byrne, David, 178

Cabral, Amilcar, 118, 141, 166

Cade, Toni, 93

Carmichael, Stokely, 99

Castro, Fidel, 84, 105

Cayton, Horace, 66

Césaire, Aimé, 117, 178

Chapman, Abraham, 93

Chaulieu, Pierre, 131

Chen, Jack, 175, 186

Chicago Defender, 1, 28

Chin, Frank, 204

Chin, Vincent, 161, 191

China, xv, 21, 22, 23, 28, 29

Chinaman's Chance, A, 174–75

China's Great Proletarian Cultural Revolution, 92, 141

China's Red Guard, 99

Chinese Cultural Revolution theory, 118

Chinese dialectics, 146

Chinese Revolution, 138

Chiwengo, Ngwarungu, 46, 55–56

Chou En-lai, 63

Christian Revolution, 123

Chrysler Workers Group, 147

Churchill, Ward, 195

CIO, 125

Cixous, Hélène, xxiii

Clarke, John Henrik, 93

Cleague, Albert, 81, 82, 90, 96, 97

Coalition of Black Revolutionary Artists (COBRA), 100

Cockrel, Ken, 107

Cold War, 64, 65–66, 67, 68, 85

Color Curtain, The (Wright), 61, 68, 71

Color line thesis, 90

Coltrane, John, 179, 182

Comintern (Soviet), 15–16, 18, 22

Committee on Correspondence, 128

Communist Manifesto, 90, 131

Communist Party, 107, 127

Communist Party of the United States (CPUSA), 121

Confucianism, 148

Congress of Afrikan Peoples, 172

Congress of Eastern Peoples, 7

Congress of Oppressed Nationalities, 59

Congress on Racial Equality (CORE), 107

Convention People's Party, 30

Correspondence, 93, 102, 108, 127–28, 134

Crisis, 7, 19, 23

Crummell, Alexander, xxxiii

Crusader, 81–90, 99, 100–102, 133

Cruse, Harold, 84

Cruz, Philip Vera, 161

Cullen, Countee, 93

Cultural Revolution, 146

Cuney, William Waring, 93

Danner, Margaret, 93, 94

Dark Princess (Du Bois), xxxvii, xlii, 1, 4, 7, 13–21

Davis, Chester, 79

Davis, Ossie, 133

Delany, Martin, xxvii, xxxiii–xxxiv

Deng Xiaoping reform, 156

Detroit, xxv, xliii

Detroit Agricultural Union, 160

Detroit Council of Human Rights, 82

Detroit Grassroots Conference, 84

Detroit rebellion, 98

Detroit summer, 160

d'Gobineau, Arthur, xxxiii–xxxiv, 11

Dialectical humanism, 116, 137–38, 140, 146–49, 151, 163

Dialectical materialism, 176

Diaspora consciousness, 69, 71

Diaspora theory, xxvi–xxxii

Dirlik, Arif, xl, xvii, xix, xx, xxiii, xxviii, 161

Dodge Revolutionary Union Movement (DRUM), 105–6, 108

Dodson, Owen, 93

Donkor, Freeman, 179

Double consciousness, 45

Douglass, Frederick, xxii, xxxiv, 73, 87

Dowell, Glanton, 100

Du Bois, Shirley Graham, 30

Du Bois, W. E. B, xii, xiv–xv, xxvii, xxix, xxxiii, xxxiv, xl–xli, 1–41 passim, 44, 47, 48, 69–71, 73, 79, 80, 90, 101, 162, 163, 168; "Africa: Roots of the War," 8, 11; *Darkwater*, 8, 10, 13; debate with Garvey on Asia, xxxv–xxxix; "I Sing to China," 32–41; "Of Work and Wealth," 13; *The Souls of Black Folk*, 21, 27; "The Souls of White Folk," 12; "The Star of Ethiopia," 4–5; "Winds of Time," 28; *The World and Africa*, 5, 7, 8

Dudziak, Mary, 79

Dunayevskaya, Raya (Freddie Forest), 121, 122, 125, 128, 132
Durant, Will, xiii, xix

East Coast Asian Students Union (ECASU), 171
East Is Red, The, 146
Edwards, Brent, xxxi
Egypt, 21
Egyptocentrism, xx, xxxii
Eldon Avenue Revolutionary Union Movement (ELDRUM), 105
Ellington, Duke, 181, 183
Elvis, 192
Embry, James, 152
Engels, Friedrich, 59
English Revolution, 121
Enlightenment, xxiv–xxv, 158
Esteva, Gustavo, 159
Ethiopia, 25
Ethiopianism, xxxiii
Ethiopia Pacific League, xxxvi
Eurocentrism, xxvii, 156, 159–60, 167, 173, 178, 185, 196
Evans, Mari, 93, 94
Evers, Medger, 86

Facing Reality, 98, 116, 129–32, 134, 135–36
Fair Play for Cuba, 79
Fanon, Frantz, 69, 84, 90, 99, 105, 110, 118, 136–37, 162, 166
Fanshen, 139, 141
Feldman, Rick, 152
Feminism, xliv, 176, 194–96
Fifth Estate, 106

Fisk University, 86, 96
Forman, James, 107, 109
Forum 66, 97
Freedom Now Party, 77, 84
Freedom Riders, 132
Freedom Rides, 133
Freeman, Don, 82, 84, 85
French Revolution, 121
Ford Revolutionary Union Movement (FRUM), 105
Fujiwara, Kityoto, 180
Furnace, Sam, 180

Gandhi, Mahatma, xiii, xxxv, 7, 14
Gandhism, 162
Garvey, Marcus, xxv, xxxiii, xxxiv; 59, 106; debate with Du Bois on Asia, xxxv–xxxix
Gates, Henry, Jr., xxxix, xxxix, 185, 192
Georgakas, Dan, 82, 94, 98, 99
Geschwender, James, 105–6
Ghadr Party, xxxv, 7
Giap, Vo Nguyen, General, 73, 76, 104, 141
Gilman, Charlotte Perking, 114
Gilroy, Paul, xxvii–xxix, xxx, 20–21, 45–46, 69; *Black Atlantic*, xxvii–xxix
Giovanni, Nikki, 97
Glaberman, Marty, 98, 105, 128, 134
Gonzalez, Marcial, xxx
Grace and James Boggs Center for Community Leadership, 161
Grant, Madison, 9
Grassroots Leadership Conference, 92, 155

Grassroots Negro Leadership Conference, 135
Grassroots postmodernism, 159–61
Greene, Ann T., 176, 195–96, 200, 204
Greenwood, Frank, 95
Group on Advanced Leadership (GOAL), 83–84
Guevara, Che, 80, 99, 104, 105

Hakutani, Yoshinobu, 46, 71
Hamlin, Mike, 105, 106, 107
Hammer, Fannie Lou, 107
Hammon, Jupiter, 5
Harper, Frances Ellen Watkins, xxxiii
Harper's Ferry, 86
Harris, Mary, 114
Hartigan, Royal, 175, 179, 182–83, 186, 189
Harvard University, 171
Havana Tricontinental Conference of 1966, 78
Hayden, Robert, 93, 94
Haywood, Harry, 17, 19
Hegel, G. W. F., xxiii, 116, 122, 125–26, 136, 151, 158
Hegelian dialectics, 116
Henry, Milton, 82, 84, 102
Henry, Richard (Brother Imari), 82, 84, 103
Hernton, Calvin, 93
Hicks, Calvin, 133
Hikida Yasuichi, xxxvi, xxxvii
Hing, Alex, 148, 161
Ho, Fred, xli, xliv, 164–204 passim
Ho Chi Minh, 21, 87, 141
Hocker, James, 152

Homophobia, 176
Hong, Pauline, 185
Hopkins, Pauline, xxxiii
Horiuchi, Glenn, 173
Horton, Willie, 190
House, Gloria, 100
House, Stu, 99
Howard, Charles, 103
Howell, Sharon, 152
Huberman, Leo, 135
Hu De-Hart, Evelyn, xx, xxxi
Hughes, Langston, 93
Huiswood, Otto, 13, 16, 22
Hungarian workers' council, 155
Hu Shih, 150
Hwang, D. H., 196
Hybridity, 178, 179
Hybridity theory, xviii, xxvi–xxxii

India, 22, 28
Indian Home Rule League, xxxvi, 7
Indian National Congress, 7, 18
Indian Nationalist Movement of North America, 109
Inner City Organizing Committee (ICOC), 77, 92–93, 96, 98
Inner City Voice, 98, 99–100, 102, 105, 106, 108
International All-Trade Union of the World, 84
International Confederation of Free Trade Unions, 67
International Conference for Solidarity with the People of Vietnam against U.S. Imperialist Aggression and for the Defense of Peace, 87

Interreligious Foundation for Community Organization, 107
Iron Curtain, 64
Iverem, Esther, 164, 170, 190
I Wor Kuen (IWK), 156, 171–73, 177, 204
Iyer, Vijay, 180
Izu, Mark, 173, 174, 180

Jackson, Jessie, 156, 173
James, C. L. R. (J. H. Johnson), xliii, 117–18, 119–20, 121, 124–25, 126–32, 134–35, 151
Jang, Gar Man, 173–74
Jang, Jon, 173, 177–78, 180, 192
Japan, xv, xxxvii–xxxvii, 7, 21, 23, 25, 28; conflict with China, 23–27
Japan Afro-Asian Solidarity Committee, 88
Japan-Russia War, xii, 1, 3
Jim Crow, 53, 56, 61, 62, 114, 121, 123
Joans, Ted, 93
Johnson, Charles, 82, 99
Johnson, Ethel, 85
Johnson-Forest collective, 118, 127–32, 135, 142
Johnson-Forest tendency, 121, 122, 125–26
Johnsonites, 121–22
Jonas, Chris
Jones, LeRoi (aka Amiri Baraka), 79, 93, 94, 100, 133, 165, 180
Jordan, Robert O., xxxvi
Journey to the West, 164, 183–85, 194, 195–97, 200, 204

Journey beyond the West Orchestra, 185

Kelley, Robin D. G., xii, xviii, xxvi–xxvii, xxviii, xl, 85, 104
Killens, John, 30, 81, 97, 100
King, Martin Luther, 133, 144, 145
King, Woodie, 93, 94
Kingston, Maxine Hong, 180
Knight, Etheridge, 94
Kochiyama, Yuri, 161
Ku Klux Klan, 17, 133
Kularts, 180

Labor Action, 121
LaGrond, Oliver, 93
Lam, Joseph S. C., 177
Last Poets, 170
Lawrence, Harold, 93
League of Revolutionary Black Workers, 81, 82, 102, 107
League of Revolutionary Struggle (LRS), 172, 177
Le Duan, 109
Lee, Eddie, 127
Lee, Harry, 127
Le Guin, Ursula K., 196
Lenin, Vladimir, xxiv, 17, 19, 22
Levering Lewis, David, xxvii–xxviii
Lewis, Marilyn, 169
Liberation News Service, 106
Liberator, 142
Lim, Genny, 175, 180
Linebaugh, Peter, xxix
Lin Piao, 90
Liu Shao Chi, 63

Long, Jodi, 174, 192
Lorde, Audre, 93
Lynn, Conrad J., 75, 79, 132–33

Mad Bear, 109
Madgett, Naomi, 93
Madsen, Peter, 180, 181
Magdoff, Harry, 156
Malcolm X, xiii, xiv, xix, xxvii, 82, 84, 91, 142–44, 145, 161, 170, 179
Mallory, Mae, 84
Manifesto for an American Revolutionary Party, 152–54
Maoism, 29, 108, 110, 118, 138–39, 142, 146–49, 156, 161
Mao Tse-tung, xxv, xliii, 74, 77, 86, 89, 90–91, 92, 94–95, 104, 105, 117, 139, 140, 146, 147–49; "Talks on the Forum at Yenan," xxv, 95–98
Marable, Manning, 67
Marsalis, Wynton, 193
Marsalis school, 184
Marx, Karl, xx–xxiv, 6, 65, 117, 122–24, 125–26, 135, 140
Marxian humanism, 151
Marxism, xvii, xx–xxiv, xxix, xxxiii, xlii, xliv, 47, 52–53, 90, 92, 115–16, 134– 36, 141, 142, 158, 162, 172, 176
Massey, Calvin, 170
Matriarchal socialism, 176
Maxwell, William, 17
Mayfield, Julian, 79, 133
Mayo, Katherine, 9
Mazrui, Ali A., xxxix

McKay, Claude, xxix, 13, 16, 17, 22, 93, 95
Mergenthaler, Audrey, 6, 28
Mexican Communist Party, 16
Michigan Citizen, 162
Mills, Irving, 183
"Miracle of Nationalism in the African Gold Coast, The," 69
Mirikitani, Janice, 176, 180, 191–92
Mobley, Mae, 133
Model minority discourse, 178, 193
Modirzadeh, Hafez, 175, 179, 185, 189
Moghadam, Val, 156
Monkey, 186–88, 196–97, 200
Monkey figure, 184–85
Monkey Orchestra, 164, 175, 185
Monkey: Part Two, 187–89
Monroe uprising, 75, 79, 95
Monthly Review Press, 81, 135, 156
Moore, Queen Mother Audley, 85, 103
Moore, William, 86
Moses, Wilson, xxxi, xxxv, 3, 4
Muhammad, Elijah, 90
Multiculturalism, 172, 175–76, 193
Multinational unity, 178
Mural Message Movement (AC3T), 161
Murotake, David, 186

NAACP, 107, 133, 152
National Liberation Front in Vietnam, 99, 103
National Negro Congress, 67
National Negro Department, 120

National Negro Labor Council, 67

Nation of Islam, xx, 170

National Organization for an American Revolution (NOAR), 152, 154–58

Native Son (Wright), 48–50

N'COBRA, 104

Neal, Larry, 77, 93, 95

Negative loyalty, 62

Negro Action Committee, 105

Negro chauvinism, 120

Negro problem, 126

Negro question, 134

Nehru, xxiv, 21

New African, 104

New American Multicultural Music, 183, 193–94, 204

New Black Aesthetic for Sale!, 192–93

New International, 124

New Left, 176

New Orleans Black Arts Movement, 191

Nietzsche, Friedrich, 47

Nkrumah, Kwame, 29, 68, 90, 104

Northern Grassroots Leadership Conference, 77, 82

Northern Negro Leadership Conference (NNLC), 82

Norton, Jim, 186

Now!, 82

Occidentalists, 159

Once Upon a Time in Chinese America, 173–74

Organic Third Layer School, 127

Organization of Afro–Asian People's Solidarity, 88

Organization of Revolutionary Socialist Sisters and Some Men (ORSSASM), 176

Organization of Solidarity of the Peoples of Africa, Asia, and Latin America, 78

Orientalism, 43, 45, 47, 57, 67, 167, 177–78

Padmore, George, 6, 29; and Dorothy, 54, 162

PAIGC (African Party for the Independence of Guinea and Cape Verde), 141

Pan-African Congress, xv, 22, 28, 43, 54, 59

Pan-Africanist, 65

Pan-African Socialism, 87

Pan-Asianism, 7, 29

Parker, George Wells, xxxiv

Patriarchy, 176

Patterson, James, 94

Patterson, Tiffany, xxvi–xxvii, xxviii, xl

Pei Sheng Shen, 185

People's Solidarity Committee, 109

Pittsburgh Courier, xxxvii, 1, 2, 25, 66

Polo, Marco, 142

Polyculturalism, xviii

Pool, Rosey E., 93

Powell, Adam Clayton, 66, 78

Prakash, Madhu, 159

Prashad, Vijay, xviii–xix, xxviii, xxxvi, 5

Protestant Reformation, 123

Ra, Sun, 170
Racial romanticism, 142
Rai, Lala Lajpat, xv, xxxv, xxxvi, 7, 10, 22
Rampersad, Arnold, 46
Randall, Dudley, 75, 93, 94, 95, 96, 101
Randolph, A. Philip, 114
Rastafarianism, xviii
Red Flag, 101, 102
Red Guard Party, 171, 172
Redicker, Marcus, xxix
Red People's Solidarity Day, 109
Reed, Ishmael, 204
Republic of New Africa (RNA), 76, 102–4, 120
Reuther era, 128
Reutherism, 128
Revolutionary Action Movement (RAM), xxv, 68, 76, 85, 86, 87–91, 99–100, 102, 105, 107, 110, 139, 151, 163, 171
Revolutionary Communist Party, 156
Roach, Max, 81, 179
Robert Williams Defense Committee, 105
Robeson, Paul, xxix, 68, 79
Robinson, Cedric, 17, 71
Rogers, J. A., xiii, xix, xxxii, 5
Romano, Paul, 122–24
Roy, M. N., xxv, 7, 16, 19, 22, 90
Russ, Joanna, 196
Russian Revolution, 137–38

Said, Edward, xiii, xxi, xxii, 45, 57
Sakolsky, Ron, 185

Salaam, Kalamu ya, 191
Sanchez, Sonia, 94, 101, 180, 191
Santo Domingo revolt, 99
Save Our Sisters and Daughters (SOSAD), 156
Schactman, Max, 134
Scientific rationalism, 158
Scientific socialism, 158
Scott-Heron, Gil, 170
Secret Circle, 68
Segal, Ronald, 73
Senghor, Leopold, 22
Seth, Sanjay, xxiii–xiv
Sexism, 176
Shabazz, Betty, 103
Shakur, Assata, 176, 196, 210
Shankar, S., 46
Shepp, Archie, 170, 179, 190–91
Shifflet, John, 186
Sei Ping-hsin, 73
Signifying monkey, 185
Signifying Monkey, The, 185
Simmons, Charles, 82
Simon, Paul, 178
Simplins, Ed, 93
Singh, Amritjit, 47
Snelling, Rolland (Askía Touré), 100
Student Nonviolent Coordinating Committee (SNCC), 107
Socialist Scholars Conference, 156
Socialist Workers Party (SWP), 80, 105, 107, 120, 122, 127–28, 134
Soul Note, 173, 177, 180, 181
Sounding Off, 178
South End, 106
Southern Land Bank, 107

Southern Tenant Farmers Union, 121

South Side Tenants Organization, 114

South Vietnam National Front for Liberation, 88

Soviet Union, xxix, 14

Spoken Engine label, 180

Stalin, Josef, 17

Stanford, Max (aka Muhammed Ahmed), xxv, 82, 84, 85–86, 92

Stanford University, 155

Stoddard, Lothrop, 11

Strategic antiessentialism, 111, 115, 124

Student Non-violent Coordinating Committee (SNCC), 81, 152

Subaltern, 56

Sukarno, 63, 65

Sun Tzu, 141–42

Sun Yat-Sen, 7, 14, 149

Sweezy, Paul, 135

Taoism, 148

Third World Communications, 191

Third World Labor Strike, 109

Third World Liberation Front strike, 172

Third World peoples' struggles, 158

Third World Summit Conference, 109, 145–46

Thomas, Bigger, 59

Thomas, Clarence, 190

Thomas, Piri, 100

Thompson, James, 93

Ting Yi Lin, 185

Tizol, Juan, 183

Tolson, Melvin, 94

Toussaint-Louverture, 109

Townsend, Willard S., 66

Transnational correspondence, 76, 110–11

Tran Van Thanh, 88

Tree Huggers, 160

Trickster figure, 185, 194, 195–96

Tripp, Luke, 82, 105, 106

Trotsky, Leon, 117, 119

Trotskyism, 52, 122, 128, 154

Tsen, Louise, 156

Turner, Bryan, 47

Turner, Nat, 109

12 Million Black Voices, xl, xiii, xli, xlii, 30, 51, 57

"Twelve Point Platform Program," 171

Tyson, Timothy, 79

UHURU, 81–82, 98, 105

United Front, 180

Unity, 172

U.S. Congress for National Freedom, 68

U.S. Labor movement, 138

U.S. Left, 138

Vaughn, Edward, 96

Vietnamese Front of National Liberation, 87

Villegas, Alma, 164, 189–90

Von Eschen, Penny, 79

Walker, Alice, 191

Walker, Margaret, 73, 93, 94

Wallerstein, Immanuel, 159–60

Wang, Cindy Zuoxin, 182–83, 186

Watson, John, 82, 98, 106, 107

Warrior Sisters, 196–204

Watts, Daniel, 97

Watts rebellion, 77, 88, 89, 90

Wehner, Martin, 186

West Bank Intifada, 159

West Coast Asian American jazz music circle, 180

West Coast Kearney Street Workshop, 173

West Virginia College, 150

White, Robert, 45–46

White Man, Listen!, 68–69, 71

Wilkins, Roy, 99

Williams, Eric, 6, 46, 99

Williams, John, 105

Williams, Robert F., xxv, xli, xliii, 30, 68, 7391, 95–96, 99, 100–104, 110–11, 132–33, 163

Williams, Veatrice, 182

Womyn, 194–95, 198, 200, 201, 204

Wong, Allen, 180

Wong, Francis, 173, 186

Workers Party, 114, 121–22, 124, 134

World Federation of Trade Unions Conference in Beijing, 63

World Literature, 102

Wright, Richard, xl, 43–71, 78, 93, 136–37, 163; *12 Million Black Voices*, xl, xiii, xli, xlii, 30

Wu Cheng, 184–85

Wu Tang Clan, xxvii

Xiaomei Chen, xvi–xvii, 159

Yale College, 149

Yellow Peril, 64

Yellow Revolutionary Nationalism, 171

Yergan, Max, 66

Young, Coleman, 160

Young, Robert, xxiii, 43

Young, Whitney, 99

Young India, xxxxi

You Qun Fu, 185

Yu Shan Min, 188–89

Zapatistas, 160

Zupan, Johnny, 128

Bill V. Mullen is professor of English at the University of Texas–San Antonio. He has also served as a Fulbright lecturer to Wuhan University in the People's Republic of China. His books include *Popular Fronts: Chicago and African American Cultural Politics, 1935–1946* and, most recently, *Left of the Color Line: Race, Radicalism, and Modern Literatures of the United States* (coedited with James Smethurst).